Critical Enthusiasm

Critical Enthusiasm

*Capital Accumulation and the
Transformation of Religious Passion*

JORDANA ROSENBERG

Oxford University Press is a department of the University of Oxford.
It furthers the University's objective of excellence in research, scholarship,
and education by publishing worldwide.

Oxford   New York
Auckland   Cape Town   Dar es Salaam   Hong Kong   Karachi
Kuala Lumpur   Madrid   Melbourne   Mexico City   Nairobi
New Delhi   Shanghai   Taipei   Toronto

With offices in
Argentina   Austria   Brazil   Chile   Czech Republic   France   Greece
Guatemala   Hungary   Italy   Japan   Poland   Portugal   Singapore
South Korea   Switzerland   Thailand   Turkey   Ukraine   Vietnam

Oxford is a registered trade mark of Oxford University Press
in the UK and certain other countries.

Published in the United States of America by
Oxford University Press
198 Madison Avenue, New York, NY 10016

© Oxford University Press 2011

First issued as an Oxford University Press paperback, 2013.

All rights reserved. No part of this publication may be reproduced, stored in a retrieval system, or transmitted, in any
form or by any means, without the prior permission in writing of Oxford University Press, or as expressly permitted
by law, by license, or under terms agreed with the appropriate reproduction rights organization. Inquiries concerning
reproduction outside the scope of the above should be sent to the Rights Department, Oxford University Press,
at the address above.

You must not circulate this work in any other form
and you must impose this same condition on any acquirer.

Library of Congress Cataloging-in-Publication Data
Rosenberg, Jordana.
Critical enthusiasm : capital accumulation and the transformation of religious passion / Jordana Rosenberg.
   p. cm.
Includes bibliographical references and index.
ISBN 978-0-19-976426-6 (cloth : alk. paper); 978-0-19-932882-6 (paperback)
1. Enthusiasm—Religious aspects—History—18th century. 2. England—Religion—18th century.
3. Economics—Religious aspects—History—18th century. 4. England—Economic conditions—18th century.
5. Religion and culture—England—History—18th century. 6. England—Civilization—18th century. I. Title.
BL980.G7R67   2011
201′.73094209033—dc22   2010029066

*For my mother, Barbara Rosenberg,
and in memory of my father, Stephen Nicholas Rosenberg,
whose kindness, intelligence, and comedic sparkle are greatly missed.*

CONTENTS

Acknowledgments
ix

Introduction: Religion, or Secularization: Dialectical Method
for the Literary Study of Secularisms
3

SECTION ONE: TIME

Chapter 1

Enthusiasm and Historicism: Mosaic Law and the Narration of History
33

Chapter 2

The Legislation of Accumulation: The Camisard Trial and Structures of Belief
64

SECTION TWO: SPACE

Chapter 3

Social Regulation and Transatlantic Accumulation
97

Chapter 4

A Cry from the Desart: Spatiality and Secularism
127

Chapter 5

Poetic Enthusiasm: The City, the Country, and Extended Accumulation
149

Notes
185

Index
209

ACKNOWLEDGMENTS

My study of the eighteenth century began at Cornell University under the direction of Laura Brown, Walter Cohen, and Neil Saccamano. Laura, Walter, and Neil provided more than an introduction to early modern study; they made an understanding of the period both possible and indispensable to an account of modernity more largely. I am grateful to them for their support during my graduate study, and beyond. Also at Cornell, Amy Villarejo was generous with her time early in her career, and she has since become a valued collaborator.

I have been fortunate to receive the assistance of a number of innovative archivists. At UCLA's Clark Library, Scott Jacobs, Derek Christian Quezada, Suzanne Tatian, and Carole Sommer all devised visionary approaches to archival hurdles. Special thanks are due to Scott and Suzanne, moreover, for making the Clark such a welcoming place since I first began using the archives there in 2003. Bruce Whiteman took time out of a busy schedule to attack from multiple angles the elusive source documents of the Camisards. Michael Widener at Yale University's Lillian Goldman Law Library also provided a great number of useful leads.

This book has received the benefit of outside support from a number of institutions and foundations. An Ahmanson-Getty Postdoctoral Fellowship at UCLA's Center for 17th- and 18th-Century Studies in 2009–2010 provided a felicitous site for research and engagement. I thank Ulrike Strasser, Christopher Wild, and Patrick Coleman for arranging a broad, provocative, and sociable program. The Marion and Jasper Whiting Foundation provided funds for travel to the Harry Ransom Center and the British National Archives. The College of Humanities and Fine Arts at the University of Massachusetts-Amherst provided crucial support during my fellowship year, and during my pretenure leave.

Portions of this work have been presented on panels chaired by Katherine Binhammer at the American Society for Eighteenth-Century Studies, Toni

Bowers at the MLA, and a third co-chaired by Sean Moore and myself at the MLA. The claims of the Introduction were sharpened through my participation in UCLA's year-long series, "Cultures of Communication: Theologies of Media in Early Modern Europe and Beyond," and through the invitation to present this project at the series' "Religious Media and the Birth of Aesthetics" conference. I am grateful to Adam Potkay for inviting me to present an early version of this project at The College of William and Mary in 2006, and to the engaged and hospitable faculty who participated in the seminar I delivered there.

An abridged version of chapter 3 appears in the volume, *Teaching the Transatlantic Eighteenth Century*; editors Cristobal Silva and Jennifer Frangos were galvanizing and accurate in their editorial advice. Sections of the Introduction and chapter 1 appear in *The Eighteenth Century: Theory and Interpretation*. I thank Tita Chico and two anonymous readers for suggestions and guidance with the articulation of complex argumentative threads.

At the English Department at the University of Massachusetts-Amherst, my first and deepest thanks go to Joseph Bartolomeo, who has served as a champion of my work from the moment I arrived, a mentor in all things pedagogical, and a bulwark of a departmental chair. My colleagues in the department have offered support and conversation that helped refine the claims of the project. In particular, Jen Adams, Joselyn Almeida-Beveridge, Joseph Black, Stephen Clingman, Suzanne Daly, Laura Doyle, Stephen Harris, and Peggy O'Brien offered useful comments during a faculty colloquium in 2008. I have been very lucky to have Aaron Winslow assist me in the preparation of this manuscript, thanks to a grant from the Dean of Humanities and Fine Arts, Joel Martin, and to support from the English Department.

I am especially grateful to Shannon McLachlan, my editor at Oxford University Press, for her keen eye for the project's potential and for her advocacy and enthusiasm throughout. Also at Oxford, Brendan O'Neill's near-immediate handling of all submission, revision, and production-related matters deserves special mention. Jaimee Biggins' production team made the final stages of editing transparent and efficient.

Over the past seven years, I have benefited from a set of exchanges with Judith Butler. For an intellectual as busy and as deeply engaged with the questions of our time, Professor Butler's assistance and conversation have been a profoundly generous act, and the essence of collegiality.

Janet Jakobsen is the contemporary scholar whose ability to illuminate the historical relationship between religion, capitalism, and sexuality is without parallel. Her reflections on *Critical Enthusiasm* have also been without parallel in shaping this project and cohering its claims. That this project has been the beneficiary of her attention and advice, is not only of great value to me, but will be felt and appreciated by any reader of this book.

I suppose it is true that when you read Marx you are never alone, but it is specifically true that when I read Marx, I do it always with Christina Crosby's crystalline redactions of the dialectical nature of the commodity-form, of labor-power, and of value, guiding my way. Since teaching me *Capital, Volume I* nearly twenty years ago, Christina has become a stalwart friend, and has talked luminously about the project with me for many years. I could not have learned Marx in the way I did, with the depth that I did, without her. And so it is also true that I could not have taken such pleasure in work without her guidance and friendship.

Friends and interlocutors who enriched the writing of this book include: David Alvarez, Nick Boggs, George Boulukos, Jennifer Charnofsky and Leslie Evans, Jack Halberstam, Grace Hong, my great friend Andrea Lawlor, Tom Lolis, Heather Love, Lisa Moore (who unstintingly edited an early version of the Introduction), Maggie Nelson, Brendan Prawdzik, my trusted friend Cornelia Reiner, Bethany Schneider, and Kate Thomas. Conversations with Hoang Phan helped hone the stakes of a historical materialist project. Carol Jennison has offered sustenance and support throughout the writing of this book.

My sister Amanda Rosenberg Hall has been an unflinching support to me, even as she roams the globe, helicoptering into remote locations to save lives. My brother-in-law Kevin Hall is also a tremendous support and a necessary resource for all things utopian and weird. My nephews, Rainer Harley Hall and Leo Edward Hall bring hilarity and buoyancy to all occasions. My aunt and uncle, Bobbie and Marvin Guter, and my cousins Avi and Lev Guter, are a greathearted and tireless team. And yes, Uncle Marvin, if they make a movie of *Critical Enthusiasm*, you can play the part of Karl Marx.

For my mother's clarity of vision in providing for my education, for her strength and resilience, and for her tutelage in comic timing, I will be always grateful.

My father, Stephen Rosenberg, passed away suddenly just as this book was nearing completion. Besides myself, he would have been the most excited to see this book in print, and it is with great sadness that I dedicate this book to his memory. My father's lessons were many; for me, they included carpentry (a skill he imparted patiently, if not always successfully), metaphysical inquiry, whistling, and the love of reading. But his pure enjoyment of research, teaching, and writing, and his commitment that my sister and I could attain lives of similar absorption and enjoyment, were, to me, his greatest and most humbling gifts.

Ruth Jennison's coruscating debate and editorial acumen have allowed me to aim for a scope and seriousness of argument that would have been impossible without her. More than this, her grasp of aesthetic form and her commitment to the stakes of historical inquiry have made thinking itself what I long hoped it could be.

Critical Enthusiasm

Introduction

*Religion, or Secularization: Dialectical Method
For the Literary Study of Secularisms*

*C*ritical Enthusiasm is a book about the historical narrative of modernity. In its broadest terms, *Critical Enthusiasm* considers the way modern culture conceives its own history as a narrative of secularization, and the processes by which this culture has generated historical doxa out of a perceived conflict between religious belief and secular epistemology. This conflict, as the product of secularism itself, cultivates a sensibility of "before" and "after," and demarcates modernity by way of a Fall: the outright unbraiding of culture from faith, a cleavage that splits time into a "now" of objectivity, and a "then" of credulous passions. Such a periodization, of course, works largely in secularism's favor. "Before," depicted as a chaos of sectarianism antagonism, enhances the allure of an "after" that ushers in rationality, dispels superstition, and renounces fiery universalism for cool, secular relativism. *Critical Enthusiasm* considers the composition of this secularization narrative in the Atlantic context of the late seventeenth and early eighteenth centuries, and sharpens our attention to the discourse and debates around religious enthusiasm.

Although scholars have found enthusiastic discourse to represent either a secularizing trend or else the persistence of religious ideology well into modernity, *Critical Enthusiasm* takes a divergent approach.[1] My study seeks to reframe the question, or perhaps to demonstrate that what appear to be two sides of a debate are essentially linked facets of a contradictory dyad. Enthusiasm is neither the hallmark of secularization nor the active remnant of a religious past; rather, the conclusion of *Critical Enthusiasm*—and I think it appropriate to anticipate this conclusion at the outset—is that enthusiastic discourse represents a uniquely dialectical encounter with the key features of early modernity. The singularity of this engagement is the result of enthusiasm's encoding, as a historicist narrative, the defining contradiction of the long eighteenth century. That contradiction is the spatio-temporal manifestation of the logic of capital accumulation.

In the following pages, the contradictions of capital accumulation will be clarified by reference to enthusiasm's mediation of the antipodean relationship between the constitution of the sovereign state and ideals of subjective freedom and autonomy on the one hand, and the transformation of the legislative apparatus to execute and regulate the extraction of profit from a work force compelled to wage labor, on the other. A perhaps less varnished way of saying this is that enthusiasm gives us an unparalleled historical window onto the intersection of early capitalism with religious discourse. The aim of this Introduction is both to offer an anatomy of this intersection, and to describe the theoretical basis of a dialectical approach to the correspondence of religion and capitalism.

****

The claim that the birth of modern historicist consciousness was coeval with the refinement of what has come to be known as the "secularization thesis," is itself nothing new. Scholars such as Talal Asad, Tomoko Masuzawa, Russell T. McCutcheon, and Gauri Visvanathan have demonstrated more or less definitively that historicism and secularization were woven together as national myth and literary fiction in an Atlantic circuit, and that this intersection not only informed social subjectivity, but the study and discourse on religion from the late eighteenth century onwards.[2] Insofar as my study departs from the extant research into secularization, it is largely to extrapolate two linked areas of concern: the formalization of enthusiastic immediacy in the ideals of the so-called "secular" sovereign early capitalist state, and the sedimentation of these processes in historicist discourse and in aesthetic form. This emphasis on form is elementary. Rather than tracing a history of religious affect in, for example, the seemingly uncanny portability of enchanted feelings, I follow Marx in a materialist understanding of religion as a "real abstraction," that is, a structure of thought and practice rooted in social relations.

Having adopted this provisional opposition between the history of feelings and the materialist exegesis of abstraction, let us now exceed it. Perhaps it would be more accurate to say that insofar as *Critical Enthusiasm* traces a history of religious affect, it does so by placing enthusiasm in the context of the onset of capital accumulation as the signal set of transformations contouring early modern life. Against this background, debate over the extent to which religious concepts were freed from or bound to their strictly theological referents becomes close to meaningless. The question, rather, has to do with the dialectical incorporation of religious forms into the logic of capitalist modernity itself. This incorporation, as we know from Marx's critique of Bruno Bauer in "On the Jewish Question," voices an eerie analogical echo between religious abstractions and the abstraction of the citizen-subject. On this point, Alberto Toscano has parsed Marx well: "Though it might transcend religious *content* by separating itself from any confessional determination, the state maintains religious *form* by embodying the alienated freedom of man in something external to him."[3] *Critical Enthusiasm* wagers that this formal integration of religious and civil abstractions makes its appearance not only in the ideology of the sovereign state, but also in the historicization and aestheticization of this state in the discourse of enthusiasm.

Scholars have tended to presume that Marx regarded religion as wholly reactionary, and secularization (so-called) as the embodiment of a progressive atheism. And yet, it was the Enlightenment *critique* of religion that received the greatest share of scrutiny over the span of Marx's oeuvre, in meticulous and passionately charged arguments against empiricist materialism and the "intrinsic contradictoriness of the secular basis."[4] If Marx unleashed a *"critique of the critique of religion,"* he did so because the Enlightenment critique of religion had taken the form of an empiricist attack on the "strangeness" of religious mythology, as if such strangeness could be simply lifted by the proper scrutiny.[5] Such, in any case, "was the kind of explanation favoured by the eighteenth century: in this way the Enlightenment endeavoured . . . to remove the appearance of strangeness from the mysterious shapes assumed by human relations whose origins they were unable to decipher."[6] For Marx, the empiricist presumption that religion could be overcome by thought partakes of an idealist sundering of intellectual production from its material context, and is as spectral and illusory as it supposes its theological target to be. This spectralizing tendency persists into even the dialectical antitheism of the Hegelian tradition, so long as the critique of religion takes the form of a conceptual rearrangement of the terms of transcendence, ungrounded in the institutional structures that buttress religious practices.

In seeking to restore the discourse of enthusiasm, in all its strangeness, to its material conditions in the milieu of capital accumulation, I offer a tripartite analysis of the relations between religious forms, aesthetic form, and the forms taken by social relations under capitalism. Here I risk an alliance with Marx's conviction, in the *Theses on Feuerbach*, that it is impossible to separate religious feelings from their institutional conditions:

> Feuerbach resolves the religious essence into the human essence. But the human essence is no abstraction inherent in each single individual. In reality it is the ensemble of the social relations . . . Feuerbach, consequently, does not see that the 'religious sentiment' is itself a social product, and that the abstract individual whom he analyses belongs to a particular form of society.[7]

The critique of Feuerbach's critique of religion zeroes in on Feuerbach's mistaken belief that religious feelings resolve themselves into secular ones. We do not need to agree with every turn of Marx's early work on religion to gain from this insight that there is no useful way to discuss a religious spirit outside the specific material contexts in which religious practices are rooted. Such a perspective does not rule out the possibility of resistant, liberationist theologies for which religion's offer of hope, communal comfort, and utopian thought has provided a real social basis for collective action and the unyielding resistance to exploitation and immiseration.[8] But it does insist that we track the often diametric tendencies of liberation and abstraction as the disclosure of another set of contradictions: the emergent contradictions of capital accumulation that characterized and shaped early modern life.

Enthusiastic Historicism

Although I will discuss the formal attributes of enthusiasm at greater length in the next section of this Introduction, for this moment we may understand religious enthusiasm in its most general sense, that is, as the passionate experience of unmediated communion with God, and as the capacity of individual subjects to know and understand divine order. "Seeing the light" is our contemporary idiom for the enthusiastic experience, and one that we will complicate considerably. This idiom, however, captures elements central to enthusiastic discourse in the early modern period, specifically the sudden experience of divine rapture that produces an instant comprehension of future events. The complex combination of immediacy and duration expressed by "seeing the light" can guide us as we specify our inquiry. Indeed, in what follows, I argue that in the period of our concern, enthusiastic discourse became a significant rubric for thinking historically, particularly in thinking through the economic transformations of early modernity. I center my analyses on moral philosophy, civil religion, legal theory, and on the structural rigor of Augustan poetry in an Atlantic context. I do so because it is in these texts, in this hemispheric circuit, and during this particular interval of time, that enthusiasm's impetuous fervor harnessed itself most explicitly to a historicist discourse. Reacquainting ourselves with this discourse and with an alliance that runs counter to canonical accounts of the coeval rise of historicist consciousness and secular rationality refreshes both our periodizations, as well as our narrative accounts, of the inception of modern culture. In doing so, I show that one of the defining features of religious enthusiasm—and one that was rearticulated in critical ways throughout the long eighteenth century—has been to some extent overlooked. That defining feature is enthusiasm's contradictory and dense relationship to historicity. The axial claim of this text, then, is that what has appeared to be enthusiasm's tempestuous, achronological relation to historical time became, in the period in question, a discursive logic that expressed not only critical aspects of this period's history, but a theory of history itself.

Enthusiasm, after all, is a temporal proposition. From the oracles of the ancients to the Dissenters of the English Civil War, enthusiastic prophesy is exemplified by an abrupt, rapturous prediction of future events, typically apocalyptic in nature. This concatenation of immediacy with an immeasurably long arc of time distinguishes enthusiasm from the timeworn truisms of priestly authority, and from the endlessly unfurling *present* of the status quo. Indeed, in some contrast to monarchical chronologies, which achingly progress at the pace of lineage reproduction and human maturation, enthusiastic politics produce uncharted, sudden transformations. If the fundamental anxiety about religious passion in the early modern period had to do both with its demonstrated threat to social order—the explosive undergirding of the English Civil Wars—as well as with enthusiasm's ongoing apocalyptic claims to thoroughly unmake the world and remake it anew, in what follows, I will show that, in the late seventeenth and early eighteenth centuries, this aspect of enthusiastic discourse began to inform a broader conception of history. Although its association with passionate prophesy and millenarian violence was not fully shed by the early eighteenth century, enthusiasm's strictly religious connotations were pried open in this period, and the term began to describe a number of other passions that shared with religious enthusiasm an expansive historical consciousness. I argue, in other words, that the putative "secularization" of enthusiasm, and, indeed, the critique of enthusiasm as well, did not eliminate or distill the force of religious passion so much as formalize enthusiasm's claims about end-times into a discourse of historical time.

Of course, from the standpoint of secularism, only a secular standpoint can grasp the movement of history correctly.[9] Religious historicism, after all, appears to be guided by a number of mystified conceptions, notably millenarian claims to history's "end" and implacable attachments to its chimerical origins. Moreover, between these arcane beginnings and cryptic ends, religious enthusiasm in particular appears to intoxicate itself on a transhistorical draught that moves by a cyclical or repetitive cadence from century to century. The synchronic peregrinations that mark "progress" for secular historicism are shattered in enthusiasm's contagious logic, which recurs rather than proceeds, so that Margery Kempe's fits of holy tears, for example, seem to leap the centuries, reappearing as the revelations of the Anabaptists, or as the street-corner testimonials of the Quakers; the passion of St. Paul refracts and ripens in Augustine's embrace of Christian virtue; the visions of the apostles are revisited and rendered in the ecstatic dancing of the Ranters. In what follows, I do not challenge this account of enthusiastic ahistoricism so much as demonstrate that its logic of recurrence and cyclical return in fact articulates crucial aspects of early modernity, specifically the development of Atlantic capitalism and the establishment of the various economic, discursive, and social apparati necessary to sustain the unprecedented accumulation and deployment of capital.

In making this argument, *Critical Enthusiasm* disputes the idea of modern history as a progressive disenchantment of spiritual meaning from the world, and it does so in the context of the humanities' recent reassessment of the longstanding split between secular and religious knowledges. A number of significant interventions have begun to unsettle the relatively uninterrupted critical dominance that the secularization thesis has enjoyed since Weber's *Protestant Ethic and the Spirit of Capitalism*. Such studies have undertaken the extensive task of negating this thesis, supplying alternate histories of the enduring forces of religious ideology, and taking the claims of religious knowledges on their own terms.[10] But while the humanities have done much work criticizing secularization narratives—complicating previous accounts of the residual nature of religious belief, broadening our conceptions of the secular, and establishing an archive of bewitching and charmed Enlightenments—we have not yet analyzed at length the ways in which secularization works *as* a narrative. *Critical Enthusiasm* supplies this analysis, not by describing the lingering enchantments of modernity—though certainly modern culture has its many enchanting facets—but rather by demonstrating that what has appeared to us as a secularization narrative would be more accurately described as the encoded history of a complex set of global and transatlantic processes of capital accumulation. The disclosure of this encoded history is a project for literary criticism, which seeks to discover, in the positive claims of historical texts, the lacunae, gaps, and resonating silences of history itself. Indeed, in order to comprehend the significance of secularization as a discursive phenomenon, we must begin to ask what the claims of secularization encoded, occluded, expressed, and transfigured.

If what was narratively encoded in the historicist logic of enthusiasm was the advent of capital accumulation, this was an occurrence that was itself dependent on a number of attendant shifts in statecraft, legal practice, economics, and culture. Linking these developments is an effort of literary-historical reconstruction, and it is so, in large part, because these connections are not immediately legible as such. In fact, as I will show, the early modern accumulation of capital is extremely difficult to comprehend, both because its processes were so vast, and because the capital that was produced was continually reinvested into the economic institutions of the Atlantic World. As tricky as this process is to recover, enthusiasm offers a unique hermeneutic. As the Atlantic World was swept into the drive for profit, and into the insistent re-employment of this profit to produce yet more profit, it was enthusiasm that came to capture the eternal return of this motion, the ghosted movements of capital across the oceans, urban landscapes and countryside, and the vanishing of profit back into the processes of production. It was enthusiasm that came to name the world-historical shifts that buffeted and reconfigured the early modern world, and it was enthusiasm—a concept that had traditionally connoted the linkage of the individual with the divine and with universal order—that came to name the subject's ability to know and understand these transformations: to apprehend the vast unseen.

Thus, although they ostensibly belong to disparate arenas of daily life, enthusiasm and economic development have long converged. The reason for this convergence is contained within the specific character of late-seventeenth- and early-eighteenth-century economic development, as well as within the conceptual history of enthusiasm. As subjects grappled with understanding the unprecedented advent of capital accumulation, along with the host of institutions that were put into place to ensure the flow of finance and profit in the Atlantic world, the historiographical conundrum that articulated itself most insistently concerned how these new systems had come to pass. Civil religion, moral philosophy, legal theory, and poetry provided the most wide-ranging models of historical change that the early eighteenth century could conceive, and, in these discourses, enthusiasm, long associated with futural, prophetic knowledges, was stretched to articulate the phenomenon of economic transformation itself. This movement of enthusiasm, from religious discourse, to moral philosophy, to economic thought, legal discourse, and on to poetry, is the general trajectory followed by this book. Such are the discursive touchstones we will use to sketch the relationships between religious ideology and the historical, aesthetic, and discursive forces of accumulation. In preparation for doing just that, a brief overview of enthusiasm is in order.

The Forms of Enthusiasm

Enthusiasm's career was inaugurated, it is said, with Socrates' concept of divine madness. Plato's redaction of Socrates in the *Phaedrus* offers a well-known and wary endorsement of this enthusiasm as a salutary, if capricious, form of inspiration that exhilarates the subject and sparks poetic production, though it does not bring forth reasoned argument. Although the poet is hardly the most vaunted citizen of the republic (this role is reserved for the philosopher) enthusiasm stirs and elevates the subject to a place "beyond the heavens." In this "beyond" the mind peeks at and develops an appetite for the Forms, and for understanding the systemic and interrelated nature of observable phenomena. Although these Forms are only revealed through philosophical labor, the inspiration to master them is an effect of enthusiastic possession.

This Platonic sense of enthusiasm proliferated throughout the classical and then the early modern periods with a shifting connotation that variously suggested scientific zeal, excessive rationality, poetic lunacy, or oracular prowess. In none of these cases, however, did enthusiasm simply denote an affect. Rather it functioned to describe an individual convoked to a state of excitement by the perception of something much larger than himself. Enthusiasm denoted a strong identification with one's object, an identification so strong that the distance between subject and object was thought to blur in an ecstasy of connotation. By invisible signs, the enthusiastic subject obtained an immediate comprehension of universal order—an order that, prior to the seventeenth century, was not confined to the religious sphere.

Indeed, in the sixteenth century, one might be called an enthusiast if one were overly identified with the abstractions of mathematics, or with the movements of the stars. In Longinian philosophy, one might experience an enthusiasm for poetry and believe oneself to be immediately in the presence of the poem's landscape or object. For centuries, enthusiasm was less a designation of spiritual meaning than it was a way of describing the acceleration of individual understanding into a kind of mania that presumed to comprehend the laws, order, or design of a complex universe. More precisely, enthusiasm named that intermediary space between subject and universal order: a charged site at which particular data are assembled into a broad-spectrum comprehension greatly in excess of any individual part.

During the English Civil Wars, enthusiasm's universal claims were amplified in the case of ecstatic communication with spirit and with the inspirations of laymen to a spiritual authority that circumvented monarch and church hierarchy. Whether one promoted religious enthusiasm as revolutionary practice—along with Abiezer Coppe, Gerrard Winstanley, and the movements for lay religion in the mid-seventeenth century or warned the populace of the dangers of religious passion—as did John Locke and Henry More—during the seventeenth century, enthusiasm became inextricable from the social context of revolution and unrest.[11] By the early eighteenth century, this immediate political urgency had dissipated to some extent, but enthusiasm remained heir to an association with subversive passions, as well as with claims to immediate, universal knowledge. As J.G.A. Pocock explains, enthusiasm was the "nearest thing to revolutionary consciousness . . . to be found in English history; and this had by no means been forgotten a century and a half after 1649."[12] In the first decade of the eighteenth century, the combination of enthusiasm's historical aura and the seductive potential of intuitive, passionate forms of understanding was explosive. With the memory of the Wars of Religion and the explosion of radical lay religions still fresh in mind, enthusiasm proliferated once again, signifying new sentiments and conceptual lineages. From the panacea for trade and consumption, to an expanding awareness of global traffic, enthusiasm became connected with an even more expansive range of references. From the experience of beauty to the self-discipline of virtue, from civic order to the faculty of judgment, enthusiasm registered a vast array of the political and cultural contradictions of the period.

Indeed, while it remained a topic of intense debate and suspicion as an inexorably dangerous force hostile to national peace, enthusiasm was reconceived as a principle of social comportment, in some cases as key to the peaceful functioning of civil society. If, at a time when the legacy of enthusiastic violence was still relatively fresh, enthusiasm took on a new life as a kind of social, regulatory passion, we might ask, how was this possible? Should it not have been the case that anything to do with enthusiasm would have been thoroughly proscribed, simply by association? Or, if enthusiasm had any positive connotations, one would imagine such connotations to be reserved for the most extreme factions, uttered in low tones in back alleys, the whispered allegiances of persecuted and paranoid sects. But this was not the case. Instead, enthusiasm was uttered loudly, by thinkers who were not back-alley prophets, but central philosophers of the Enlightenment. For the Third Earl of Shaftesbury, for example, enthusiasm became the foundation of a social ethics, and for him it underwrote concepts of individual sovereignty and market freedom. For Hume, enthusiasm came to describe the process of Parliamentary democracy. For Henry Stubbe, enthusiasm was key to reconstructing a history of Islam that operated in contiguity with Christian history rather than as its foil and supplement.

This explosion of enthusiasms marks the moment at which enthusiasm's seventeenth-century stigma of religiosity gave way, at least partially, to new aesthetic and epistemological projects. As Shaun Irlam has argued, enthusiasm embarked on an expansive journey throughout the century, eventuating in a poetics of the Romantic sublime, a worldly version of religious passion whose end was not spiritual ecstasy per se or even revolution, but rather "the positive accumulation of knowledge."[13] We may glimpse such an enthusiasm in Wordsworth's "Tintern Abbey," as the speaker's passion for nature quickens into a passion for his own mind and its processes:

>...And I have felt
> A presence that disturbs me with the joy
> Of elevated thoughts; a sense sublime
> Of something far more deeply interfused,
> Whose dwelling is the light of setting suns,
> And the round ocean and the living air,
> And the blue sky, and in the mind of man;
> A motion and a spirit, that impels
> All thinking things, all objects of all thought,
> And rolls through all things. Therefore am I still[14]

The progression from the positing of an unpicturable object, one that itself does not disturb the speaker, to the object's "presence", produces the disturbing joy of "something far more deeply interfused." Far more deeply than what, we wonder? But this is just one layer of wonderment that unfurls in strata of landscapes made simultaneously more material—the light of the setting sun in which something (a presence? an elevated thought?) might dwell—and more ethereal at once, teetering to a provisional halt at the subject, "still," at the edge of a line break, about to tilt over into something else, but posited here, amidst the congested radiance of light, sun, ocean, air, sky, mind of man.

This enthusiasm harmonizes more closely, I wager, with our contemporary sense of enthusiasm than, for example, the Platonic climb to the Forms. But such an enthusiasm is still in the future for our study. This is, after all, a Romantic enthusiasm, and one that, as Jon Mee has recently reminded us, was as problematic in the late-eighteenth and early nineteenth century, as bound up with the political-revolutionary subject and the heritage of Civil War, as it was embraced as an aspect of the transcendental subject.[15] If Romanticism brought to the foreground the epistemological drive of enthusiasm, in the early eighteenth century the knowledge accumulated under the banner of enthusiasm was of a different variety. Prior to the abstracted enormities of the Romantic sublime, enthusiasm was enlisted to another epistemological project: to provide an account of historical transition. Indeed it was, in critical ways, through the discourse of enthusiasm that early modernity came to represent itself as a specific period in time, to describe itself as occupying a temporal break with the past, and to generate a sense of what that break consisted of.

To reconstruct this discursive transformation we will have to abandon the misty fields of Romantic poetry and embed ourselves in the somewhat drier genres of the early Enlightenment. Committing ourselves thusly will not only deliver us a greater historical purchase on the problem of enthusiasm's capaciousness in these later periods, but will open up seemingly austere Enlightenment genres to a number of prismatic problematics. Although it is not without precedent, such work runs against the grain of traditional approaches to both religious and economic history. Scholars of secularization often consider the transformation of religious thought as separate from the history of capitalism, while scholars of economic development often fail to account for the tenacious force of religious ideas, except as the residuum of an obsolete social order. Aside from the considerable oeuvres of Christopher Hill and J.G.A. Pocock, who take quite opposite positions on the period, this schism has been a longstanding one within the humanities. This book parts company with a standard account of the relationship between religious history and economic history, in which the rise of a modern, secular capitalist society is accompanied by a decline in religious enthusiasm. Instead, we will ask: Why did enthusiasm undergo the kinds of discursive proliferations just described? What historical conjunctures gave rise to this shift, and how can we begin to reconstruct them?

Entry Points: Secularization Studies and Postsecular Historicism

The humanities' reconsideration of the Enlightenment has provided a number of methodological options with which to consider the question at hand. Recent work has begun to allow for more dynamic relationships between religious passions that have been coded as nonmodern and the rational, scientific methods we have come to associate with modernity. In re-historicizing modernity, we have admitted entrance to these religious passions, not as bearers of an obsolescent past, but as critical formations that act in concert with industrialization, nation building, and the refining of the modern subject. Contemporary scholarship in the history of feeling reflects the centrality that questions of affect, affinity, and the supra-empirical have taken on within the disciplines.[16] Building on such work, we may engage the problem of enthusiasm from a metahistorical angle, and argue that, not only does feeling have a history, but that the discourse around feeling has framed the way we think about history since the early Enlightenment. The exemplary instance here, of course, is Weber's celebrated argument that capitalism only truly established itself once religious enthusiasm had been converted into an enthusiasm for capital accumulation. But Weber's conjuncture of enthusiasm and capitalism was not new, even in the nineteenth century. Thus, we may ask why religious enthusiasm is the key—not just for Weber, but for seventeenth and eighteenth-century thinkers as well—to periodizing modernity? Why is it, in other words, that we have come to conceptualize Western history in general, and the economic transformation of modern culture in particular, in terms of a category of ecstatic feeling?

One potential, though partial, approach may be to narrow the terms of the question, and note that, in the late seventeenth and early eighteenth centuries—a period during which religious ideologies maintained a powerful hold over the national psyche, over aesthetic conventions, and over the theorization of reason itself—the discourse of enthusiasm became a way of thinking about the very concept of historical change. This approach does not aim to invert the Weberian tradition as such; it does not disclose the incomplete secularization of the world, or describe alternate processes of modernization that leave religious frameworks intact.[17] As I noted earlier, a number of recent studies have begun to amass enough critical force to sway academic opinion significantly in this direction, and to open up the disciplines to a rapprochement between religion and modern culture. Instead, I wish to historicize the central claims of the Weberian tradition itself. I wish to argue, not so much that enchantment persists, but that the discursive force of enchantment has been a defining framework for Western historicist thought since the early Enlightenment.[18]

In the past decade or so, a subfield or tendency has emerged within the humanities, commonly recognized as secularization studies. Although secularization studies approaches the problem of modernization and secularization from a number of disciplinary angles, a starting point common to the range of its practitioners is that modernity is much more complexly enchanted than previous accounts have posited, and that this state of complex enchantment constitutes a challenge to social histories, literary studies, and political theories that have binarized empiricist and supra-empiricist techniques of knowledge production.[19] Dipesh Chakrabarty encapsulates the central claim of this approach, noting that historical work itself has been hampered by our inability to think modernity and enchantment together: "The moment we think of the world as disenchanted . . . we set limits to the ways the past can be narrated."[20] Grounding secularization studies' reconsideration of the history of the passions is the understanding that such reconsideration ultimately entails and makes possible an overturning of the history of history itself; it upends the presumption that as history "proceeds," so does the progress of secularization, of disenchantment, and of the stripping of magic from the world.

This book takes as its point of departure the openings cleared by secularization studies for the serious investigation of enthusiastic passion as an object of study. Such work has made it possible to describe the contexts that give form to the passions at any given period in time, such that *enchantment* now ceases to mean simply some vague superfluity of feeling, and has come to reveal its concrete, defining attributes. This book takes seriously not only this call for the historicization of passion, but also, and more importantly, the need for some account of the causes of the shifts in meaning experienced by passion. Accordingly, *Critical Enthusiasm* advocates broadening our focus from the phenomenon of enthusiastic feeling to the formal qualities of enthusiastic discourse. In inquiring why enthusiastic passion appears to recur from one period to another, we thus ask: What social relationships and historical phenomena are encoded in this recurrence? What was specific to the late seventeenth and early eighteenth centuries such that *enthusiasm* came to articulate these relationships and events in the particular ways that it did? How can the study of enthusiasm in a number of generic encodings reveal these relationships and their structuring role in the early modern period? And finally, how is it that enthusiasm and economic transformation form such a uniquely productive friction, and what were the historical reasons for the discursive detonations generated by bringing these two concepts together?

Hermeneutics of Accumulation

My proposition that we consider religious, economic, and cultural concerns together is in itself not particularly controversial. The complex historiographical question of recovering the traces of these conjunctures in the discourse of enthusiasm, however, demands the resources of a variety of disciplinary approaches. In registering the conditions that underwrote the transformations and innovations of this period, the discourse of enthusiasm became complexly interwoven with the acts of imperialist aggression and the institutional transformations and economic sea changes that accompanied the opening strains of commercial society. Accordingly, *Critical Enthusiasm* draws on a number of intellectual traditions in order to recover this history. I begin with the tradition of moral philosophy, which, more than any other Enlightenment discourse, envisioned the possibility of expanding enthusiasm's range and application. As the discursive keystone to which the book returns to over the course of the argument, moral philosophy represents the period's most capacious epistemological field, reaching back to the origins of political theory, and stretching forward to morph into aesthetics, ethics, political economy, and jurisprudence. The focus on moral philosophy allows us to move between these disciplines and to historicize them at the same time. Indeed, returning to moral philosophy's transformation of enthusiasm returns us to the discourse that formed the seeds of ethics, jurisprudence, aesthetics, and political economy—all of which I treat in what is to come.[21]

In compiling this interdisciplinary compendium of enthusiastic thought, I create what we may think of as a *hermeneutic of accumulation*. As I will show, the advent of capital accumulation was dependent on a host of attendant structural shifts in eighteenth-century politics, economics, and culture. We thus need a hermeneutic adequate to the sprawling world of eighteenth-century finance and economic development, and one that gives an account of the particularly volatile transitions taking place at the levels of cultural discourse, economic change, and statecraft. With this hermeneutic, I will show that capital accumulation is accompanied by a number of other major transformations: the shift from common to statute law (and the corresponding centralization of Parliamentary power), the racialization of labor, urbanization, and the development of agrarian capitalism. All these shifts come to be mediated, in one way or another, in the discourse of enthusiasm. *Critical Enthusiasm* traces this complex history across the Atlantic and back again, and through the underbelly of England's urban and agricultural transition zones: those areas most rapidly changed by the forces of economic modernization.

Such an expansive perspective places *Critical Enthusiasm* within a vibrant field of hemispheric study that has emerged in the past several decades within the humanities. The spreading of literary, historical, and intellectual study beyond the confines of the nation-state has been an energizing and indispensable movement forward for humanistic research. Enthusiasm is primed for such an energization, since this discourse has long been a transatlantic concept. In studies that span the English Civil Wars to the Great Awakening, enthusiasm has allowed scholars of religion to chart the movement of concepts, beliefs, and practices between England and America.[22] Building on this work, I show that the movement of enthusiasm across the Atlantic registers other such movements that are perhaps more occluded and harder to track.

The Secret of Capital Accumulation

We might best describe these occluded movements under the banner of capital accumulation. The action of capital accumulation flouts the borders of nation-states, as the expansion of global tracks of labor, production, and circulation describe new boundaries and territories, on land and at sea. As Giovanni Arrighi, Samir Amin, Ian Baucom, and David Harvey have shown, capital accumulation is the signal material condition that made possible the establishment of the modern world system. Thus, while a grasp of the history and procedures of capital accumulation can be a demanding task—one that requires a deciphering of early eighteenth-century history and culture from a number of angles—such a grasp will be critical to our understanding of transatlantic economic and political development. Moreover, because accumulation itself often takes place in hidden or occulted ways, and because accumulation is made up of a complex interweaving of financial, social, ideological, and structural transformations, it can be very difficult to discern when or where an act of accumulation is taking place.

Let us then begin this inquiry with what appears to be a simple question: what is capital accumulation? Immediately, we are a bit confounded, because accumulation includes and yet is in no way limited to the simple accumulation of goods. Ian Baucom explains accumulation as a process that far exceeds the simple act of exchange:

> [W]arehouses and shop windows are but one of the two fundamental types of place in which capital accumulates, that, indeed, the accumulative protocols of commodity capitalism alternately precede and follow another practice of accumulation, an accumulation of value not in the factory zones and the shopping and consumption districts of capital, but in its quarters of high finance, its stock exchanges, its bond, credit, and currency markets, the money zones that Arrighi, following John Ruggie, calls capital's "spaces-of-flows."[23]

More than a simple pile of commodities, accumulation denotes the endless movement of capital—within the nation-state, across the Atlantic, around the world. In what follows, I follow scholars like Arrighi and Baucom in arguing that accumulation is a powerful and necessary hermeneutic for literary study of the eighteenth century. And I build on their work to show that the history of these "spaces-of-flows" is uniquely legible in the debates around enthusiasm and through the imprint of religious thought in literature, poetry, philosophy and political theory.

Critics who research "spaces-of-flows" understand the movement of history, at least in part, through tracking the movement of money. This approach has contributed as much to our understanding of the eighteenth century as it has to our grasp on the twentieth and twenty-first. One of the great virtues of this approach, in fact, has been to open up the field of eighteenth-century studies to a transatlantic milieu of accumulation that exceeds the history of any one particular nation-state. In following these exciting new histories of the movement of money, however, we come to recognize that the spaces-of-flows themselves support and are supported by a vast array of other institutions and forces. Along with the spaces-of-flows—those vertiginous movements of high finance—capital accumulation depends upon the forces and relationships that are put into place to make this breathtaking movement possible. From the legal apparati that serve to protect the burgeoning institution of private property to the racialization of labor, capital accumulation requires an array of interconnected practices in order to establish itself.

The mechanisms of capital accumulation, both within the nation-state and extending out from it, are a complex bundle of institutions, ideologies, and the application of sheer force. These institutional markers are what we will use to track the movement of capital accumulation, as this movement is not itself particularly self-evident. Capital accumulation does not necessarily produce lavish edifices or luxury goods. It is not visible as the surface appearance of wealth or the development of trade routes. In fact, in the early eighteenth century, the intensification of luxury and lavishness could just as easily have described the heights of Spanish or French colonial rule, or late imperial China—empires that had flourished without a resultant large-scale capitalist transformation of the home country—as the economic ascendance of England.[24] This forces us to re-pose the question: If capital accumulation is not necessarily or immediately the accretion of wealth or goods, what is it?

At the most basic level, capital accumulation is the complex manner in which profit is reinvested back into the means of production. As Harvey and other have pointed out, Marx was the first to articulate the ephemeral quality of accumulation. And while Marx's economic analysis has been superseded in many respects, his account of accumulation stands as a viable description of one of the fundamentals of capitalist profit-production: the first and most significant condition of accumulation is that the capitalist must "sell commodities" and "reconvert into capital the greater part of the money received from their sale."[25] Accumulation is not the establishment of a pile of wealth, but rather the constant movement of profit in order to make more profit. In this way, accumulation relies on money's apparent vanishing, its expeditious transfer and reinvestment back into the processes of production. In reconverting money into capital, enterprising eighteenth-century proto-capitalists were able to realize more profit from the labor-power of their employees than they paid out in both wages and raw materials. Additionally, they began to invest in innovations in production in an effort to increase their own rates of profit. The effects of this innovation were impossible to avoid; such changes in production propelled England toward its Industrial Revolution. But the constant process of reinvesting money into the processes of production—a process that, to the naked eye, appeared to make profits disappear—made accumulation *itself* hard to track or visualize.

Fugitive Accumulation

"Fugitive accumulation" is a mnemonic we might use to understand the evaporative action of accumulation, and the kinds of analytic work required to distill it from the record of the past. One of the ways we can do this work is to reconstruct the process of accumulation by the historical marks that it leaves. Indeed, accumulation links far-flung nations and territories in the singular but often contradictory drive toward profit. As Arrighi explains, from the retrospect of the twentieth and twenty-first centuries, the history of spaces of flows is hidden within the vast internationalization of markets that occurred during the early modern period. Our conventional understanding of early modernity as more territorially grounded than postmodern capitalism is thus, for Arrighi, a habit of thought that obscures the complexity of early modern capitalism:

> [T]he conventional spaces-of-places ... are wholly inadequate to describe, let alone explain, the development of the singular spaces-of-flows engendered by the 'internationalization' of international relations within the organizational structures of world capitalism. Given this inadequacy, non-territorial spaces-of-flows may have existed unnoticed alongside the national spaces-of-places throughout the history of the modern world system.[26]

The spaces-of-flows that comprise the system of circulation—no matter how "non-territorial" they may appear—are themselves supported by an array of other institutions put into place to transform geographies, relationships, and forms of labor.[27] We are reminded here of John Brewer's important intervention in liberal histories that depict Britain as a "lightly administered" state. Against such accounts, Brewer showed us that the British state was not just guided by flows of money, but it was a true force, centralized in critical ways as early as the seventeenth century, and maintained by a standing army and a vast colonial enterprise.[28]

Brewer's conclusions are echoed by Robin Blackburn, who eloquently describes the ways in which accumulation was ultimately inextricable from the strengthening of the state:

> [T]he consolidation of capitalist relations ... required the protection and patronage of a concentrated social power, the state, with its Acts of enclosure, its labour statutes

> and Poor Laws, armed bodies of men, contracts for supply . . . Only with the sponsorship of the state could incipiently capitalist forces find the scale and stability they needed to make the transition to industrial accumulation proper.[29]

This intersection of political and economic might was, furthermore, profoundly transatlantic:

> Mercantile initiative and credit could, given the transatlantic slave trade, directly sponsor the expansion of the plantation, enabling the planter to ignore any restraint which natural reproduction would have imposed. Thus . . . the planter . . . was goaded further down the path of accumulation by the eager demands and exactions of merchants who were also suppliers and creditors.[30]

As critics such as Saree Makdisi, Peter Linebaugh, and Marcus Rediker have argued, in order to reinvest surplus profit back into the means of production, capitalism established a transatlantic system of expropriation and plunder, a coercive system of wage labor, an ideological imaginary that seized and transformed the language of faith and belief, and a state-legal apparatus that ensured and protected the flow of profit.[31] It was this system of exploitation that was not yet naturalized to the early eighteenth century. And it was this system that depended on the institutionalization of an entire matrix of domination and development in order to begin to function.

The onset of capital accumulation marked nothing short of a massive historical break at every level of eighteenth-century society. However, this was a historical break that, in important ways, covered its own tracks. As capital continually disappeared into the production process, eighteenth-century poets, authors, philosophers, and political theorists reached for the language and the conceptual frameworks to describe what had begun to happen. Looking back on the eighteenth century, it was clear to Marx that the political economists and moral philosophers had made a mistake in confusing "capitalist production with hoarding"[32] or with a quantum of wealth that is immediately graspable either physically or conceptually.

And yet some of these "mistakes" blossomed into ornate formulations in the eighteenth century. From fabrications about the despotism of the ancients or the mythic native industriousness of the peasantry, from gothic novels conjuring the opulence of the East to nationalist poetry lauding the sacrifice of natural resources to the glories of British trade, the century's writers developed quite a roster of apocryphal accounts to describe the cultural shift that they sensed themselves to be occupying. In this sense, the "mistakes" of the political economists (and the novelists, poets, and philosophers) were not errors so much as rich symptomatic mediations of the real historical conditions of capital accumulation. It will be our analytic task to read backward from the imprint of these "mistakes" to the record of accumulation that they conceal and encode at once. For this project, enthusiasm provides a unique guide.

Enthusiastic Encodings I: The Mediation of History

As we can see just from the brief sketch of the term's changing significations, enthusiasm is a historically dense term. By this I mean that it both absorbs the contradictions and relations specific to a particular historical conjuncture, and that it tends to trail the residue of these associations with it as it passes into new circumstances and absorbs new relations. Enthusiasm's signification is thus extremely specific to its historical moment, while it suggests a long historical arc, a sort of lariat of significations. We might think of this motion in the following way: For a term such as *enthusiasm* that undergoes strong periodic iterations, meaning is configured via loops of contextual connotation, accrued at various moments, and coiling into distinct architectures at different points in time. Each coiling knits arcane iterations of enthusiasm together with emergent ones, so that the significance of the term, at any given moment, is a heterogeneous accumulation. This lariat structure requires an analytic strategy sensitive to the historical density of discourse formation, and recalls Fredric Jameson's definition of genre critique as the analysis of discourse's "formal sedimentation." Form, argues Jameson, "is imminently and intrinsically an ideology in its own right. When such forms are reappropriated and refashioned in quite different social and cultural contexts, this message persists and must be fully reckoned into the new form."[33]

Jameson's approach is opened further by Baucom, who sees genre critique as

> a general theory of historicist interpretation, a historicist hermeneutic which allows us to honor the Lukácsian injunction to situate literary texts within the "historical peculiarity" of the "age" in which they are produced while simultaneously to recognize that such historical situations (or ages or periods) are not sui generis but host to prior such moments, not autonomous but invested by a range of pasts which are not, in fact, past.[34]

This book intends to analyze the formal sedimentation of the discourse of enthusiasm in the late seventeenth and early eighteenth centuries, and to uncoil the peculiarities that accreted to this term in this period. To do so will require a considerable effort of contextualization and reconstruction in order to recognize the forces registered by enthusiastic discourse in the early modern period. It will also require some discipline in estrangement. Enthusiasm as we know it today is enrobed in a set of historical inscriptions and specific to our own situation in such a way that these inscriptions cannot be interpreted directly. The current traits of enthusiasm have much to teach us about enthusiasm's historical significance, not because the term has remained static over the centuries, but because the sedimentations and wrinkles of meaning accrued by the term work as a suggestive cipher for us as we begin our investigations.

As we embark on this work of estrangement, then, let us ask ourselves what enthusiasm signifies at present. Though *enthusiasm* evokes an expansive, unreserved comportment, we find that the term itself is generally reserved for relatively specific instances. Individuals or groups that are categorized as enthusiastic within the twentieth and twenty-first centuries generally fall into one of three camps: the love besotted, the political, and the religious. In the first case, one would almost undoubtedly turn to the language of affect in an effort to capture this essence of enthusiasm. The love of a particular hobby to the exclusion of the fulfillment of other needs—indeed, an animating passion that exceeds reason—exemplifies this application of enthusiasm.[35] As the description of an absorbing interest, the designation "enthusiast" seems endlessly portable, and is applied in common parlance to any number of passions. The sheer number of special-interest magazines and web sites that qualify *enthusiast* with a prodigious litany of objects—such as *Game Enthusiast, Chess Enthusiastt, Rod-and-Reel Enthusiast, Starry Night Enthusiast*, and so on—bears out this claim.

The enthusiastic subject might be besotted with anything in particular, from starry nights, to recreational drugs, to another human, but in any case the designation of an enthusiastic love suggests that the subject feels for the object what Colin Jager has described as an "existential commitment."[36] Such commitment is not simply analogous to a religious emotion; love for the object does not resemble a religion because it is a similar sort of feeling—namely, a rapture that is equivalent to spiritual rapture—but rather because, like religion, it takes the form of an "enacted discipline."[37] Enthusiasm structures the life of the enthusiast and, religious or not, all enthusiasts tend to accrue the designation "fanatical" for precisely this reason: the enthusiastic object's structuring role for the enthusiast.

Whereas the lover (or the chess-player, or the astrologer) might find himself classified as an enthusiast based largely on the degree to which his "existential commitment" structures his life, in the case of today's religious enthusiast, there is another mitigating factor. Here, the "enthusiastic" designation tends to depend not only on the level of commitment, but also, and centrally on the distance between the religious group in question and state support in the form of funding and official recognition. This is not an encyclopedic definition of enthusiasm but rather a working definition that seems to capture with reasonable accuracy the current application of the term in reference to religious practice and belief.[38] As we study the heritage of enthusiasm, we will perhaps reflect that the distance between a religious group and the designation of enthusiast echoes in provocative ways enthusiasm's early modern articulations.

For the field of the political, this distance from the authorizing hand of the state is repeated, and uncannily so. On this topic, there has been a renaissance of critical attention, and recently scholars have highlighted the centrality of enthusiasm to the philosophical tradition. In addressing Kant's *Conflict of the Faculties*, Slavoj Zizek, for example, describes revolutionary passion as a critical instance of enthusiasm. The French Revolution's "true significance," argues Zizek, "does not reside in what actually went on in Paris . . . but in the enthusiastic response that the events generated in the eyes of sympathetic observers all around Europe."[39] Zizek goes on to argue that Kantian enthusiasm represents the critical potential of political feeling, that sublime and incalculable enthusiasm awakened "in the heart of all spectators," that represents the true historical content of revolutionary action. Similarly for Alain Badiou, enthusiasm describes the revolutionary subject's "commitment to a truth . . . [his] absorption in a compelling task or cause, a sense of elation, of being caught up in something that transcends all petty, private, or material concerns."[40] In Jean-Francois Lyotard's account—also drawing on Kant—enthusiasm represents a political spectatorship that coheres around unanticipated or incalculable historical events. In these works, enthusiasm describes a relation between the self and the larger social world, that is, an account that exceeds the private, and mirrors religious passion as a universalizing structure of thought.

Zizek, Badiou and Lyotard draw not only on the Kantian conception of political sentiment, but also on the Hegelian tradition of enthusiasm as an "immediate action"[41] that precedes and inspires ethical comportment. For Hegel, rather famously, enthusiasm represents the longing of the mind for an immediacy of knowledge and identification with Spirit—a longing that must be sublated into dialectical thought. En route to scientific knowledge, the immediate, or primitive, stage of sense-consciousness is overcome, that "sort of ecstatic enthusiasm which starts straight off with absolute knowledge, as if shot out of a pistol."[42] Although we do not have the space here to enter into a lengthy analysis of the *Phenomenology*, it is worth noting that Hegel exposes what he understands as the epistemological conditions that underlie the subject's attraction to enthusiastic immediacy. Indeed, the pistol trope functions as a guiding shorthand for the project of the *Phenomenology*; in transposing enthusiasm's revolutionary violence to the analytic setting, Hegel resignifies the violent immediacy of enthusiasm as itself a mediated form of knowledge. This resignification is crucial to Hegel's critique of religion, and it is not insignificant that such a critique zeroes in on enthusiasm as a fantasy of immediacy that relies on a set of conjectures and subjective intercessions in order to be apprehensible.[43]

The current uptake of enthusiasm in theoretical discourse is rooted in a Hegelian tradition for which enthusiasm furnishes a critical mode of thinking through the complex graftings of subject and world. It is precisely this tradition that Marx upends and refunctions for a materialist dialectic that finds new resonances in Zizek, Badiou and Lyotard, albeit in markedly different ways. To parse the distinctions between these strands of thoughts would take us significantly off course. Let us instead return to Marx's critique of Hegel's theory of mediation itself. In this critique, Marx takes his distance from Hegel largely around the question of the mediator. For Hegel, the subject mediates all knowledge; no knowledge is immediately transparent without the intervening presence of the subject. For Marx, however, it is the signal contradictions of capitalism that comprise the preeminent mediations of modern social life. Discourse, knowledge, and the disciplines are all based in the foundational contradiction of the commodity form, in which qualitative differences between objects are suppressed in rendering equivalent all commodities to money, and in the contradictions of labor power, in which qualitative differences in human production and output are rendered equivalent in wages. This correction of the Hegelian idealist mediation is indicated by Marx in his famous pronouncement that he will stand Hegel "on his head":

> The mystification which the dialectic suffers in Hegel's hands by no means prevents him from being the first to present its general forms of motion in a comprehensive and conscious manner. With him it is standing on its head. It must be inverted, in order to discover the rational kernel within the mystical shell.

Scholars have not infrequently interpreted Marx's inversion as a kind of deadening of the allure of metaphysics, or at least they have presumed that such an inversion, with its routing out of the glittering "mystical" climes in favor of the seemingly dogmatic and dry "kernel," could not have much to add to a study of religious concepts. But this "rational kernel" presents the possibility of a much richer engagement with the problem of secularization and with its material contexts than has been previously thought. To elucidate this engagement, let us flesh out a bit further the relationship between religious discourse and the contradictions of capitalism.

Enthusiastic Encodings II: The Commodity Form

I argued earlier, in the section titled "The Secret of Capital Accumulation," that capital accumulation was not necessarily legible in "the surface appearance of wealth." This claim is largely true. Capital accumulation is not equivalent to the appearance of wealth. And yet, an anatomic relationship does obtain between the appearance of wealth and the processes of capital accumulation. Let us take some time to illuminate this rapport.

Capital accumulation is a counterintuitive construction: insofar as the cardinal rule, for the capitalist, is to reinvest profit back into the means of production, the all-too visible onslaught of commodities that capitalism generates represents both a vanishing point of profit and the product of an ongoing process of capital accumulation. Such, at least, was Marx's classic formulation: "The wealth of societies in which the capitalist mode of production prevails appears as an 'immense collection of commodities.'"[44] At first glance, we may be tempted to read this declaration as the announcement of a simple, representational relation that obtains between the capitalist mode of production and the commodity. The commodity is not, however, equivalent to capital accumulation; it is the *form of appearance* of the capitalist mode of production. It is so, not because the commodity is the product of capitalism, but more precisely because, as the product of capitalism, the commodity's phantom-like objectivity[45] obscures the real social relations upon which its production is based:

> The mysterious character of the commodity-form consists therefore simply in the face that the commodity reflects the social characteristics of men's own labour as

objective characteristics of the products of labour themselves, as the socio-natural properties of these things . . . Through this substitution, the products of labour become commodities, sensuous things which are at the same time supersensible or social.[46]

The fetishism of the commodity—what Marx terms the commodity's "secret"—is the result of this substitution of the commodity's autonomy for the relations between persons, and for the relations of production that undergird capital accumulation.

For Marx the ghostliness of a culture populated by objects that appear to interact of their own animate accord, is an index of the advancement of capital accumulation. And yet, the ghostliness of capitalism cannot be simply taken apart by empiricist attack or analyzed into mundanity. This is because the ghostliness of capitalism is *real;* it is a real abstraction. Under capitalism, an object is attributed a supernatural aura, or worth, through a process that extinguishes its material specificity while generating its value. "As use-values, commodities differ above all in quality, while as exchange-values they can only differ in quantity, and therefore do not contain an atom of use-value."[47] The contradictory relation of use and exchange is the basis of the form of value, and thus, although it is an abstraction, it has actual social substance and significance. Harvey parses this key contradiction as a conceptual aporia at the heart of the commodity: "Everything has to be material in order to be validly considered as real, but . . . the materiality of the commodity can[not] tell you anything you might want to know about what it is that makes [all commodities] commensurable."[48]

Commodification binds the specificity of the object to its exchange-value in a tense, dialectical suture that results not only in the violent eclipse of qualitative differences between objects, but also the celestializing of the object *qua* commodity. And while we might have imagined religion as the last place to look for a clarification of this process, it is religious language precisely that functions to expose the mechanisms upon which the apparently self-evident, self-sustaining forms of market value depend: "A commodity appears at first sight an extremely obvious, trivial thing. But its analysis brings out that it is a very strange thing abounding in metaphysical subtleties and theological niceties."[49] Scholars have at times interpreted these lines as an outright denigration of the commodity and religion at once. But this is a reduction of Marx's argument. For here, as in many analytical turns of *Capital*, Marx draws on religion as the only and most apt analogy to explain the abstraction of persons and labor, and the autonomization of things, under capitalism. Toscano reminds us that Marx's understanding of the commodity form allows us unique purchase on the question of secularization. Via a return to Derrida's *Specters of Marx*, Toscano provides an unambiguous account of the role of Marx's religious analogies in understanding the uncanny animation of capitalism's object-world:

> If we are to follow Derrida, religion itself can be regarded as paradigmatic of the processes of autonomisation mercilessly pursued by Marx throughout the domains of ideology and abstraction. As Derrida notes . . . "only the reference to the religious world allows one to explain the autonomy of the ideological, and thus its proper efficacy, its incorporation in apparatuses that are endowed not only with an apparent autonomy but a sort of automaticity . . . as soon as there is production, there is fetishism: idealization, autonomization . . . dematerialization and spectral incorporation."[50]

The commodity appears autonomous as a result of the antinomies of its form; it attains value to the extent that both its qualitative specificity and the real social relations by which it is produced are suppressed. This commodity fetish, furthermore, is the autonomization on which capitalist abstraction in general ("idealization . . . dematerialization and spectral incorporation") is based. Via Toscano, we see that this process of fetishism is formally religious, that is, commodity fetishism can be comprehended only via the abstraction and supernaturalization formerly proper to religion: ". . . there is considerable truth to Jacques Derrida's indication regarding 'the absolute privilege that Marx always grants to religion, to ideology as religion, mysticism, or theology, in his analysis of ideology in general'; at least if by privilege we understand the necessity of the religious 'analogy,' for grasping the process of autonomisation that characterizes a society—that of capitalism—in which men are dominated by abstractions."[51] Alongside Toscano, and following Derrida, then, we can say that the commodity abounds in "theological niceties" exactly to the extent that its supernatural autonomization is the *real appearance* of the social contradictions of capitalism. The religious analogy is more than a figurative adjutant; it is the form taken by the antagonisms that structure capitalist production.

In *Critical Enthusiasm*, I strive to give the religious analogization of abstraction a historical context in the early eighteenth century. To that end, we can return Derrida's argument to Marx's assertion at the outset of *Capital* that the "wealth of societies in which the capitalist mode of production prevails appears as an immense collection of commodities." Not only is the fetish itself actual, but the autonomization of the fetish is the form of appearance of the vanishing action of capital accumulation at large. Throughout this book, we will study both the commodity-logic and the capital-accumulative logic of the discourse of enthusiasm. And it will be the argument of *Critical Enthusiasm* that the autonomization of the fetish finds its echo—in an uncanny discursive reuptake—not only in the language of religion, but more specifically in enthusiasm. As we have shown, enthusiasm classically connoted an autonomous relation between the subject and divine—or universal—order. In a curious redundancy, with the onset of early modernity, enthusiasm becomes the discursive-aesthetic carriage of not only the processes of religious autonomization, but also the autonomization of commodities, and the abstraction of persons, in the context of capital accumulation. Put another way, the formally religious secret of the commodity form finds its echo, perhaps perversely, in enthusiasm's own fantasies of autonomy and immediacy.

If this nexus feels counterintuitive, Raymond Williams's well-known formulation may assist us in comprehending the contradictory ways in which the residual language of religious autonomization comes to code the emergent logic of capital accumulation. What appears residual in moments of great cultural transition, argues Williams, is in fact an integral part of the dominant order. Indeed, this residue conditions the dominant order "as an effective element of the present. Thus, certain experiences . . . which cannot be expressed . . . in terms of the dominant culture . . . are practiced on the basis of the residue."[52] Drawing on a Williams-esque lexicon, we can say that the fantasies of immediacy long articulated in the rhetoric of enthusiasm, give shape to the ideologies of autonomy that attend the birth of commodity culture and the relations of capital accumulation. Furthermore, these fantasies, as I will show, are discursively reconfigured to articulate ideals of state sovereignty and the autonomous, self-regulating subject of that state. All of these topics—the commodity, the sovereign state, the autonomous subject, and the aesthetics mentioned earlier—will receive exegesis in the chapters that are to come, and will be placed in the context of the vanishing tendencies of capital accumulation.

In what remains of this Introduction, I provide redactions of the chapters that follow. I have divided the body of this work into two sections called simply "Time" and "Space," and they seek to elucidate the spatio-temporal dimensions of capital accumulation. In the portion titled "Time," I describe the intersection of capital accumulation and enthusiastic historicism. I pay particular attention here to both the historicization of comparative monotheisms and the legitimation of state sovereignty via the changing status of belief in legal discourse of the late-seventeenth and early-eighteenth centuries. In the second half, "Space," I work with poetry as well as archival materials—religious manifestos, statute laws, and documents of colonial policy—to describe the territorial and architectural transformation and production of the Atlantic circuit, as well as the mediation of these processes within the aesthetic innovations of enthusiasm.

Section 1: Time

Chapter 1: Enthusiasm and Historicism: Mosaic Law and the Narration of History

The central claim of chapter 1 is that much early eighteenth-century historicist thought has been woefully overlooked because its historicist logic is couched in the language of religious tradition. In drawing our attention back to the early eighteenth century, I highlight the ways in which historicist thought has been presumed to take the form of a secularization narrative, and I challenge this assumption by arguing that the terms of historicism cohered in important ways in the early eighteenth century, even in texts that appear more explicitly concerned with religious ideology than with historical narrative. I show that Deists, political theorists, moral philosophers, and freethinkers historicized their present specifically in terms of the twinned problematics of religious sentiment and economic development. In readings of the Third Earl of Shaftesbury, John Locke, David Hume, John Toland, and Henry Stubbe, I show the ways in which religious historicisms were simultaneously histories of capital accumulation, and I argue that one of the critical ways that these authors documented the economic development of Britain was by generating religious histories centered on the problem of competing monotheisms. I show the ways in which historicizing monotheisms—Islam, Judaism, Christianity—allowed philosophers and political theorists to think through the often-contradictory relations between religion and national identity, as well as the uneven development of global economic systems and relationships. Although these histories do not function as empirical historical records, they are a crucial example of the development of periodizing discourses in the early part of the century around the dual forces of religious ideology and economic change. Finally, I deploy Marx's concept of "primitive accumulation"— or the severing of the population from the land and from the means of production— in order to demonstrate the interweaving together of these historicizing discourses with political-economic genesis myths about the inception of wealth under capitalism.

Chapter 2: The Legislation of Accumulation: The Camisard Trial and Structures of Belief

In Chapter 2, I review the upheaval of eighteenth-century legal discourse and practice to accommodate the advent of capital accumulation, and demonstrate that the concept of enthusiasm reflected these transformations in unique ways. I focus this legal history on a series of debates surrounding the Camisards, religious enthusiasts who immigrated to London following Louis XIV's revocation of the Edict of Nantes, and who were subsequently tried for public displays of enthusiasm. In readings of the Camisard Prophets, Shaftesbury, Bernard Mandeville, and the legal theorists Edward Coke and Matthew Hale, I demonstrate the ways in which enthusiasm yoked an ideal of the "free market" to that of enthusiastic self-government. I examine these figural pairings in terms of changes to the legal landscape and to the politics of policing religious sedition in the early eighteenth century. I argue that the Camisard trial reflects a larger shift in English legal theory and practice from the feudal construct of common law to the rise of Parliamentary statute law. I show, further, that this shift entailed an attendant transformation of what J.G.A. Pocock has described as the historicism of early modern legal discourse; if common law depended on the authority of custom, statute law authorized a kind of speculative historicism based on generalizable principles. This legal historicism recalls what Mary Poovey has described as the "conjectural history" that undergirds the bureaucratization of the early modern state.[52] I argue that this shift in legal historicism accommodated a new set of debates around capital punishment, and the relation of capital punishment to not only the exercise of state sovereignty, but also refinements in the productivity of the state. I show how this shift in conceiving statute was central to the intensification of capital accumulation, and I describe how this shift was transfigured in moral philosophy into an enthusiastic aesthetics of social order. Just as the free market is imagined to adjust its own excesses, so too does the enthusiast. Like enthusiasm, the market shores up its own potentially boundless powers by a delicate balancing act of exchange and circulation.

If the market's regulation is exemplified in the democracy of enthusiastic self-regulation, however, the apparent democracy of enthusiasm drives moral philosophy toward the intractable contradiction that haunts all of free market ideology in this period, and well into modernity: that of the irreconcilability of social regulation and market freedom. The solution to this irreconcilability is the subject of chapter 3.

Section 2: Space

Chapter 3: Social Regulation and Transatlantic Accumulation

Chapter 3 builds on critical accounts of race and capitalism to argue for the influential force of colonial contexts on British moral philosophy. Though much transatlantic work has tracked the impression that British political theory and philosophy made on colonial and Early American ideals, I invert this relation. In chapter 3, I show that the racial dynamics of the colonies influenced the articulation of moral philosophy in striking ways, and I demonstrate the transatlantic, colonial, and racialized conditions of moral philosophy's core concepts. Building on historian Robin Blackburn's account of the integration of plantation slavery into British capital accumulation, I suggest ways in which moral philosophy reflects the role of New World slave and indentured labor in the processes of accumulation that laid the basis for the Industrial Revolution.

For eighteenth-century moral philosophy, the tension between social regulation and market freedom is addressed through the intensification of two ideological and material apparati: that of institutionalized racism and the development of the law, particularly the expansion of property law. Where chapter 2 addressed the former context, Chapter 3 concentrates on the organization of theories of racial difference in relation to the seemingly "democratic" freedoms of the market and of enthusiastic subjectivity. Here, I read Locke's *Fundamental Constitutions of Carolina*, Shaftesbury's letters concerning both the management of his estate in Dorset and Indian policy in the Carolina colony, and metaphors of market regulation in *Characteristics*, to show how racialized blackness functions to secure an ideology of market self-regulation.

I focus in particular on the Carolina Colony as the critical theater for a number of conflicts: the conflict of the ideals of the *Fundamental Constitution* and the material constraints of Indian policy and wars; the conflict of the ideal of freedom and the ongoing realities of the slave trade and indentured labor; and the conflict of religious practices and local, colonial competition for resources and profit. I show further the ways in which the institutionalization of racial oppression as a transatlantic form of social control served the development of capital accumulation. In a concluding reading of "Sensus Communis," I build on David Harvey's concept of the "spatio-temporal fix" to argue that the Atlantic circuit produces a "spatio-temporal secular fix" in the historicization, narrativization, and aestheticization of an enthusiastically sovereign market. Ultimately, I show that race operates as both the material precondition for and the ideological limit to this enthusiastic self-regulation that the moral philosophers seek to ascribe to market practice. Chapter 3 thus connects the racialization of labor in the colonies to the conceptualization of "enthusiastic" market autonomy in England.

Chapter 4: *A Cry from the Desart*: Spatiality and Secularism

In Chapter 4, I focus on the archive of John Lacy, a London lawyer and convert to Camisard Protestantism. The key texts of this archive are Lacy's 1712 Camisardist assessment of modern geography, *An Ecclesiastical and Political History of Whig-Land*, Lacy's Preface to the French Camisard Maximilien Misson's, *A Cry from the Desart*, and the *Prophetical Warnings of John Lacy*. In readings of these works, I demonstrate the ways in which religious ideologies often ran counter to the emergent logic of capitalism, and can thus help us uncover otherwise cloudy aspects of the spatial dynamics of capital accumulation. In Lacy's archive, I discover a counter-hegemonic theorization of geographical, political, and psychic space, that is, a theorization derived from Camisardist enthusiastic ecstasies and prophetic declarations. Building on the work of Raymond Williams and Henri Lefebvre, I extend the argument of chapter 3 to show that Lacy's enthusiastic geographies capture the simultaneously productive and devastating unevennesses of capitalist development. I further these claims via David Harvey's conception of "accumulation by dispossession," or the extension of primitive accumulation around the globe, to show the interlocking of the de-development of the British countryside, the plunder of Camisard enclaves in rural France, and the expansion of urban productive capacities in the English core. Furthermore, I argue that this "interlocking" relation becomes uniquely visible under the lens of a nonsecular understanding of space. This is an understanding that exceeds the bare, empirical data of statistics in favor of a theoretical, speculative approach to the dynamic interrelationships of capital accumulation that, in slipping out of view, condition the visible worlds of urban and rural life.

Chapter 5: Poetic Enthusiasm: The City, the Country, and Extended Accumulation

Chapter 5 describes the intersection of moral philosophy and poetics, and it uncovers what we might think of as an "enthusiastic aesthetics of history." The guiding question that I ask here is: How did the discourse of enthusiasm come to inform the ways that poetic form represented history and historical change?

I approach this question via a return to the history of legal transformation, and an extended engagement with the social, historical and material context of urban development. In readings of seventeenth-century statutes concerning sewer management, I describe the concentration of British law around problems of commodity exchange and the protection of property. I return to the discussion begun in chapter 2 about capital punishment and state formation, and show how a legal area as seemingly mundane as sewer management expressed key aspects of nation building and of the development of the legislative character of Britain. Uncovering this history adds a crucial chapter to our understanding, not only of how capital development proceeded in the early eighteenth century, but how aesthetic form registered these historic processes.

Jonathan Swift's poetics, I argue, aesthetically reformulate the occlusion of these spatial histories from casual view. In readings of "Stella's Birthday" and the urban georgic, "A Description of a City Shower," I argue that Swift creates an "enthusiasm of history," a poetic argument about the complex nature of historical change. In the place of a historical narrative about urban development, Swift offers the promise of a poetic mediation of the histories that are sedimented within the streets, sewers, and subjects of the city itself, as well as those that are embedded in the changing relationship of the city to the countryside. Swift's work reflects the intersecting histories of capital accumulation, the transformation of legal theory, and the shifting fates of religious enthusiasm. Swift's sensitivity to the various imbrications of the law with religious doctrine makes his work a particularly acute register of the coordinated fortunes of statecraft and belief structures during the early eighteenth century.

I produce this reading in the context of the recent intensification of interest in the "City Shower." Indeed, the "City Shower" has become a touchstone for transatlantic study, in large part due to its central figure of water. Building on Laura Brown's proposal that the sewer connects with what she calls the "fable of oceans and floods,"—a pervasive eighteenth-century trope of fluidity that registers the expansion of transatlantic trade routes and the growth of the British empire overseas—my chapter seeks to connect this transatlantic focus with a return to the interior of the nation-state, and to the question of national infrastructure in a transoceanic age.[53] Swift's poetics thus provide a crucial closing chapter, and they open out onto a consideration of how the hermeneutic of accumulation might be expanded to treat problems in British and transatlantic study, and in the literary study of secularization more broadly.

Section One

Time

Chapter 1

Enthusiasm and Historicism

Mosaic Law and the Narration of History

Secularization's title to modernity is vast. In disburdening itself from the universalizing predilections of religious ideology, and in detailing the ethical capacities of the sovereign subject, secular modernity laid claim to a present unbound from the religious conflicts of the past. Or so it is said. This rather familiar narrative of secular advancement announces the cultivation of a reasonable, Enlightened present from a past imagined to be theocratic, violent, and soaked in religious terror. More important than this apocryphal narrative, however, is the discursive twist marked by the advent of secularization *as* a narrative. In periodizing itself around the mark of religious passion, the long eighteenth century established religion itself as an object of knowledge. It is this epistemological shift that indicates the onset of Enlightened thought, characterized by the ethical subject's ability to recognize the universalizing claims of any religion as simply one particular worldview among a host of worldviews.[1]

The starting point for our analysis of the transformation of enthusiasm in the late seventeenth century will be the uptake of this term into the discourse of moral philosophy. The very concept of the *historical period*, with its attendant claims to self-reflexivity and chronological consciousness, owes much to this development. Indeed, moral philosophy, which fastened historicism and ethical discourse together in the narrative logic of secularization, found in enthusiasm a supple guiding concept for sovereign self-management. This was, moreover, a reciprocal process: Just as modern culture composed religious histories with the engines of empirical knowledge, religious tradition informed the historicization of modernity's present.

In the early eighteenth century, the key conjuncture in need of explication by such historicisms was the advent of commercial society: the forces that gave rise to it, and the past out of which such a culture emerged. As the eighteenth century moved toward an expansive industrialization, moral philosophy began to give narrative shape to its own prehistory. This is a process that produced such major works as Hume's *History of Natural Religion* and Gibbon's *Rise and Fall of the Roman Empire*. More than this, however, the drive to define and communicate, not just the historical past, but the bewildering and forsaken temporal category of the *transition* from the past to the present, permeated texts that were not ostensibly large-scale historical reconstructions. The paradigmatic text that I will explore in this chapter is the Third Earl of Shaftesbury's "Letter Concerning Enthusiasm," but his argument is part of a much larger disciplinary movement. Henry Stubbe's *An Account of the Rise and Progress of Mahometanism* John Toland's *Letters to Serena*, Locke's *Essay Concerning Human Understanding*, and Hume's *History of England* will all receive mention in what comes. These texts combined the force of enthusiastic discourse with a drive to comprehend and narrate the emergence of modern culture at a number of levels. In seeking to explain the basis for modern historical development, such work produced rich narrative efflorescences and unexpected argumentative leaps that bear further analysis. In analyzing them, we are able to witness, not only how historicism itself developed, but how the driving concerns of historicism informed the disciplinary evolution of a range of discourses: ethics, aesthetics, jurisprudence, and political economy all drew from the terms established by moral philosophy's wrestling with the problem of periodization.

In this chapter, I will not review recent claims regarding the forging of modern consciousness in the context of religious tradition. A number of recent studies have addressed these questions, and quite well.[2] For such studies, the shifting fortunes of enthusiasm functioned as a kind of shadow-narrative for the complex history of secularization, in which the transubstantiation of religious fundamentals into liberal principles reveals the contouring force of religious ideologies well into modernity. Although I do not address these studies at length, I am indebted to their reintroduction of the problem of enthusiasm into Humanistic study. In raising the question of historicism and enthusiasm, however, I mean to describe what I take to be a critical and rarely interrogated coupling between religious passion and economic development. I do so in order to demonstrate the co-ordination of enthusiasm and economic transformation in the production of historicist thought. In what follows, I aim to elucidate the intersection of enthusiasm and capital accumulation, and I will argue that the rise of the concept of secularization, and the periodization of modernity around the pivot point of enthusiasm, can be best understood in terms of the more general historicist tendency underpinning the narrativization of the onset of accumulation.

As background, a brief summary of modern accounts of this onset is in order. Clearly we would be remiss not to review the positions of Marx and Weber as the pre-eminent annalists of the emergence of modern social order. However, although the topic itself demands a book-length study—and has occasioned many—for our purposes, a short précis will have to suffice, one that zeroes in on a critical point of convergence between these traditions. Indeed, for all their differences, we know that Marx and Weber agreed, at least on this one thing: that the foundational event of modernity, the event that signaled the transformation of the world of work, of national identity, international relations, and daily life, was the accumulation of capital. Marx regarded this process as having begun with the requisition of church lands for proto-capitalist agriculture; from the "spoliation of the church's property," incipient accumulation continues, through the "robbery of the common lands" and "the usurpation of feudal and clan property."[3]

If, for Weber, accumulation was the result of Protestantism's ascetic compulsion for thrift, rather than capitalism's inexorable drive toward profit, this makes his understanding of the centrality of accumulation no less noteworthy for our project than Marx's. Weber's claims about the inverse relationship of enthusiasm and accumulation will be familiar to many of us: "The full economic effect of those great religious movements, whose significance for economic development lay above all in their ascetic educative influence, generally came only after the peak of the purely religious enthusiasm was past. Then the intensity of the search for the Kingdom of God commenced gradually to pass over into sober economic virtue."[4] Thus it is, for Weber, that the "*summum bonum* of this ethic, the earning of more and more money," comes to pass as a variety of enthusiastic religious calling.[5]

Weber's account of bourgeois economic life has been supplemented by even more complex sociological, economic, and literary histories that recognize the crisis-driven complexities of market logic (along with a still wider spectrum of religious residua).[6] However, the frequent appearance of the Weberian formula—which yokes religious enthusiasm into a historically critical relationship with accumulation—in Western philosophy and social thought suggests the fruitfulness of its further consideration. Indeed, Weber's constellation—enthusiasm, capitalism, accumulation—is not unique to Weber; it predates the *Protestant Ethic* by at least a century. If the variables that compose this constellation shift in relation to one another, a significant number of political thinkers from Hobbes to Locke, Mandeville to Smith, along with radical theologians such as John Toland, Charles Blount, and Pierre Bayle, argued, in one way or another, the usefulness or detriment of enthusiasm to the project of statecraft and to the development of a new, commercial economy.[7]

From Locke's critique of enthusiasts to Hobbes and Boyle's debate over enthusiastic knowledges, from Mandeville's enthusiasm for the beauty of the division of labor to Smith's enthusiastic sympathies for material wealth, enthusiasm and accumulation seem to magnetically find their way back to each other in political theories of social order, specifically those theories that seek to account for the origins, development, and transformation of that order.[8] What sets the terms for Weber's inquiry, in other words, is a much earlier conjuncture, one that defined a great deal of political and theological debate in the Enlightenment period. This conjuncture saw the conjoined application of conceptual traditions of religious enthusiasm and the pressures of capital accumulation to the theorization of social order, and to the narrativization of historical change.

What the Weberian constellation makes clear to us, then, are the ways in which Weber's own social history of religion and accumulation is premised on a prior articulation of social discourse around just these nodal points. In what follows, I will show that early modern political theorists, Deists, and religious historians continually returned to the problematic of enthusiasm in conceiving narratives of social development. In making this claim, I want to stress that it is not simply that enthusiasm took on new significations within the eighteenth century, although it did amass a compendium of new meanings. It is much more accurate to say, however, that at this point, enthusiasm became a *meta-concept*: Beyond signifying a host of new referents, enthusiasm captured something about the contradictions specific to the early-eighteenth-century moment—contradictions, for example, between a negation of the radical religious expression associated with civil unrest, and a support for radical freethinking—that produced a historicist narrative *about* that moment.

In what follows, I will explore the enthusiastic discourse of social order in two parts. I reserve the first half of this chapter for an overview of the conceptualization of social order via the tradition of enthusiastic passion. This strategy is most cultivated in Shaftesbury's pivotal work on the topic, and as such I focus on his *Characteristics*. But I will discuss the intersection of enthusiasm and social order in other works of moral philosophy and political theory, as well, beginning, in fact, with a brief review of enthusiasm in Locke's *Essay*. The second half of this chapter explores the question of enthusiastic historicism. Here, I focus on moral philosophy and Deist theology, and argue that their combined forces forged a historicist discourse of early capitalism that relied heavily on a radicalized conception of religious history. In the late seventeenth and early eighteenth centuries, the problems attendant upon the development of a new economic system were imagined in terms of a historical apparatus still largely indebted to the formal structures of Anglican and Trinitarian theology. Under pressure to account for new economic and social formations, the bounds of this theology were stretched and mutated into new alignments and innovative formulations. I describe the efforts of theologians and political theorists to reconcile divine and secular history through a renewed orientation to the problem of Mosaic law, and through a refutation of priestcraft and the doctrine of the Trinity. Repudiating Trinitarianism and priestly power was a conceptual move that allowed for renewed historical connections between a monotheistic Judaism, Islam, and "primitive" Christianity. In literalizing Biblical history, early-eighteenth-century thinkers were able to draw on an expansive range of historical precedents for grappling with the phenomenon of economic transformation. These historical allegories are the subject of this chapter's second section.

At present, I return to the question of enthusiasm via Locke, whose refutation of enthusiasm set the terms of debate for political theorists and moral philosophers that followed. His distaste for enthusiasm, furthermore, stands to this day as the archetypal Enlightenment overturning of religious superstition. The case, we may not be surprised to find, is in fact somewhat more complex, and beginning with Locke, will allow us to root our inquiries into enthusiastic discourse with a sense of the dense rhetorical claims enthusiasm

Enthusiasm: The Shadow of a Thought

Scholars rarely discuss the development of Enlightenment rationality without invoking the Lockean critique of enthusiasm as a turning point in the advancement of secular reasoning. The importance of Locke's critique for histories of secularization has much to do with his appraisal of blind-faith revelations as unsatisfactory. Indeed, Locke argues that faith alone—that is, faith without an accompanying reason-based empiricist process—cannot confirm the truth of a proposition. The difficulty with enthusiasm is twofold. First, it is tautological: the proof of enthusiasm is only the experience of enthusiasm itself. Second, enthusiasm is a falsely immediate form of knowledge. An enthusiast clings to a revelation on the basis of a perceived communication with God, rather than what even Locke concedes is the distinctly boring experience of arriving at a conclusion through the application of rigorous testing. Enthusiasm is a faulty derivation of truth because it is immediate and does not subscribe to the "tedious and not always successful Labour of strict Reasoning."[9] Enthusiasm lacks the necessary reflexivity and commitment to duration that is integral to the empirical process. These two epistemological mutations—immediacy and tautology—effervesce in the ecstasies of revelation. To this, Locke famously objects: If the enthusiasts "say they know it to be true, because it is a revelation from God, the reason is good: but then it will be demanded how they know it to be a revelation from God."

For some time, this kernel of Locke's critique has marked the key moment at which Enlightenment secular rationality damns enthusiastic belief to the far side of history—as part and parcel of a murky mysticism that characterized prescientific thought, and that ended more or less definitively with the Restoration. Scholars have thus debated the relative merits or shortcomings of the critique of enthusiasts accordingly. And yet, when Locke issued his now infamous critique, he did so in the context of a larger, metacritical project to subject human understanding to empiricist principles. The critique of enthusiasts is, in many ways, consistent with this larger project, which is not to demystify religion, but rather to theorize the consistency of the subject over time, and to propose a methodology by which the subject comes to know himself as a thinking being. This much we know from the opening assertions of the *Essay*, which announce nothing less than the great reflexive project of the Enlightenment: analyzing the faculties of analysis themselves. "The Understanding, like the Eye," says Locke, "whilst it makes us see, and perceive all other Things, takes no notice of it self. And it requires Art and Pains to set it at a distance, and make it its own object."[10]

The subject's comfort and consistency is in peril at precisely the point at which Locke proposes to trace the putative integrity of self-conception, as the

"Art and Pains" of analysis signal the exacting antinomies of empiricism. And yet, although the estrangement that attends the putatively natural unfurlings of perception is uncomfortable, it is a beacon of discomfort nonetheless, one that guides us through an investigation of the processes of perception. Indeed, pain and tedium mark the processes by which we come to knowledge. In the end, it is not that the subject is entirely consonant with this history or is even expected to be. Rather, empirical method is a training in assessment—a training that transpires using the data of the subject's own perceptions, and the subject's ability to recognize the processes by which he or she has come to these perceptions, resulting in a faculty of judgment that can then be applied to phenomena in the world.

In issuing his critique of enthusiasts, then, Locke did not seek to interrogate the legitimacy of Protestant revelation per se, but rather to examine the principles of empiricism at their limit. Consider that, by Locke's own assertion, as far as revelation itself goes, "the reason is good." In other words, if an individual were to come into possession of information communicated by God regarding possible future events, the imprimatur of godliness would, itself, be sufficient to vet the legitimacy of that information. Later in this chapter, we will see Locke apply this logic to the case of Moses. For now, however, let us note that, as strange as this claim may seem, Locke did not directly dispute either the history or the possibility of prophesy. The problem, rather, has to do with the historical nature of enthusiastic knowledge. The question, for Locke, is *how* the subject has come to a proposition, and if the subject can account for the means by which he or she has come to know that this is a revelation. The peril of enthusiasm, as Locke sees it, is not that the enthusiastic subject has an overly passionate relationship to divinity, but rather, that this subject has an insufficiently empirical relation to himself. This latter is, we are assured, a historical problem, because the enthusiast does not know and cannot account for how he has arrived at particular revelatory knowledges.

The ability to narrate one's own historical relationship to understanding is the cornerstone of the *Essay* in general. Here let us recall Locke's discussion of the tedium of empiricist research. Much has been made of Locke's acknowledgment of the labor invested in empiricist practice. But, frequently enough that it bears further consideration, Locke explains this labor in terms of its duration: its boring quality, its temporal stretch. When Locke inveighs against enthusiasm, we see the inaugural strains of a great transformation—a transformation by which the question of enthusiasm shifts from a focus on its verifiability to a focus on its relationship to temporality. This is, of course, a shift that comes to true blossom in Hegel's dismissal of enthusiastic knowledge as the antithesis of the "long and laborious journey" of true science. For Hegel, enthusiasm is dangerously abrupt: "the rapturous enthusiasm which, like a shot from a pistol, begins straight away with absolute knowledge" produces the mirage of instantaneous understanding.[11] As I noted in the Introduction, this is not the place to begin an inquiry into Hegel at any length. But Hegel's final determinations on enthusiasm notwithstanding, in the *Phenomenology* enthusiasm summits its philosophic climb to become a cipher of temporality itself—more properly, of the intersection of knowledge with time.[12] This process begins, however, with Locke, for whom enthusiasm demonstrates, if by negative example, the historical quality of knowledge, and of subjects as well.

The *Essay* is devoted to describing the ways in which individuals come to master the reflexive nature of association, and thus to know themselves, over time, as thinking subjects. By invoking the danger of ideas taken out of temporal context, Locke redefines enthusiasm as a problem, not of secularization as such, but rather of temporality. The critique of enthusiasm is a demonstration of the perils of a de-historicized relationship of the subject to his own epistemological formation. Without memory, without an account of how one has come to know a proposition, we are nothing more than children, for whom the mind is heedless of perceptions, and thus incapable of forming ideas, the latter of which are, for Locke, the aggregated, metabolized data of repeated sense impressions. Without memory, the "Ideas in the Mind quickly fade, and often vanish quite out of the Understanding, leaving no more footsteps or remaining Characters of themselves, than Shadows do flying over Fields of Corn; and the mind is as void of them, as if they had never been there."[13] For Locke, the bearer of history is the subject himself, and without his recollections, all ideas are as shadows—nonreflective, unselfconscious, not even as substantive as a wind—flickerings over a landscape that leave no trace. The material world cannot register the impact of an idea except by the impression that it leaves upon the mind. And enthusiasm is thus the shadow of a thought, an idea without a history.[14]

Hume's England and the Historiography of Transition

I turn to Locke in order to open up the general proposition of this chapter, namely, that in the late seventeenth and early eighteenth centuries, enthusiasm not only expanded its range of significance, but became a conceptual framework in Enlightenment accounts of the origins, development, and structures of social order. Indeed, Locke's *Essay* exemplifies the early modern deployment of enthusiasm as a way of thinking, not just about history itself, but of how historical transitions are made. The frequency with which enthusiasm comes to articulate a sense of history is, in part, a reflection of the impact of Locke's *Essay* on the period as a whole. It is also, however, the case that, in linking historicity with the category of enthusiasm, Locke carries through a much longer association between religious thought and the question of historical period. As Michael McKeon has explained, the sense of occupying a rupture with the past was first elaborated during the Renaissance, but codified during the Reformation, "especially in countries like England, where the political and institutional marks of reform were deep and pervasive."[15] This geographical and political context is one reason, McKeon argues, "for the revival of apocalyptic historiography in Reformation thought".[16] It is, in other words, via the religious tradition of ecclesiastical history that the concept of the historical period is introduced into Reformation discourse.

By the later eighteenth century, of course, Hume's magisterial *History of England* had codified the marriage of enthusiasm and history to some extent. Hume's *History* gives an account of the Reformation and the rise of the English state in which superstition and enthusiasm were recognized, not just as a problem of statecraft, but a problem of statecraft in an era during which the state needed to balance the tendencies of market practices with the at-times contradictory ideological forces of religious belief. In Hume, the Lockean formulation—which builds from a critique of enthusiasm to carve an account of history from the sheer toil of empiricist thought processes—is formalized into a historical methodology in itself. In the Humean account, the state supplements those areas not addressable as simple human desires, but which nonetheless comprise the realm of human and social needs, such as "armies, fleets, and magistracy": offices that the people will not volunteer to monetarily support. As J.G.A. Pocock has argued, for Hume, in any society, "the arts, trades, and professions can often, though not always, be supported by the prices which those receiving their benefits are willing to pay for them ... But there are some professions which are 'necessary in a state' but do not supply individuals with commodities for which they are willing to pay."[17]

Pocock sees the church in competition with state power, hoarding its riches and holding "them on the basis of a claim to independence of and competition with the civil power."[18] Whether or not we agree with Pocock's analysis of the political structure of Britain at this time, his account of Hume's preoccupation with the struggle between theocracy and Parliamentary monarchy is instructive. This struggle undergirds the narrative of history itself for Hume, who argues that, in order to break from the forces of theocracy, the people must lay aside the superstition that keeps them bound to the hierarchical structures of the church. Hume's account of Elizabethan Parliamentary history bears out this claim: "Actuated by that zeal which belongs to innovators, and by the courage which enthusiasm inspires, they [the Elizabethans] hazarded the utmost indignation of their sovereign; and employing their industry to be elected into parliament; a matter not difficult, while a seat was rather regarded as a burthen than an advantage; they first acquired a majority in that assembly, and then obtained an ascendant over the church and monarchy."[19] To build the civil order, subjects must act enthusiastically, which is to say, as independent conveyers of universal truths. This latter does not lead to a state of anarchy but rather extends an enthusiastic logic to the structures of Parliament and to the intensification of Parliamentary governance.

Shaftesbury's Enthusiasm: The Historical Conjuncture

If Hume's massive history is the better-known account of the convergence of enthusiasm with the economic transformation of the English state, another eighteenth-century tome adumbrated Weber's constellation of historicist terms and in so doing, anticipated, as well, that Weberian methodological aim to trace, in the signifiers of religious belief, the economic transitions experienced by early modernity. This tome is Shaftesbury's *Characteristics*, in particular his two essays, "A Letter Concerning Enthusiasm" and "Sensus Communis: On The Freedom of Wit and Humour."

The "Letter" and "Sensus Communis" arrange themselves around a central philosophical claim: that enthusiasm constitutes a necessary social passion by which civil society regulated itself in the classical period, and that this model of civil self-regulation ought to be replicated in the present day. The essays also arrange themselves around a specific historical referent: the appearance, in London, of three French Protestant refugees and religious lay preachers—otherwise known as "enthusiasts." I will introduce the refugees' impact on London in just a moment and describe this impact at considerably greater length in the ensuing chapters, but before I do so, it is worth noting that the anxiety raised by enthusiastic religion was, itself, an anxiety about historical transformation. This, too, I will discuss in more detail shortly. For now let us recognize that the fear expressed in nearly all anti-enthusiastic rhetoric is the fear of a total collapse of social order. In this sense, the enthusiastic millenarian wish—for the end of the world and the coming of the new—is strangely consonant with the anti-enthusiastic critique of millenarianism: that enthusiasts indeed represent an apocalyptic threat to the world as it is. Here, Francis Hutchinson's vision of the refugees' potential impact on London may be instructive: "When they have railed against us Ministers, till they have the Rabble about them, then the leveling Principle is always taken up, and from preaching against Priests, they turn their Doctrines against the Rich."[20] The term "leveling" is a direct invocation of the Levellers' efforts during the English Civil War to overthrow major institutions such as private property. As Michael Heyd explains, "the ministers were never tired of insisting that the enthusiasts' claim to direct divine inspiration did not threaten merely the authority of the Church. It also endangered the social order as a whole, economic, political, even familial"[21] It was in the context of such debate, a debate that circled around the question of the social order as a whole and the dangerous potential of its radical transformation, that Shaftesbury joined the conversation.

As Heyd has argued, Shaftesbury's work on enthusiasm was "undoubtedly" the "most famous text of the early eighteenth century dealing with enthusiasm"[22] The significance of Shaftesbury's work may have something to do with the fiery historical context in which he wrote it—as a response to the actions of three Camisard prophets recently emigrated from the Cevennes region of southern France in 1706, twenty-one years after Louis XIV's revocation of the Edict of Nantes. The revocation, as is well documented, spurred the flight of thousands of Protestant Dissenters from Catholic France to Amsterdam.[23] And yet, if the Huguenot diaspora has received a great deal of critical attention, the Camisards—a millenarian peasant contingent of the Dissenters that remained behind in southern France—are considerably less well known. From 1702 to 1705, radicalized by more than twenty years of post-Edict repression, the Camisards embarked on an organized guerilla resistance to Louis XIV's draggonnades. Animated by what historian Hillel Schwartz calls "the spirit of martyrdom," the Camisards countered the royal army with military tactics and endured three years of intense mountain fighting.[24] After their surrender, three of the original Camisards took their religious vision to London where they provoked debate by issuing flamboyant predictions of the Second Coming, proclaiming miracles, and speaking in tongues.

The Camisards attracted only a small number of converts in London and did not advocate violent action against the English state. Nonetheless, their public presence became a focal point for anxiety about the recursion of religious radicalism. Controversy around the Prophets returned repeatedly to the dangers to national stability of mass sociality. The Civil Wars' merging of communitarian ideals, religious radicalism, and violence loomed large in discussions of how to approach Camisard prophesy, and shortly after their arrival in London these religious refugees were prosecuted for generating public disturbances—brought to trial for "blasphemy, sedition, and causing tumults among the queen's subjects."[25] The Camisards' actions were coded as infectious and generative of panic and mass raptures. These raptures were derided as "enthusiasm." In 1707 three Camisards were fined and sentenced to the pillory by the Queen's Bench Court.

The Camisard controversy was untimely in many ways. In the early eighteenth century, the threat to the state by lay religions was comparatively small when set against the upheavals of the English Civil Wars. Moreover, any direct Camisard action had been taken against the French, not the British. And yet the Camisards sparked a complex and important set of debates. This section takes up the Camisards' untimeliness, and asks what the tenaciously controversial nature of enthusiasm in the early eighteenth century can tell us about the period more largely. The case of the Camisards very clearly highlights enthusiasm's longstanding association with radicalism and its capacity to incite debate throughout the eighteenth century. More importantly, however, the Camisard controversy raises the problem, not just of the infectiousness of religious ecstasy, but of the correlation of individual feeling with the limits of state power in a capital-accumulative age.

In 1706, the degree to which enthusiasm was still perceived as a threat to English civil order is evinced by the spectacular retributive measures Camisard prophesy occasioned from the courts. The extent of enthusiasm's continued relevance in public culture is likewise evinced by the considered attention the trial received in print. On the occasion of the trial, Shaftesbury wrote two renowned essays, "A Letter Concerning Enthusiasm," and "Sensus Communis: On the Freedom of Wit and Humour." In 1711 these pieces were collected, together with Shaftesbury's other published and unpublished works, as *Characteristics of Men, Manners, Opinions and Times*.

Characteristics was enormously popular. Of philosophical works published in English, only Locke's *Second Treatise* was reprinted more frequently in the eighteenth century. In his couplings of classical rhetoric and religious tradition, and in his seductive descriptions of the passions, Shaftesbury appealed across a wide spectrum of readers, and his work captured much about the contradictory and variable imagination of the early eighteenth century. We can begin to register the broad relevance of Shaftesbury's "Letter" simply by reviewing the ideologically varied list of its respondents. The nonjuror Samuel Parker; the Bishop of Gloucester; Edward Fowler (a notorious opponent of the nonjurors); and the High Anglican layperson, Mary Astell, all wrote responses. Unlike these contemporaries, who in their separate ways responded to the French Prophets by insisting on repressive measures, Shaftesbury advocated countering the dangers of enthusiasm by allowing it to run its course.[26] Enthusiasm, Shaftesbury argued, is not itself problematic. The repression of enthusiasm by the state, however, is quite a hazard, because to punish enthusiasm is to fan the flames of religious zeal. It is worth quoting Shaftesbury's opposition to the Huguenot trial of the Camisards at length here:

> There are some, it seems, of our good brethren, the French Protestants who . . . have set afoot the spirit of martyrdom to a wonder in their own country, and they long to be trying it here, if we will give them leave and afford them the occasion—that is to say, if we will only be so obliging as to break their bones for them . . . blow up their zeal and stir afresh the coals of persecution. But no such grace can they hitherto obtain of us. So hard-hearted we are that, notwithstanding . . . the priests of their own nation would gladly give them their desired discipline and are earnest to light their probationary fires for them, we Englishmen, who are masters in our own country, will not suffer the enthusiasts to be thus used. Nor can we be supposed to act thus in envy to their phoenix sect, which it seems has risen out of the flames and would willingly grow to be a new church by the same manner of propagation as the old one, whose seed was truly said to be 'from the blood of the martryrs'.[27]

In this opening polemic of the "Letter Concerning Enthusiasm," Shaftesbury seeks to de-escalate the Prophets' spiritual aura while circumscribing the jurisdictional power of the monarch. The argument here may sound familiar to us, since it appears to anticipate a liberal progress narrative about the self-secularization of religious zeal, which, left to its own devices, is presumed to dissipate in the face of reasoned argument to the contrary. So, too, for Shaftesbury, repressing enthusiasm only makes its fanatic version more productive by confirming the enthusiasts as martyrs and thus reifying fanatacism's claims to truth. An overly "solemn" approach to religious enthusiasm is precisely what produces its truth-aura, whereas an enthusiastic raillery, and the just application of "good humour," exposes fanatacism's ridiculousness.

Beyond simply arguing for the dangerousness of censure, however, Shaftesbury defended the Prophets by redefining enthusiasm as a principle of sovereign self-management. The religious subject's direct relation to God models the Enlightenment subject's capacity to intuit and regulate his relation to the social whole. For Shaftesbury—who draws here on a famous and much-cited passage from John 4:1—the passions raised in the subject are the same ones that we use to sculpt ourselves into moral beings: "'to judge the Spirits whether they are of God,' we must antecedently judge our own Spirit . . . This is the first knowledge and previous judgment"[28] Judgment is not exemplified by Hobbesian force of law; nor is it ultimately a matter of divine provenance. Rather, the experience of enthusiasm is an act of self-training in the faculty of judgment:

> when men find no original commotions in themselves, no prepossessing panic which bewitches them, they are apt still, by the testimony of others, to be imposed on and led credulously into the belief of many false miracles . . . But the knowledge of our passions in their very seeds, the measuring well the growth and progress of enthusiasm, and the judging rightly of its natural force and what command it has over our very senses, may teach us to oppose more successfully those delusions which come armed with the specious pretext of moral certainty and matter of fact.[29]

In distinctly Lockean fashion, judging oneself becomes the basis on which one judges in general. In some contrast to Locke, however, the name for this faculty of judgment is *enthusiasm*. For Shaftesbury, the real danger is not that one might be too enthusiastic to calibrate reasonably with the social order at large, but that, without enthusiasm, one will never learn how to judge at all.[31] In this way, the concept of enthusiasm functions as a general principle of ethical comportment. The religious subject's direct relation to God and to universal order models the Enlightenment subject's ability to directly understand and implement ethical codes of civic life and social order. In the transmutation of religious ideology, the self-authorizing passions of the Dissenting tradition began their conversion into the enthusiastic self-authorization of the modern subject. This process was linked inextricably with the articulation of a general theory of social order.

Enthusiasm and the Social Whole

In Shaftesbury, the intertwined influences of religious and economic thought set the terms for ethical, political, and aesthetic discourse with a force that surpassed any moral philosopher of the century, at least until Smith. But it was his renovation of the religious tradition of enthusiasm, and his grounding of the British ethical tradition in the language of enthusiastic experience, that placed Shaftesbury's work at the ideological center of early modernity; and places it, consequently, at the core of the argument of this book. Indeed, for Shaftesbury, enthusiasm is a gauge of ethical experience itself, and without the barometer of enthusiasm, individuals are adrift in evaluating right from wrong. This is because, in sensing one's own processes of cognition and sensation, the subject senses something larger than himself. In Shaftesbury, the dynamism of the social world is mediated through the magnificence of the sensorium and through the subject's ability to experience and enjoy the complexity of the sensorium through the workings of his imagination. The ethical subject senses the play of historical forces through the experience of pleasurable reflection.

This sumptuous process is itself formally reproduced within the magisterial *Characteristics* as a whole. Shaftesbury's rich text pursues the problem of social order over a range of essayistic and literary modes, ranging from Platonic dialogue to diaristic contemplation, and this large volume brings together free-form meditations on diet, comportment, proprioception, and world history with polemics on virtue, beauty, religion, law, and the self—a range of inquiries that strikes us now as frankly unmanageable. In its time, however, *Characteristics* exemplified moral philosophy's totalizing tendency—described by John Guillory as the "theoretical foundation" for the discipline of jurisprudence—in constellating classical ethics, empiricism, theology, aesthetics, and political discourse.[32]

The totalizing aspect of enthusiasm warrants further attention. It is not just that, like almost any cultural phenomenon, enthusiasm registered the contingencies of its specific moment. More than this, the discourse of enthusiasm itself provided a universalizing account of its present conditions and of their historical development. As enthusiasm's supernatural dimensions were rechanneled toward the end of the seventeenth century, the concept retained elements of transcendental significance that were harvested by moral philosophy to theorize and to aesthetically chart the dimensions of social order. As J.A.I. Champion explains, "In eschewing Lockean individualism, theorists like Harrington, Toland, and Shaftesbury promoted more holistic conceptions of the relationship between individual and community. This conflation of ethics and politics can be more readily identified if we take seriously the radicals' religious opinions."[33] Enthusiastic passion, in other words, became a way of describing the individual's relation to the social whole itself.

But what did it mean, precisely, for Shaftesbury to claim enthusiasm as a kind of passion? To the modern reader, passion seems to be the very substance of the psyche. But for Shaftesbury the passions mark individual subjects' calibration with an objective order that exceeds them. The passions, in other words, are not the mark of the idiosyncracies of individual taste, or even the tip of an iceberg of subjective "depth," but are rather meant to be a sign of the co-ordination of the subject with a larger order. The passions in Shaftesbury are, in this sense, admittedly sentimental but only in the very strict early eighteenth-century sense that they rely on the data of felt relations. More importantly, they are universal; all individuals experience enthusiasm, and, with the proper judgment performed upon them, enthusiastic passions gesture toward the larger social order:

> Something there will be of extravagance and fury when the ideas or images received are too big for the narrow human vessel to contain. So that 'inspiration' may justly be called 'divine enthusiasm', for the word itself signifies 'divine presence' and was made use of by the philosopher whom the earliest Christian Fathers called 'divine' to express whatever was sublime in human passions ... So that almost all of us know something of this principle. But to know it as we should do and discern it in its several kinds, both in ourselves and others, this is the great work and by this means alone we can hope to avoid delusion.[34]

By straddling the sentimental and the rational, and in conceiving a social totality in the particulars of the self, *Characteristics* makes a methodology of the popular eighteenth-century concept of the *je ne sais quoi*. The *je ne sais quoi* is not itself either an idea or a sensation; the *je ne sais quoi* is that faculty that mediates between cognition and sensation. As against the Hobbesian model of conformity to the law out of fear, and the Lockean thesis of the rational derivation of social institutions, Shaftesbury proffers the mediating capacities of enthusiastic fervor. Through the *je ne sais quoi* of enthusiastic passion, the subject senses the syncopation of his or herself with the social order in general. As John Guillory puts it, for early-eighteenth-century moral philosophy, social order was "an order of the sensible rather than the intelligible."[35] Just as the subject divines the right relation of sensation and cognition in order to produce correct moral judgment, so, too, does the social order at large exhibit this simultaneously intuited and mathematical model of harmony. One senses one's own processes of cognition and sensation and, in sensing them, senses the social whole. As J. B. Schneewind explains, "[t]he moral sense, when well educated, does indeed reveal objective harmony to us. But our moral assessments do not derive from our possession of objective knowledge. They come from the procedure of reflecting on our own direct desires and passions and noticing the special feeling we obtain from such reflection."[36] For Shaftesbury, the *je ne sais quoi* opens out onto a much larger epistemological and social field; indeed, through the *je ne sais quoi*, the subject positions himself or herself in relation to a universal order that coordinates part to whole. This order is not a creation of custom or human design, but, instead, guides human judgment. What we perceive as beautiful is a sign of this universal order, and our assent to its structuring role allows us to form ourselves as moral beings.

The aesthetic implications of this theory are quite clear. When we perceive something beautiful, we perceive a correspondence to universal order. We do not need to be scientists to be able to perceive such correspondences:

> All things in this world are united. For as the branch is united with the tree, so is the tree as immediately with the earth, air, and water which feed it . . . Thus, in contemplating all on earth, we must of necessity view all in one as holding to one common stock. Thus too in the system of the bigger world. See there is a mutual dependency of things, the relation of one to another, of the sun to this inhabited earth and of the earth and other planets to the sun, the order, union and coherence of the whole! And know . . . that by this survey you will be obliged to own the universal system and coherent scheme of things to be established on abundant proof, capable of convincing any fair and just contemplator of the works of nature.[37]

When we see something beautiful, we see "'not a beauteous body but that from whence the beauty of bodies is derived, not a beauteous plain, but that from whence the plain looks beautiful.'"[38] Sense experience and aesthetic appreciation both exist by virtue of a larger structure that guides the parts into their proper places and *is* the placement of these parts. The subject's introspection, in Mary

Poovey's words, "yields understanding of the proper relation between the self and the whole, of which the individual is but a part"[39]

Shaftesbury's theory of the enthusiastic correspondence of subject with social order presses us to complicate our extant accounts of the term's secularization—presses us, indeed, to recognize that we cannot understand the secularization of enthusiasm as the simple negation of religious worldviews. Against those histories of secularization that track the withering away of religious thought and belief, enthusiasm in moral philosophy retained the archaic connotation of an immediate correspondence between subject and universal order, but located the center of that order in the various and intersecting apparati of civil society and the self. Lawrence Klein's extensive work on Shaftesbury comes closest, in this regard, to what I want to argue regarding the implications of Shaftesbury's social thought. For Klein, Shaftesburian politeness is a measure of the subject's integration with the social field, and thus functions as an incipient theory of social order. In addition to reviving Shaftesbury's *Characteristics* in a vital new edition, Klein's work has reconfigured how literary studies regards the history of "politeness."

Enthusiasm and Historicism in the Philosophical Tradition

In the literature on the political and ethical tradition, the problem of the social whole has largely been treated as a problem of "cognitive mapping"—the modern subject's increasing inability to picture the social world as it is made increasingly complex by capitalism.[40] Guillory and Poovey represent the best of recent scholarship on this subject, and in large part, they regard the problem of the whole in terms of its ability to be imagined as such. In other hands, this approach has a tendency toward anachronism, however, and bears perhaps too deep an imprint of the twentieth-century problem of the social whole, particularly late modernity's production in the subject of an anxiety about the world's vast unrepresentability. In the early eighteenth century, the question of the social world was not confined to the problem of its cognition by the subject.[41] Rather, in this period, the problem of the social world was perhaps more saliently encountered as the problem of its genesis. Indeed, as the question of social order detached from a primarily religious framework, it bound with theories of the inception of the practices and structures of modernity. As Suvir Kaul has shown, this drive—which we can fruitfully describe as a *periodizing* one, latent within the texts and culture of the early eighteenth century—meant that describing the contours of the social world at this time necessarily entailed metabolizing, expressing, or repressing the problem of its inception.[42] As a master concept by which the early eighteenth century filtered the contradictions of its historical moment, the discourse and debates around enthusiasm became one way in which the early eighteenth century imagined the historical breach it occupied. In the thick of an early modern crisis of secularization, but prior to the transcendental turn at late century, enthusiasm was part of that interstitial discourse that inherited the task of developing a theory of the modern social world's inauguration.

As critics have argued, the eighteenth century saw the rise of historicist thought and the drive to periodization.[43] This is the drive to develop, first, a sense of "contemporaneity," and next, a historical account of the present moment's difference from previous periods. The literary histories generated by Ian Balfour, James Chandler, and Clifford Siskin have done much to describe the contours of Romantic and late eighteenth-century historicism. Building on such work, but extending backwards, I wish to demonstrate the ways in which a historicist logic coalesced with philosophical tradition and natural law in the language of religious history.[44] If we are surprised to find a good dose of Christian theology and Biblical argument in Hobbes, Mandeville, and Locke, we ought to recall that the late seventeenth and early eighteenth centuries generated an urgency around the question of historical transformation, and that the extant discursive framework for thinking about history was not in any way a secular one. We can re-enter this question via a return to Locke, for whom, as we know, the acquisition of knowledge about the self functioned analogously to the acquisition of historical knowledge in general. If the Lockean proximity of the personal and the historical is, imminently, a radical subversion of ecclesiastical authority, this subversion operates not only in the *Essay*, but—for example—in Locke's *Reasonableness of Christianity* as well. The assertion, in *Reasonableness*, that the single requirement for Christian salvation was belief in Jesus as the Messiah, was, in effect, part and parcel of a re-imagined history of primitive Christianity that centered on the many miracles by which Christ signified to his disciples and to all believers his eminence. This history concludes with a "proof": "We have above observed, from the words of Andrew and Philip compared, That the Messiah, and *him of whom* Moses *in the Law and the Prophets did write*, signifie the same thing."[45]

If, for Locke, reading an argument, and "comparing" words, has now merged with an empirical "observation," this is both because Locke's empiricism constantly bleeds out at the edges, becoming increasingly mediated as his argument intensifies, and an effect of the convergence of the new category of fact-based historicity with the literalization of a Biblical history that would be theoretically accessible to any reader.[46] This private, readerly relationship to the text—and thus to history, Biblical or otherwise—made Locke himself something of an enthusiast; indeed, it was on the basis of this self-authorizing historical hermeneutics that Locke elicited the censure of anti-enthusiasts like Francis Fullwood. The enthusiastic empiricist is one who, in his dismissal of enthusiastic revelation, rewrites Biblical history around the monotheistic triad of Moses, Christ, and Mohammed. This was a category, furthermore, that included all "fanatical" forms of belief that were not based in "patristic interpretations": Socinians (of which Locke was a supposed member), papists, and "Mahometanism."[47]

Islam, Anti-Trinitarianism, and Enthusiasm

The above grouping, although it may appear strained to us today, follows a logic common to eighteenth-century discourses about religion, which often turned to Islam as an exemplification of the dangers of enthusiasm. Indeed, the enthusiastic association with Islam was at the forefront of theological debate in the late seventeenth century. As early as 1641, a "sect of Mahometa[n]" converts was reported within London. Though it is unlikely that such a sect existed—the report is more likely to have registered the Muslim population within London—the presence of the sect was presumed to be the result of the upheaval of the Civil Wars and the influence of enthusiastic religions.[48] As a reflection of the presence in London of significant numbers of Muslim sailors, ambassadors, and merchantmen largely as a consequence of Queen Elizabeth's granting the charter of the East Indian Company in 1600, the text goes on to imagine the mechanisms of Islam's persuasiveness: "This sect is led along with a certain foolish beliefe of Mahomet, which professed himself to be a Prophet, and this was his manner of deceiving: He taught a pigeon to pecke a pease from forth his eare, bearing the ignorant in hand that the Holy Ghost brought him newes from Heaven."

By and large, the conversion to Islam was represented in the seventeenth century as an act that involved the combination of seductive deception with some degree of force. As Nabil Matar has argued, "conversion to Islam was described as a predicate of Muslim power: whether the power of forcing children or enslaving sailors, of extending cultural and religious hegemony or of alluring the 'small' men of Christendom with employment opportunities and the promise of a better life."[49] Although there were numerous reports during the seventeenth century of conversion to Islam, more often than not these reports reflected the proliferation of anxiety about sectarianism, and were specifically responding to fears about the combined force of religious enthusiasm with a theocratic state. Moreover, as a number of scholars have argued, most extant records attest to the voluntary nature of conversion to Islam, as well as to the nonconversion of many Christians, captured during sea battles, who returned to England unharmed and frequently still Christian. There has been a great deal of work documenting why anxieties around Muslim conversion were articulated with such urgency in the late seventeenth century, despite the empirical evidence to the contrary.[50] We might profitably consider here the question of how the depiction of Islamic enthusiasm transformed during the period of our concern, and to what ends.

If, figuratively, Islam amplified fears about the return of enthusiastic theocracy in England, as the seventeenth and eighteenth centuries progressed, this figuration became even knottier as it was recruited to new discursive and ideological campaigns.[51] The consolidation of trade with the Muslim world during and as a consequence of the Glorious Revolution, and the intensification of Britain as a financial world power, expanded the field of debate and, in some cases, this expansion produced a simultaneously orientalist characterization of one of

Britain's preeminent rivals in financial dominance, while—seemingly counterintuitively—idealizing Islam as a positive historical marker for an increasingly secularized Biblical history. The contradictory suturing of a xenophobic characterization of Islam with the periodization of a monotheistic Britain in terms of Islamic history is exemplified in the publication and popularization of Henry Stubbe's *An Account of the Rise and Progress of Mahometanism* (1671). In Stubbe, we see the ways in which freethinkers and Deists began to construct a historical account of monotheism that traced the prophets in a lineage from Adam, through Moses, Christ, and Mohammed.

In *An Account*, Stubbe refunctioned a long-standing association of Islam with anti-Trinitarian thought. During the mid-seventeenth century, "Mahometan" could signify almost any anti-Trinitarian thinking, even forms of belief and theology that did not explicitly state an affiliation with Islam.[52] Building on this panreligious historical basis, Stubbe countered dominant accounts of Mohammed as a false prophet who had manipulated the people with duplicitous visions. For Stubbe, Mohammed's enthusiasm was legitimate, in that it "correctly" perceived the divine presence, and so established him within a trajectory of genuine prophets. Against the claim that Mohammed perpetrated false prophesy or simply suffered from epilepsy, Stubbe countered, "I grant he might either naturally or by some other unknown causes frequently fal into Extasies, and lye intranced, but as this differs much from the falling Sickness, so neither could it be an accident in the lest strange or incredible among the Arabians, who doubtless had learn'd examples of the like from the Jews and Christians concerning the Extasies of the old Prophets and of Paul. It has been believed in other Countries, as wel as Arabian, that some men might fall into such Raptures and might converse with Angels."[53] These approving representations of Islamic enthusiasm seemed to some to be almost Lockean ecstasies of inwardly turned self-relation. Indeed, as scholars have argued, this was but one of the many associations by which Locke—whose ownership of a copy of the Koran was public knowledge—came to be associated with freethinking radical theologians.[54]

The connection between Locke and the radical theologians, however, exceeded the simple fact of his interest in Islam and Islamic history. Indeed, Locke, along with Stubbe, John Toland, Spinoza, Charles Blount, and John Spencer, shared an interest in the interlocked histories of monotheistic religions and in demonstrating the roots of civil theology in these traditions. To some extent, then, the connection between anti-Trinitarianism and Islam was a reflection of the very real historicist tendency to reimagine Biblical history. This historic-political argument hinged on the legitimacy of Mosaic law as inherited by Christ, Adam, and Mohammed, and it articulated a positive valuation of enthusiasm, at least as it pertained to these prophets.

Stubbe's work had a great influence on John Toland's work in *Nazarenus, or Jewish, Gentile, and Mahometan Christianity* (1718), in particular Toland's argument that Mohammed and Moses did not just receive the word of God, but functioned as "believers" to establish a society based in civic virtue. This connection between enthusiasm and civic virtue, in fact, pervades Stubbe's *Account*. The text displays this connection quite forcefully in the many anecdotes attesting to the power of Mohammed to incite virtuous behaviors in Moslems. Central to these is the recurrent discussion of the prohibition on drinking wine, which Stubbe takes as an allegory for Islamic virtue more widely. Mohammed's abstaining from alcohol, Stubbe relates, was persuasive enough to convert unbelievers, not just to Islam, but to a virtuous life in general: "Tho' all the Topics that Rhetorick its self could yield would not have persuaded them so powerfully as this single Apologue [for abstention] . . . [indeed] the abstinence from Wine . . . [was] of so great importance to the preservation of Civil and military Discipline, mutual friendship, Obedience . . . [etc.]." Islam is described by Stubbe repeatedly as a provocation to a virtuous comportment that fluidly extends from body to temperament. The Islamic "Minds," Stubbe claims, "sympathized with their bodies . . . in an equality of temper and uniformity of disposition, and would render them more firm in their Religion, fixed in their friendship, equal in their Humours, and tractable in their Passions"[55]

The holistic aspect of Islam is not strictly a curiosity to Stubbe, but rather the model for a rational, civil theology. More importantly, however, it was this civic model that explained for Stubbe the success of Islam, not just in the Medieval world, but into the seventeenth century: "The Original and Progress of Mahometanism was one of the greatest Transactions the World has ever been acquainted with, wherein a new Religion was introduced which hath now maintain'd itself above a thousand years, & hath increased its extent, & spread its Proselites, over more than a fifth part of the known Earth, to which Judaism, including all its colonies, was never equal, nor perhaps Christianity itself."[56] Here in his opening salvo, we see the kernel of Stubbe's reconfiguration of the question of enthusiasm: rather than focusing on the verifiability of spiritual vision, Stubbe deploys enthusiasm to posit a world history of religions. Indeed, the example of Islam's durability allows Stubbe to consider simultaneously the question of historical transition—the "introduction" of "new Religion" into the ancient world—with the question of historical continuity—Islam's "maintainance" of itself as the dominant world religion.

The convergence of empiricist epistemology with a tripartite history of monotheism that included Judaic, Christian, and Islamic foundations meant that enthusiasm had become both a hermeneutical question—a question about the legibility of history and historical documents without the mediating forces of church hierarchy—as well as a historical one—a question about the "true" origins of Christianity. More than this, the binding of civil theology to the history of monotheism meant that, as the association of enthusiasm and Islam functioned to perpetuate orientalist stereotypes of fanaticism, this conjunction also recoded enthusiastic discourse. This is not to argue that enthusiasm shed its association with theocracy entirely. Rather, it retained and transfigured this association: enthusiasm began to signify the relationship between individual belief and political order more broadly as, in the monotheistic trajectory, the prophets' enthusiasm established an order of civic virtue and political stability. In this way, enthusiasm's stigmatized connotation of theocratic fanaticism began to expand into a seemingly contradictory association with the politics of rational, civic virtue.

We should pause here to note that, as enthusiasm's contradictory significations intensified, the term did not become illegible or nonsensical. How was this possible? I will venture that what the existence of such contradictions tells us is that enthusiasm had begun to become a metadiscourse, that is, it began to connote the myriad and often oppositional significations that collected around the relationships of individual sovereignty, religious history, and social transformation. For enthusiasm, that is to say, the stakes were no longer limited to the specific question of whether the believer was "correct" in his apprehensions. As enthusiasm expanded into a methodological approach to ecclesiastical history, it also began to allegorize the knowability of both the immediate historical past and the social order of the present.

To grasp what might be at stake in making this claim, we may turn to any number of well-researched studies treating the foundational role of radical theology in Enlightenment thought and political theory; Jonathan Israel and Margaret Jacob's works define what has been a decades-long, interdisciplinary inquiry into the overlapping histories of religious thought and political theory.[57] Their work, along with that of Christopher Hill and J.G.A. Pocock, obviates the need for me to rehearse the surprising pairings of theology and Enlightenment political ideals that elaborated themselves throughout the period. Now that we have moved past debates in which it is incumbent upon us to demonstrate that Enlightenment theology strove equally with Enlightenment science toward the accumulation of knowledge, we can, at least momentarily, bracket the issue of whether that knowledge was excavated using the tools of religious tradition, secular analysis, or some composite of both. The question I wish to ask here, rather, is not so much what sections of Enlightenment knowledge were propped on theological foundations, but rather, what sort of knowledge was accumulated and produced by such composite engines and, more importantly, what historical phenomena such knowledge mediated. We have already begun to answer this question by tracking the development of historicism in Locke, Hume, and Stubbe. In what follows, I will argue that the advent of new, unaccountable economic practices and relationships produced a turn to the history of world religions, and to a radicalized Christian history that functioned as an allegory for the more contemporary problem of historical transition. Indeed, I will show that this radicalized Christian history served as an allegory for the cyclical nature of the economic transformations associated with early capitalism. Perhaps it is not particularly surprising to claim that the transition from Judaism to Christianity worked as a figure for the transition from feudalism to capitalism.[58] But why, we may ask, was it that, at this point, the combined forces of Enlightenment empiricism and radical theology turned their attention so passionately toward the question of the origins of social order? Moreover, in doing so, what historical specifics did this juncture articulate?

The anonymous author of the *29 Sects*—no less than Stubbe and Toland—provides us with a clue. The turn to Islam as historical examplar of the relationship between prophesy and state building was one way to metabolize—through allegorical identification—England's relationship to the vast Muslim trading empire. In this way, we can read the figure of Islamic empire as at once a direct negotiation with Muslim power, and also as a figure for Britain's Atlantic expansion. As Ian Baucom has eloquently argued, the early eighteenth century in England was "a moment in which a globalizing finance capital begins to develop those stock, bond, and paper-money networks, those circuits of debt and credit financing, that Pocockian world of imaginary and mobile property, which inaugurate an Atlantic cycle of capital accumulation."[59] The Muslim world functioned as a flickering figure for this transformation, one that does not match up exactly to the English case, but which is that much more figuratively powerful for this mismatch which allowed England to discursively differentiate itself from the kinds of force that accompanied the undertaking of empire—indeed, the empire-building represented by the Muslim world is fontasized as a feature of the historical past—while allegorizing the cyclical nature of historical transformation that serially enshrined new regimes in what Giovanni Arrighi has called "systemic cycles of accumulation."[60] If it appears counterintuitive to call on ancient Islam as a figure for contemporary England, consider Arrighi's assertion that these cycles have the effect of producing curious fastenings of residual to emergent figurations: "The system seems to be moving 'forward' and 'backward' at the same time . . . Old regimes do not just persist [or vanish] . . . Rather, they are repeatedly resurrected as soon as the hegemony that superseded them is in its turn superseded by a new hegemony."[61] In the late seventeenth and early eighteenth-century England, as England began to replace Holland as the leading "regime of accumulation," the marking of this interstitial space with the figure of Islamic law confederated religious enthusiasm, state power, and civic virtue into a historicist allegory of the birth of British economic might.

Mosaic Law and the Narration of History

This articulation of civic virtue as a flight from the threat of theocracy is nowhere more evident than in the version of historicism to which Shaftesbury's *Characteristics* repeatedly returns as it ranges over topic and argument. Shaftesbury, of course, was Locke's best-known critic on the subject of enthusiasm, and his embrace of enthusiasm has long been understood as an overturning of Locke's original negation. If we understand Locke as having opened up enthusiasm to the problems of historicism, however, then Shaftesbury's embrace of enthusiasm must be valenced differently.

Turning to Stubbe has allowed us to see that Shaftesbury's embrace of enthusiasm has its intellectual precedent in a range of historical thought. Such a contextualization is crucial because Shaftesbury is frequently taken to have rebirthed enthusiastic discourse by linking it with the potential for civic virtue, or at least by resuscitating the classical linkage of these two concepts.[62] If Stubbe's history of Islam can be said to have articulated this connection before Shaftesbury did, of what, exactly, did Shaftesbury's innovation consist? Later, I will show that innovation is largely in the connections that Shaftesbury's work articulates between ideals of civic virtue and the problem of accumulation that underpinned the early eighteenth century. How this unfolds we shall now see.

As we argued earlier, Shaftesbury takes up the Deist and empiricist engagement with Jewish and Christian history in an effort to revive the value of enthusiastic thought and belief for a modern social order. Like the Deists, Shaftesbury engages monotheism and biblical history to conceptualize the modern political sphere; and, like the Deists, Shaftesbury's account of Mosaic law can be contradictory and vexed—at times disdainful, at times venerative.[63] Deism extends the Christian tradition of idealizing the Mosaic republic as a model for the English republic, but it strips this republic from its association with Judaism's purported reliance on superstition.[64] Unlike either the Deists or Locke, however, for Shaftesbury, Judaism exemplifies the ill-effects of a lack of enthusiasm and serves as a warning example of the dangers of censure exacted by a theocratic force. He introduces this approach to religious history in the "Letter." In arguing for enthusiastic passion as a mainstay of civic order, Shaftesbury claims that, without the mediating force of enthusiasm, Judaism created the conditions for its own obsolescence:

> The Jews were naturally a very cloudy people and would endure little raillery in anything, much less in what belonged to any religious doctrines or opinions . . . The sovereign argument was 'Crucify, crucify!' But with all their malice and inveteracy to our Saviour and his apostles after him, had they but taken the fancy to act such puppet-shows in his contempt as at this hour the Papists are acting in his honour, I am apt to think they might possibly have done our religion more harm than by all their other ways of severity.[65]

Shaftesbury sets the crucifixion against the English satires of the French Prophets. In palimpsesting an account of the birth of Christian history over the contemporary context of Camisard millenarianism, Shaftesbury makes an argument about the composition of social order in the present. In contrast to the inquisitorial style of the French and the Jews, the English "deny these prophesying enthusiasts the honour of a persecution." Rather than persecute the Prophets, the English are already "delivering them over to the cruelest contempt in the world . . . they are at this very time the subject of a choice droll or puppet-show at Bartholomew Fair"[66]

For Shaftesbury, the model enthusiast is Christ, and yet nothing to do with Christ's theology enters into Shaftesbury's account of the rise of Christianity. Rather, it is the exercise of repression that confirms Christ as a martyr. This, in some ways, conforms to a traditionally Deist argument, because it recognizes the immanence of the spirit while discounting the role of Christ and the significance of miracles: Christ is a martyr, not because he performed miracles, but because social forces have made him so. For Shaftesbury, as for the Deists, religion itself is not capable of proffering positive truths. But unlike the Deists, Shaftesbury's solution to this lapse does not rely on a rational derivation of immanence, but rather on the processes of social calibration. In the place of positive truth, Shaftesbury proposes performance by way of puppetry. Much like the model of enthusiastic adequation between the subject and the social, the puppet shows dramatize the possibility of a one-to-one relation that leaves no remainder, a fantasy of perfect adequation.

The adequation of subject and social order is, however, not ultimately a tenable pairing. Consider that the main appeal of the puppet show is the promise that, through puppetry, the state will not have to "try its strength" by enforcing a legal determination on the enthusiast. In the place of force, satiric performance allows the public to self regulate. Puppetry stands in for, while utopically displacing, state power. At the core of self-regulation lies the specter of the political apparatus, and it is worth noting at this point that Bartholomew Fair took place at Smithfield, the site of public execution and of animal slaughtering. In celebrating puppetry as the obverse of juridical force, Shaftesbury replaces the bloody juridical present of Smithfield with a bloody theocratic history of Judaism. In this way, he periodizes. The oscillation between pleasure-fair and public slaughterhouse (human and animal), is recoded as a schism between a modern, self-regulating social order and brutal, ancient theocracy.

Shaftesbury's fixation on what he sees as the degenerate nature of Jewish tradition is, in many ways, based in a sense of the differential modernizations of world history. This structural logic anticipates Smith's, Hume's, and even Kames's developmental thought. The violence of Mosaic law, which demands a nonreciprocated investment from its subjects, serves both as a developmental foil to Britain and as a mirror for the developmental delay of the contemporary French state. Against the "Papists," who are "at this hour" enacting barbaric show trials of the Prophets, Shaftesbury fantasizes a truly reciprocal British public culture regulated by enthusiastic self-regulation and balanced social exchanges. We are reminded here of Bartholomew Fair's function as a commercial and trade center, as Shaftesbury substitutes the apparent equivalences of British exchange—the mimetic pleasures of the summer "fair"—with the "unfair" apparatus of theocratic power. Whereas the French would be willing to "stone" the Camisards as punishment for enthusiasm, the British apply a kind of aesthetic neutralization: the power of imitation. Shaftesbury returns to the classical context to develop this point.

In fact, it is not just any classical text that Shaftesbury turns to, but Lucretius, a notorious antagonist of religion. Shaftesbury quotes Lucretius's transcoding of Epicurus as an example of the historical relevance of an enthusiasm severed from religious hierarchy. Even the atheist, Epicurus, believed in supernatural phenomena, and required the services of enthusiasm to manage the social whole:

> "Many likenesses of things wander in many ways in all directions, delicate likenesses, like spider web or gold leaf, which easily join with one another in the breezes

where they meet . . . And so we see centaurs and the limbs of Scyllas and the dogs face of a Cerebus and likenesses of those whose bones the earth embraces after death has come their way, since all kind of likenesses are borne about everywhere—some spontaneously come into being in the air itself and some are shed from all sorts of things."[67]

Here, Shaftesbury calls into service the well-known Epicurean atomic thesis: that all matter emanates simulacra, which enters the eyes and causes a perception of the object. According to Klein, Shaftesbury does so in order to advance his argument that even atheism is a kind of enthusiasm, and that the only guard against false enthusiasm is the moral development of the self through enthusiastic experience. To this, we might add that Shaftesbury stakes this argument on a somewhat desperate positive claim: that the social whole is fueled by the magnetism of likeness—"all kinds of likenesses are borne about everywhere"—rather than by the profitability of unequal exchanges. For Shaftesbury, this claim represents the fantasy of equality that marks the "Letter" from the start: that the subject's experience of himself might map perfectly onto the social whole more generally. This dreamscape of balanced, even social circulation elaborates a kind of magical equivalence that threads through the world, just as those likenesses that "spontaneously" come into being. The *je ne sais quoi* of "spider web or gold leaf" is that space of an unsayable, perfect adequation of subject and social.

Egypt, the Hermetic Tradition, and the Figure of the State

If Shaftesbury's "likenesses"—the puppet shows for which he finds classical support in Lucretius—are the figural foundation for the fantasy of rational British exchange, the force of Mosaic law haunts the "fair" exchanges of the puppet show, and the aesthetically pleasurable "spider web" and "gold leaf" give way to the somewhat more gruesome "limbs of Scyllas" and "dogs face of a Cerberus." We uneasily come to realize that these things, too, "easily join with one another." Indeed, even in this imaginary landscape of equivalence and harmony, mimetic breakdowns and imbalance shadow Shaftesbury's efforts to describe a world of semblances that magically spring into being. This tense proximity of self-regulation and the threat of incongruity is highlighted further in Shaftesbury's meditations on the origins of Judaism in his *Miscellany II*.

The *Miscellanies* are best understood as appendices to the more formal essays of the *Characteristics*. *Miscellany II* reflects the Deist revival of interest in the Hermetic Tradition, which traces the Egyptian origins of Mosaic law. Here, Hermeticism allows Shaftesbury to introduce the question of accumulation in thinking through why and how imbalances and exploitations come to haunt the social order. Shaftesbury borrows Deism's critique of priestcraft, and takes it further, arguing that it is impossible for any State or Monarchy to withstand the Encroachments of a growing Hierarchy, founded on the Model of these Egyptian and Asiatick Priesthoods. No SUPERSTITION will ever be wanting among the Ignorant and Vulgar, whilst the Able and Crafty have a power to gain Inheritances and Possessions by working on this human Weakness. This is a Fund which . . . will prove inexhaustible. New Modes of Worship, new Miracles, new . . . Saints . . . (which serve as new Occasions for sacred DONATIVES), will easily be supply'd on the part of the religious Orders; whilst the Civil Magistrate authorises the accumulative DONATION, and neither restrains the Number of Possessions of the Sacred Body.[68]

The reference to Egyptian and "Asiatick" (likely Persian) priesthood metaphorizes both Catholic France as well as High Tory Anglicanism. The Hermetic tradition held that the Egyptians were the first to articulate a monotheistic system of belief, and that this *prisca theologia* was passed on to the Jews either through force or through the influence of Moses's priestly training in Egypt. Authors like John Toland and Anthony Collins had turned to the Egyptians and the Jews as an exercise in comparative religious history, and to construct a model of historical transformation by which the pristine nature of primitive religions are conceived as always subject to priestly corruption, and thus in need of continual reform. For the Deists, Moses "was inspired not by revelation, but by his training in the Egyptian priestly tradition of esoteric knowledge . . . [and] a rational lineage of civic lawgiving."[69] As Toland argues in *Letters to Serena*, "The most ancient Egyptians, Persians, and Romans, the first patriarchs of the Hebrews, with several other nations and sects, had no sacred images or Statues, no peculiar places or costly fashions of worship; the plain easiness of their religion being the most agreeable to the simplicity of the divine nature."[70] Joel Reed points out that Toland's rescripting of Biblical history "undermines the foundation of Judeo-Christian exclusivity by substituting secular history for biblical claims about revelation";[72] in his Trismegistan history of comparative religions, Toland extends the kind of monotheistic historicism exemplified by Stubbe's *Account*. These variables, however, are arranged quite differently by Shaftesbury, who builds on the Deist project of severing Christ from the conception of God, but does so not to produce a history of comparative religions, but an allegory of the asymmetrical relations of political spheres, present as well as past.

The figural availability of Egypt as a dangerous model of theocracy, we might argue, represents a secularizing drive in that the rationality and equality of a fantasized present are contrasted to the religious tyranny and exploitations of the past. However, if read symptomatically, this secularization narrative reveals a set of surprising encodings. Consider that, for Shaftesbury, the Deist trajectory appears as a "servile Dependency of the whole Hebrew race on the Egyptian Nation,"[73] a figuration that, as Adam Sutcliffe notes, "cast the Egyptian priesthood in purely negative terms, as utterly ridden with magic and superstition."[74] By compounding a fetishized ancient orient with the figure of accumulation (the "Civil Magistrate authorizes the accumulative donation") Shaftesbury presents not only the historical past as a threat, but also casts France's absolutist policies as arcane and diabolical. In so doing, the trial of the Camisards becomes the focal point for a debate about state power, a debate that is allegorized in the historical relationship between religious traditions. Britain is posited as a realm of equivalent exchange, whereas the Egypt-France figural dyad illustrates the dangers of theocratic rule. Indeed, in Egypt—an Egypt that Shaftesbury severs from the fashion for Hermeticism by allying it with an equally primitive and nonmodernizing Persia—Shaftesbury finds a figure for historical forms of "accumulation" engineered through a political apparatus unable to resist the hierarchical force of the church. Priestcraft feeds on an "inexhaustible fund" (of superstition) in the people, resulting in an "accumulative Donation"[75] that is unrestrained. This secularization narrative posits a distinction between a dangerously religious past and a rational, ideal present. But the point to take from this is not so much that the early eighteenth century was invested in secularization in and of and for itself. Rather, because this narrative is organized around the figure of accumulation at the level of the state, what it does is simultaneously allegorize *and occlude* the contemporary accumulative conditions of British development as an attribute of a distant and violently religious past.

As Dipesh Chakrabarty has argued, this sort of historicism, which draws discursively on anachronistic figures to compose a theory of world development, had its origins in the eighteenth century.[76] For Shaftesbury, the figure of Egypt works particularly well to locate Britain within a long view of world history because the Egypt of the Deists had come to embody the contradictory quality of an impossibly remote past *and* a past that had been recently renovated to function in occulted contiguity with a Deist Christian lineage—a lineage that was conceived as continuing into the present. In pathologizing accumulation as symbolic of a distant past, in other words, Shaftesbury periodizes the contemporary English state. That this periodization unfurls around the co-ordinates of the state and the violences of accumulation reflects the historical context of England as it began to grapple with regulating vast accumulations of wealth, both at home and in the colonies. As Robin Blackburn eloquently describes, accumulation was complexly interwoven with the development of the English state:

> [T]he consolidation of capitalist relations . . . required the protection and patronage of a concentrated social power, the state, with its Acts of enclosure, its labour statutes and Poor Laws, armed bodies of men, contracts for supply . . . Only with the sponsorship of the state could incipiently capitalist forces find the scale and stability they needed to make the transition to industrial accumulation proper[77]

For Shaftesbury, the fascination with theocracy registers the increasing influence of commercial interests over England's political interests, but displaces this influence to an imagined past, warped by the forces of religious tyranny.

I want to put a little more emphasis on this point, because, although Shaftesbury fashions his attack on the Tory imbrication of High Church and State in seemingly noneconomic language, it is worth dwelling on the fact that he introduces the concept of accumulation as key to placing England within world history. His position on enthusiasm notwithstanding, *this* may be Shaftesbury's true departure from the Lockean tradition. In direct contradiction to his tutor, Shaftesbury does not see labor as the source of value. Rather, accumulation is posited as the foundation of wealth. In making this claim, I do not mean to argue that Shaftesbury was, in his time, regarded as a specifically economic thinker (although this is in large part because the discourse of moral philosophy had not narrowed its focus to what we now consider the economic sphere as such). Shaftesbury does not explicitly refine any economic principles; indeed, he is not interested in the creation of any one commodity's value or in calculating the proportion of labor invested in an item for exchange. Yet, although Shaftesbury does not calculate the creation of any one commodity's value, his historicist anecdotes raise a number of questions about the historical preconditions for the creation of value in general, questions that he answers, in somewhat strained fashion, with "accumulation." This is without question a signal moment in the self-periodization of the early eighteenth century: the generation of a history of forms of state that centers on accumulation as primary. This history is, furthermore, a distinctly nonsecular one.

In Shaftesbury, then, the narrative of secularization converges with the chronologies of an unevenly developing world to generate a fantasy of the contemporaneity of Britain in contradistinction to the imagined barbarism of theocracies. This process is our key—as I promised in my Introduction—to understanding how secularization worked *as* a narrative. Such an approach draws on Fredric Jameson's conceptualization of narrative as the encoding of history itself, and of the problem of historical transition more specifically. On how to read narrative as the encoding of history, Jameson argues

> There is . . . a synchronic version of the problem: that of the status of an individual "period" . . . and a diachronic one, in which history is seen in some "linear" way as the succession of such periods, stages, or moments. I believe that the second problem is the prior one, and that individual period formulations always secretly imply or project narratives or "stories"—narrative representations—of the historical sequence in which such individual periods take their place and from which they derive their significance.[78]

To turn to the narrative dimensions of this secularization story will allow us to articulate why it is that accumulation gets yoked together with secularization in the ways that it does here, and to understand how this pairing allegorizes the diachronic architectures of historical transition in early capitalism. Such an exposition is the subject of this next section.

Secularization as Primitive Accumulation

To visualize how the preceding concepts work together, we would do well to turn to Marx, who may seem an unlikely touchstone in an investigation of religious discourse. This is, however, in large part because the Marxist oeuvre has been frequently taken as an outright negation of the pleasures and consolations of religious belief. For Marx, however, religion is far more complex than the hallucination—or the compensation for the miseries of the world—with which his work has been routinely associated. I will not enter into a lengthy discussion of Marx on religion here, because that would draw us significantly away from our argument. I will, however, direct the reader to Marx's lengthy diagnosis of religion in the *Contribution to the Critique of Hegel's Philosophy of Right*: "Religion is the general theory of this world, its encyclopaedic compendium, its logic in popular form, its spiritual point *d'honneur*, its enthusiasm, its moral sanction, its solemn complement, and its universal basis of consolation and justification. It is the fantastic realization of the human essence . . ."[79] Far from the one-sided view of religion with which Marxism has been charged, religion—the "general theory of the world," its "logic in popular form"—represents a capacious effort to conceptualize the systemic nature of the social world. We cannot fail to notice the turn to *enthusiasm* as the name for this process; indeed, enthusiasm functions as the only unqualified signifier of human potential and social logic "in popular form," in Marx's litany. If we provisionally accept that Marx does not truck in ecstatic tropes to lampoon them, but rather to delve deeper into the material conditions that create and sustain these ecstasies, we can use his analyses to contextualize Shaftesbury's deployment of enthusiasm.

For Marx, the answer to the question, not only of how capitalism's dominance began, but of how this rise to dominance has been narrated, lies in the concept of primitive accumulation. And it is primitive accumulation, I offer, that can guide us in understanding Shaftesbury's turn to Jewish and Christian history and to the Hermetic tradition as a framework for thinking through the Camisard trials and the problem of enthusiasm. For Marx, primitive accumulation is two things at once. First, it is that set of events that replaced feudalism with capitalism. This process includes but is not limited to the historical complicity of the state with the economic initiatives that created a mass of free labor for capitalist exploitation. Capital accumulation is dependent on the extraction of surplus value from laborers; the transformation of feudal serfs into wage-laborers through legislation that removes them from the land and from any hope of reproducing themselves otherwise is the necessary condition for this extraction.[80]

But primitive accumulation is also the discursive matrix by which moral philosophy and political economy imagined and gave form to this transition. As the eighteenth century moved away from the initial severing of traditional relations of production, and into full-fledged capitalist accumulation, moral philosophy began to give narrative shape to its own prehistory. In doing so, it sought to explain the basis for its own historical development. This is what Marx understands as the *narrative* of primitive accumulation: that genesis myth that capitalism must generate in order to explain to itself (and explain away) its initial accumulation of profit. Primitive accumulation is deemed "primitive" by Marx, not because accumulation took place in primitive ways, but because early modern philosophy and political economy have mythologized the modern phenomenon of free labor as the result of primeval and fantastic forces. This mythology is created through the discourse of primitive accumulation, which does not accurately identify the real conditions of economic transformation, but rather mystifies these conditions as having taken place in a primitive past. In the mythic past produced by the political economists, religious terror and theocratic tyranny—rather than the transformation of the countryside, the inauguration of the imperial nation-state, the creation of the plantation system, and the birth of commercial capitalism—produced the initial accumulations of profit.

Although Shaftesbury certainly does not provide us with a Marxian account of capitalist development, his text reflects the pressures and forces of this development by producing a narrative of primitive accumulation. For Shaftesbury, what this means is that the mythic history of accumulation is not just analogous to a theological account of original sin. Rather, this mythic history is an allegory for the conditions of incipient imperial capitalism. Shaftesbury's narratives of prior histories of accumulative regimes that were explicitly theocratic in nature— in which the origin of accumulation was the result of the application of state force—stage the modern conditions of capitalist accumulation in the theological lexicon of primitive accumulation. Marx has provided us with an analysis appropriate to this literary or tropic character of primitive accumulation in a chapter that is titled "So-Called Primitive Accumulation." The "So-Called" is Marx's way of pointing up the category error made by the political economists. Political economists regard as primitive what is only apparently so because it constitutes the inaugural moment in the formation of capitalism, the often-invisible ground for the conditions within which the political economists live and write. To political economy, the moment of accumulation seems impossibly far away because it is nothing less than the occluded historical substratum of modernity. For Marx, however, this mystical moment constitutes precisely the separation of the producer from the means of production:

> The capital relation presupposes a complete separation between the workers and the ownership of the conditions for the realization of their own labor. As soon as capitalist production stands on its own two feet, it not only maintains this relation but reproduces it on a constantly expanding scale. The process, therefore, which creates the capital-relation can be nothing other than the process which divorces the worker from the ownership of the conditions of labor; it is a process which operates two transformations, whereby the social means of subsistence and production are turned into capital, and the immediate producers are turned into wage-laborers. So-called primitive accumulation, therefore, is nothing else than the historical process of divorcing the producer from the means of production. It appears as "primitive" because it forms the pre-history of capital, and of the mode of production corresponding to capital.[81]

Where the political economists see a fantastical build-up—the mystical amassing of capital necessary for historical transformation—Marx sees the prior condition of a separation: that of the laborer from the means of production.

Where the political economists regard history as simply progressive, telic, and cumulative, Marx exposes the precondition of capital as the negation of already-existing conditions—the divorce of the worker from the means of production—and the scandalously profitable extraction of surplus value from the labor of the worker.

In political economy's narratives of primitive accumulation, the event of accumulation is described as having taken place in the distant past, and responsibility for the violence of accumulation is foisted off on a mystified history that appears primitive for this reason. This narrative is a necessary ideological handmaiden to the development of concepts of the free market and liberal equality, because this mythic history, in which the pathologically unequal forces of accumulation are attributed to a savage and distant past, promotes the ideal of British "equal" exchange in the eighteenth-century labor and commodity markets.

For Marx, Adam Smith is the *locus classicus* for the mystification of accumulation, and the critique of the classical political economists centers on Smith's theory of the "prior" accumulation of "stock necessary for capitalist production." For Smith, conditions are ripe for accumulation due to the diligence and frugality of the capitalist class themselves, who increase "capitals" by "parsimony, and dimins[h] [them] by prodigality and misconduct." For Smith, the ethical act of saving lends a magical quality to the matter of money, and thus "[p]arsimony, and not industry, is the immediate cause of the increase of capital."[82] By saving, Smith figures, the capitalist class has more money to reinvest in hiring more laborers, who produce profit. But by Smith's calculation, capitalists would not have the money to buy the labor that they need unless they saved. So "parsimony" is the "prior" act that births accumulation.

Marx, of course, vehemently disagrees. Smith's primitive accumulation, he writes,

> plays approximately the same role in political economy as original sin does in theology. Adam bit the apple, and thereupon sin fell on the human race. Its origin is supposed to be explained when it is told as an anecdote about the past. Long, long ago there were two sorts of people: one, the diligent, intelligent and above all frugal elite; the other, last rascals, spending their substance and more, in riotous living. The legend of theological original sin reveals to us that there are people to whom this is by no means essential. Never mind! Thus it came to pass that the former sort accumulated wealth, and the latter sort finally had nothing to sell except their own skins. And from this original sin dates the poverty of the great majority who, despite all their labour, have up to now nothing to sell but themselves, and the wealth of the few that increases constantly, although they have long ceased to work.[83]

Scholars of the period have tended to regard Marx's critique of Smith as an attempt to overturn the Smithian account of economic development, and have debated the merits—or shortcomings—of this critique accordingly. However, Marx is not exactly chastising Smith for poor economic analysis, but rather identifying a *narrative tendency* within the discipline of political economy. This narrative tendency is consonant with the elaboration of secularization as a narrative, and precedes Smith by some decades. In jettisoning a past steeped in religious tyranny, moral philosophy and political economy embedded, within the narrative of secularization, an allegory of, not only their contemporary historical moment, but of the conditions that gave rise to that present, and out of which that present emerged.

Shaftesbury's mythologization of Egyptian accumulation, French barbarism, and the freedom and civility of enthusiasm may be understood in this light: as a specifically narratological historicism that deploys secularization as an allegory for the violence and inequality of the economic conditions of early-eighteenth-century Britain. Indeed, although Marx's account of eighteenth-century history may have fueled even more complex and historically informed analyses of the period than his own, we can retain from his observations this important, strikingly *discursive* one: the eighteenth century developed narratives that corresponded to the phenomenon of capital accumulation. These narratives attempted to come to terms with the transformations of early capitalism by imagining that these transformations took place in a barbaric past dominated by a brutal religious state. These are historicizing narratives, not because they accurately identify the ways in which capital accumulation transpired, but because they assemble a large-scale world history that revolves around a contemporary condition—capital accumulation—that is assigned historical relevance.

As we close this chapter, we may reflect that the rise of the concept of secularization in the early modern period may be best understood in terms of the perhaps more general historicist tendency underpinning the narrativization of primitive accumulation. Because narratives of primitive accumulation assign responsibility for the accumulation of capital to a mythic past, often theocratic in nature, they dovetail with the rise of narratives of secularization. The concept of primitive accumulation allows us to re-encounter the problem of secularization from the perspective of the drive toward accumulation more generally. For literary study of the eighteenth century, therefore, Marx's theory of primitive accumulation is critical. By uncovering Smith's ideological blindspot, Marx delivers, not only a prehistory of capitalism, but a literary model of demystification. Indeed, in the chapter on primitive accumulation, we have a hermeneutic approach to a historical problem: so-called primitive accumulation is the narrative by which the eighteenth century regards and institutionalizes itself as a distinct historical phenomenon. It is the discursive basis by which the eighteenth century narrates itself as a particular historical moment predicated on—but divorced from—the actions of long-ago historical actors. In subjecting Shaftesbury to a hermeneutics of accumulation, we thus expose the hitherto unexplored narrative logic at the core of his theory of enthusiastic social order. This is the logic of periodization.

Chapter 2

The Legislation of Accumulation

The Camisard Trial and Structures of Belief

"Like Delphick Priests, the Prophets Swell
Of Ruins, Blood and Judgements tell;
But this we're well aware on;
The War is fierce, and Trading low,
Our Wants and Taxes tell us so"[1]

"Accumulate, Accumulate! That Is Moses
and the Prophets!"[2]

The arrival in London of the three Camisard prophets from the Cévennes, Elie Marion, Durand Fage, and Jean Cavilier was not a particularly well-publicized event in June of 1706. The trials of the French Prophets (as they came to be called) and their associates one year later, however, occasioned a proliferation of broadsides, news reports, and satires. Tried first at the Huguenot Court at Savoy, and then the Court of Queen's Bench, Guildhall on July 4, 1707, Marion and two comrades, the English Prophet John Lacy and the Swiss mathematician, Nicolas Fatio de Duillier, were found guilty of printing and publishing the compendious *Prophetical Warnings of Elias Marion, heretofore one of the commanders of the Protestants, that had taken arms in the Cévennes*. On November 6, 1707 the three were charged with blasphemy and sedition, but due to clerk's error, on November 10, 1707 the case was retired. On November 22, 1707, the case was revived, and Fatio, Lacy, and Marion were sentenced to the pillory, where they stood in public view for two days, charged with "creating tumults among the Queen's subjects."[3]

The trial of the Prophets appears to fall squarely in line with the practice of censuring religious enthusiasts for sedition, a practice that came to a peak during and just after the Civil Wars and Restoration, when fears about religious militancy ran high and when the history of unrest allowed Parliament to write into law an unprecedented and extensive jurisdictional reach. The "tumults" of which the Prophets were convicted drew on a history of struggle between religious radicals and the English state, and they were largely a reference to the Levellers' strategy of large-scale demonstrations and organized recruitments—a strategy that was met with the 1648 Parliamentary decision to arrest anyone "raising tumults" near the Parliament building. Such decisions were codified in the Tumultuous Petitioning Act of 1661, which ostensibly legislated against twenty or more persons presenting a petition to Parliament, but which also had the effect of proscribing meetings—religious or otherwise—of more than ten people on the "evidence" that such a petition might be generated.[4] This not inconsiderable history meant that, by the early eighteenth century, sedition laws were worn closely into the legislative fabric of religious passion.

This correlation was only reinforced by Marion's militant self-description as a "commander," a title that was made much of in the literature surrounding the trial. Marion's *Warnings*, moreover, did nothing to lessen the blow of this association. Close to 200 pages of vivid predictions closed with this invitation,

> O Sinner tremble now. Behold your incensed Judge;
> behold his Wrath doth kindle . . . Where are, my child, those
> dumb Dogs? Let them come now; let them come; let them
> draw near . . . Draw near, you Bulls of the Earth, who have
> pushed at mine Inheritance, who have pursued my Lambs.
> Come, that I may deliver you unto Satan.[5]

The Camisards' history defending the peasantry—or "Lambs"—of the Cévennes from Louis XIV's incursions had certainly been cause for concern for the French monarchy, which battled them for over three years and suffered numerous losses. The monarchy's road-building "improvement" project in the early eighteenth century allowed the dragoons to enter and patrol the area with great regularity and ease, and for the peasant Camisards, who lacked financial resources for emigration or conversion, survival depended on a well-wrought military program of resistance. In the context of the struggle against the French monarchy, these warnings would have certainly reflected an extensive program of guerilla warfare.[6] In England, however, the Camisards did not develop a military orientation. More than this, during their tenure in London, the Camisard strategy had begun to shift as it took on characteristics of the burgeoning English evangelical movement. The Camisard tradition, heavy with insurgent tactics, came to absorb an English approach directed at gaining converts and emphasizing virtue over violence.[7] Few Londoners, moreover, would have read Marion's lengthy and expensive work, a single collection edited and published by Fatio. And while the Prophets were something of a sensation in London, their followers did not at any time exceed 500, according to the Prophets' own bookkeeping.[8] In all, the dangers of Marion's *Warnings* were relatively limited. It is fair to say, then, that the Prophets' sensationalism was greatly enhanced, if not generated almost entirely, by the numerous trials, and it was not largely a reflection of their threat as a religious movement.

In introducing the preceding caveats, I do not mean to dispute the Prophets' contributions to English, and, indeed, transatlantic, millenarianism.[9] Their works aroused interest and gained converts from various layers of English, colonial and Continental society. The attendance rolls from Camisard meetings in London, for example, list equal parts laborers, tradesmen, and merchants.[10] In England the Prophets counted Fatio,—a scientist whose theory of gravity was approved by Newton—and Lacy, an esteemed lawyer, among their cohort, but their ability to attract followers should not, itself, have been cause for alarm. Inasmuch as they trailed a history of confrontation with the French state, the Prophets articulated positions that were in many ways consonant with official English political ideology. After all, the Prophets had emigrated at the height of the War of the Spanish Succession, when it would seem that the Camisard perspective on the Bourbon monarchs concurred neatly with that of the British. Of what, then, did their perceived threat consist? The author of the "Satyr" on the Prophets offers us a clue:

> Like Delphick Priests, the Prophets Swell
> Of Ruins, Blood and Judgements tell;
> But this we're well aware on;
> The War is fierce, and Trading low,
> Our Wants and Taxes tell us so

By cunningly yoking together prophesy's supernatural aura with the very material concerns of "Wants" and "Taxes," the author demystifies the oracles while contextualizing the content of the Prophets' claims by way of a perhaps counterintuitive pairing. It was not only the Prophets who "Swell[ed]" in the early years of the eighteenth century, but also, and perhaps more importantly, the power and the reach of the English government. Legal historian David Lemmings summarizes this development:

> In this century of semi-continuous warfare the government raised more revenue from taxation than ever before, increasingly in the form of intrusive customs and excise regulations, and maintained unprecedented numbers of soldiers and sailors, including many Englishmen who were recruited against their will, sometimes under statutory powers. Naturally an expanded bureaucracy was needed to organize such an extensive fiscal-military effort, and there were complaints about the unparalleled bureaucratic power associated with the new 'army' of state servants, especially the officers of the burgeoning revenue departments, who represented the bogey of centralized direct administration.[11]

As Lemmings points out, the growth of the English bureaucratic state was made possible by the explosion of statute laws put into place to ensure the ability of the government to enforce an across-the-board extraction of revenue from citizens and to discipline laborers to ensure a compliant workforce. The war effort exacted massive demands on the English subjects, ranging from forced conscription to a host of workplace legislations designed to maximize profit at home. As these demands swelled, the threat of general discontent grew. In order to build and sustain a high level of English productivity, as well as a lengthy war on the continent, these two aims were laced together in English law, most notoriously in the Act of 1708, which outlined exactly who could be forcibly conscripted: those with "no lawful calling or employment." This sealing of workplace legislation with the stamp of wartime exigency meant that employers could "use the threat of call-up against recalcitrant workers" to keep demands low and output high.[12] Our "Satyr" articulates this baleful conjunction in a play on the status of prophesy. Rather than debate the legitimacy of the Prophets' predictions, the author points out that no prophesy or prophet is particularly exceptional in an increasingly bureaucratic age. This was a time, after all, during which the inequitable calculus of profit made it increasingly easy to predict what would happen next: more taxes, more wants. If prediction had become, so to speak, *more predictable* under the expanding bureaucracies of the early eighteenth century, then, in an extremely mundane sense, anyone could become a prophet.

In this chapter, I will examine at greater length the ways in which the longstanding association between religious enthusiasm and national stability was contoured by the rise of statute law and legislation of economic, social, and cultural life. I draw our attention here to Shaftesbury's articulation of enthusiasm in the text of "Sensus Communis," for it is in "Sensus Communis" that Shaftesbury most explicitly situates the Prophets' trials as a recodification of enthusiasm as self-regulation. In doing so, "Sensus Communis" illuminates the cross-pollinations of moral philosophy and legal discourse, a pollination that was articulated, both conceptually and in practice, in terms of the problem of sovereignty.

Reading "Sensus Communis" in a jurisdictional light reveals a number of complex formulations. Indeed, the conceptualization of enthusiasm as a kind of sovereignty had a number of contradictory effects, foremost among these the conceptually untenable nature of competing sovereignties. If enthusiasm had begun to describe an ideal of autonomy, the legal apparatus, the autonomy of which was increasingly supported by the framework of Parliamentary statute, mediated the calibration of this individual with the state to a large degree. Although these two autonomies might mirror each other figuratively, their coexistence, in practice, was often fraught. In the final section of this chapter, I show that the friction between individual and state sovereignty is resolved, for Shaftesbury, through a meditation on capital punishment. In this, Shaftesbury's work expresses a larger shift at the level of statecraft, and one by which the state's sovereignty was conceived not just through spectacular displays of its power, but also, and perhaps more importantly, through the intensification of strategies for hidden extractions of profit that were both mundane and macabre. The debates around capital punishment in the early eighteenth century, which I discuss in some detail, reflect this changing nature of the bureaucratic state. In tracing this history, I read Shaftesbury not only alongside Bernard Mandeville's

Fable of the Bees—a text that has been considered in conjunction with *Characteristics* from the early eighteenth century onwards—but also in terms of Mandeville's *An enquiry into the causes of the frequent executions at Tyburn*. As we investigate the bureaucratization of capital punishment in Shaftesbury and Mandeville, we will bring together the framing concerns of this chapter: enthusiastic historicism and legal transformation in the context of capital accumulation. Indeed, the dynamic relationship between the highly visible enforcement of the law, and the occulted, inexorable production of profit, was bound inextricably to the intensification of statute. This is a point to which we will return. For now, a brief review of legislation and sovereignty will lead us into a reading of Shaftesbury.

Sovereignty and Secularization

As legal historians have chronicled, during and after the Restoration, there was a striking increase in the quantity and applicability of Parliamentary legislation over the feudal construct of common law. David Lieberman, in his study of the British legal system post-1688, explains that there was "a surprisingly neglected consequence of the consolidation of Parliamentary government in the years following the 1688 Revolution. Accompanying the establishment of a regular annual Parliamentary session was the dramatic increase of the King in Parliament's exercise of its constitutional powers to make law."[13] This explosion of statute laws and of a judicial system that, with increasing frequency, ruled on cases without common law conventions of trial by jury, overwhelmed the populace. As Matthew Bacon argued in his *Abridgement of Law and Equity*, "The jurisdiction herein given to justices of peace by particular statutes, is so various, and extends to such a multiplicity of cases, that it were endless to endeavor to enumerate them."[14] In what follows, we will ask how the discourse of enthusiasm came to naturalize this sort of jurisdiction and control, and inquire after the host of social relationships upon which the sovereignty of statute relied.

The preceding question returns us to the problem of the untimeliness of the Camisard controversy in London, and of the ambiguous significance of Camisard prophesy at a time when the threat of religious unrest was relatively low, and the English military mission on the continent dovetailed with the Camisards' own antagonistic relationship to the French monarchy. I want to propose that we understand the untimeliness of the Camisard trials in terms of the dual purpose that the trials represented. On the one hand, religious enthusiasts continued to be tightly patrolled in the early eighteenth century due to enthusiasm's long-standing association with threats to national stability. On the other hand, and importantly, what the Camisard trials—and highly publicized trials around religious dissent more generally—did was to enrich the sense of imminent threat to the state and, thereby, augment an atmosphere in which Parliament might put into place statutes that addressed the perhaps more pressing concern, not of religious unrest per se, but of the potential for unrest over the simultaneously increased demands (in the form of taxes) and privations (in the form of "wants") exercised by the state over its citizens. One of the effects, in other words, of the publicity around religious enthusiasm as a threat to state sovereignty, was the ideological authorization of Parliamentary Acts that had themselves no direct relationship to religious dissent and its punishment. Although certain high-profile cases such as the Prophets' would continue to be tried at courts such as Westminster and Savoy throughout the eighteenth century, far more cases were being decided in summary jurisdiction at lower-level tribunals that adjudicated the minutiae of property law and the bureaucracies of daily fiscal management.[15] It is in terms of this relation between loudly advertised assize cases and the quiet but unmistakable proliferation of laws decided by statute in county courts that we need to understand the spectacular nature of the Camisard trial and its debates.

Let us be clear about what the expansion of the legislative power of statute meant in the early eighteenth century: the increased ease with which justices were able to prosecute the laboring poor. As Douglas Hay has explained,

> The expansive definitions of rogues and vagabonds . . . allowed justices to whip and commit to the house of correction a wide variety of transient and suspect poor . . . Most of this legislation was enacted to make criminal, and to punish summarily, acts which were not crimes at common law. The most common prosecutions were for vagrancy and other poor law offenses, breach of contract (master and servant), poaching offences under the game laws, wood theft, vegetable theft, and embezzlement in materials in industry.[16]

Statutory powers meant that defendants could be tried without jury and committed or fined without testimony or evidence.[17] The intensification of statute ranged from large-scale legislation around international trade to the criminalization of nearly all forms of customary appropriation. From the parceling of the workday to the custody of waste, from the insuring of the national debt to the survival strategies of the poor, from taxation to conscription, the law not only began to regulate a range of areas in increasingly microscopic and previously unimaginable detail, but the practice of law underwent a radical transformation. After the Restoration, Charles II's burst of statutes put into place Acts authorized in large part by the national memory of religious violence, but by no means confined to the sphere of legislating religious practices.[18] Instead, rooted in a foundation largely defined by religious unrest, statutes multiplied and spread, centralizing and regulating commerce and exchange at every step, from production to purchase. Francis Bacon's legendary reflection on the causes of sedition registers this shift:

> The causes and motives of seditions are, *innovation in religion; taxes*; alteration of laws and customs; breaking of privileges; general oppression; advancement of unworthy persons; strangers, dearths; disbanded soldiers; factions grown desperate; and whatsoever, in offending people, joineth and knitteth them in common cause.[19]

The discursive history of enthusiastic sovereignty, I wish to argue, can guide us in understanding the ways in which religious discourse and economic transformation were—to borrow a phrase from Bacon—*knitted* together in the legal language of the early eighteenth century. Indeed, this knitting suggests that the putative sovereignty of statute is more complex than it at first appears.

The second of my two epigraphs, Marx's biblical rendering of the law of capitalist accumulation—"Accumulate, accumulate! That is Moses and the Prophets!"—puts a finer point on this process. At first glance, Marx's formulation might seem a somewhat glib diagnosis of the religious fervor for money making, in which the passion for God is transubstantiated into a passion for profit. But let us understand the citation as the provocation that it is. For Marx, accumulation is not like the Mosaic law; it *is* the Mosaic law. Accumulation is the watchword of modern culture, and this is not because an analogous relation between the passion for money and the passion for God prevails, but because accumulation's religious cast recalls the intertwined histories of religious belief and the economic modernization of England. This intertwining relied on the apparatus of the law—more specifically the intensification of statute—to not only extend its powers to address the threat of religious violence, but, more importantly, to *generalize* these powers to a range of other applications. In this way, the transformation of the law depended on the continued and even escalated perception of the dangers of religious fervor in order to develop its particular jurisdictional character. In casting religious passion as the hallmark of a barbaric past, and one that required constant and decisive punishment, Enlightenment culture appeared to "secularize" the public sphere through the policing of fanaticism. At the same time, however, as modernity appeared to inexorably extricate itself from the seductions of religious enthusiasm, the sovereignty of statute took root in the soil of this putative secularization, in order to bring to full flower the powers of Parliament to police property and economic life. What this double movement means for us is that the apparent secularization of fanaticism, a process that has been frequently conceived as a broadening of the application and relevance of religious language, was in many ways the reflection of another broadening: the extension of legislation around religious passion to an array of other situations. Whether such a development dampened religious fervor or whether it fueled this fervor (as Shaftesbury had argued in the "Letter") is to some extent beside the point. In either case, what this discursive motion did was to authorize and reinforce other prerogatives of state, specifically the proliferation of statute to protect and enhance the economic gains of early modernity. How enthusiasm and the aesthetics of enthusiastic passion came to register this process will be the focus of our chapter.

Sovereignty and Historicity

Much has been written about Shaftesbury's recoding of enthusiasm. Enthusiasm has been hailed as the inauguration of an ethics of secular magic, a holistic, passionate aesthetics, and a theology of social calibration. Preceding all these classifications, however, is one simple but critical historical fact: Shaftesbury's work on enthusiasm was written in direct response to a notorious string of trials, and, as such, his work operated a critical interpenetration of moral philosophy and legal theory in the early modern period. In considering this interpenetration, we will ask exactly how moral philosophy functioned as an analytic testing ground for theorizing the limits and character of jurisdiction, as we attempt to situate these specifics in terms of the transformation of the British legal apparatus in the eighteenth century.

The aforementioned transformation—one which promoted the accumulation of capital and protected the gains of landowner and state—has been well documented by legal historians.[20] Accompanying this transformation, moreover, was the ideological reconfiguration of English national identity. The transition from conceiving an England defined by common law to conceiving a state characterized by statute was a task that drove to the heart of the conception of a specifically English national temperament. Common law's domination of historical accounts of English legal character had reached its peak in the seventeenth-century works of Edward Coke and Matthew Hale. Coke, Lord Chief Justice of England from 1613–1616, delivered passionate descriptions of common law, most famously as natural reason refined by wisdom. For Coke, common law, broadly speaking, is the

> expression of the ultimate order of things: its total self-consistence and inner harmony bespeak the coherence and continuity of social life itself . . .' . . . for as in nature we see the infinite distinction of things proceed from some unity, as many flowers from one root, many rivers from one fountain, many arteries in the body of man from one heart . . . so without question *Lex orta cum [ex] menta divina*, and this admirable unity and consent in such diversity of things, proceeds only from God the fountain and founder of all good laws and constitution.[21]

Here, English sovereignty is embodied in the harmonious operation of common law; and, in a self-authorizing tautology, common law derives its authority from the harmony of English sovereignty and social order. Common law's sovereignty prevailed over monarchical right, and inasmuch as this law ideally reflected the habits and customs of the people, Coke's rulings argued for the precedence of judicial interpretation over the provisions of statute.

The dominance of common over statute law was not, however, simple or uncontested. In fact, Coke's writings frequently worry at this relationship, and famous decisions like *Heydon's Case* exemplified the dexterity required to negotiate the often fraught relation between common and statute law. In *Heydon's Case*, Coke insisted on the necessity of common law, even (or especially) given the increasing prominence of statute. Here, he argues that statute may be required to compensate for gaps in common law, but this compensatory quality does not detract from the value of common law. In fact, statute, Coke showed, should be interpreted as the supplement to common law and not as superior to it. The key here is the interpretive force that common law provides:

> For the sure and true interpretation of all statutes in general (be they penal or beneficial, restrictive or enlarging of the common law), four things are to be discerned and considered: (1st). What was the common law before the making of the Act? (2nd), What was the mischief and defect for which the common law did not provide. (3rd), What remedy the Parliament hath resolved and appointed to cure the disease of the commonwealth. And, (4th), the true reason of the remedy; and then the office of the judges is always to make such construction as shall suppress the mischief, and advance the remedy, and to suppress subtle inventions and evasions for continuance of the mischief, and *pro private commodo*, and to add force and life to the cure and remedy, according to the true intent of the makers of the Act, *prop bono publico*.[22]

Coke defines common law as superior to statute in flexibility, application, and contemporaneity. This is because statute law can always be circumvented through "inventions and evasions." By some contrast, the sovereignty of common law consists in its ability to subtly address such "inventions," which, because they are ongoing, will inevitably fall outside what Coke sees as the static letter of statute. Even as Coke argues for the superiority of common law, however, we wish to note that common law's sovereignty is contingent on a dynamic, corrective relation to statute. In a two-step motion, common law congeals customary practices into the rule of law, and it is continually reconfigured through the courts to address the inevitable shifts of criminal practice—shifts that are themselves produced as a response to the prescriptions of statute.

Matthew Hale, Chief Justice of the Court of King's Bench from 1671–1676, also favored common law over statute. And, like Coke, Hale's evaluation of the preferable nature of common law continually reveals its magnetic connection with statute. Hale refined the distinction between common law and statute law in terms of the relationship of both to the written word:

> ... for although (as shall be shown hereafter), all the laws of this kingdom have some monuments or memorials thereof in writing, yet all of them have not their original in writing; for some of those laws have obtained their force by immemorial usage or custom; and such laws are properly called *legis non scriptae*, or unwritten laws or customs. Those laws ... that I call *legis scriptae*, or written laws, are such as are usually called statute laws, or Acts of parliament, which are originally reduced into writing before they are enacted or received any binding power.[23]

This discursive refinement of common and statute law was not absolute. After all, Hale acknowledged, much of what his contemporaries considered custom were the result of statute laws put into practice and forgotten over time. Such erstwhile statutes, he argued, "are now accounted part of the *lex non scripta*, being as it were incorporated thereinto, and become part of the common law; and in truth, such statutes are not now pleadable as Acts of parliament (because what is before time of memory is supposed without a beginning, or at least such a beginning as the law takes notice of) but they obtain their strength by mere immemorial usage or custom."[24]

With the passage of time, statute becomes common law. For Hale such a claim is, in part, a justification for the role of the Justices at a time during which the increase of Parliamentary statutes was beginning to threaten the Justices' decision-making capacities. The claim, however, is somewhat ambiguous. On the one hand, Hale argues that common law continually engulfs and subsumes statute. On the other hand, his claims demonstrate that common law is not built purely on a foundation of social convention and customary practice, but rather on the artificial apparatus of statute, an apparatus that is naturalized and forgotten over time. In either case, what Hale brings to the foreground is a logic that was at the heart of legal theory in the early modern period: the historical nature of the law. The particulars of this historical logic may appear curious to us now, for while it would seem inarguable to modern readers that the written word had greater historical purchase than social custom within Enlightenment culture in general, and for legal theory in particular, Hale regards the relationship of custom to historicity differently. For Hale, writing may be a sort of "memorial," but custom is an "immemorial" force that supersedes the seemingly self-evident power of the written law. Custom is the living memory of a time "before the time of memory," a time that is inaccessible through the written law, which loses its legal force because it references a past that is not cognitively accessible. This past, however, is apprehensible through the continuously reiterated usages of common law and custom.

The historicity of early modern legal discourse has been argued at length by J.G.A. Pocock in his *Ancient Constitution*.[25] In brief, Pocock asserts that the denial of the Norman Conquest allowed English legal theorists and ordinary subjects to imagine themselves part of a continuous flow of history in which common law functioned as an eternal truth; as such, Pocock argues, the "common law mind" dominated historicist thought in the early modern period. In Alan Cromartie's summary, for Pocock the dominance of this form meant that, "because the English denied the Norman conquest, and had no sense that they had been feudal, or that feudalism was an import, they were imprisoned in the common law mind. They presumed (because lawyers told them) that the present developed out of a past that was related and continuous. Common law was immortal, and this 'ruled out 'catastrophic' breaks, and excluded a view of the past as essentially foreign.'"[26] The debates around Pocock's claims are extensive and do not need to be rehearsed here.[27] The point upon which we may expand, however, has to do with how a theory of history was embedded in the debates around legal discourse and practice in this period. As Cromartie points out, there existed historically significant divergent opinions on common law and on the Norman Conquest, notably that of radicals such as the Leveller William Walwyn, who had no difficulty admitting the Norman Conquest, and who used this historical reference point to argue for the necessity of overthrowing the rule of law and of the monarch. The common law, Walwyn insisted, was "'French garb or clothing which the Conqueror and his successors, by main strength, forced our forefathers to put on."[28] If the sovereignty of common law had become a kind of historicist discourse in the seventeenth century, the rise of statute was a challenge not only to the practice of common law, but to the historicist forms associated with it.

Wit: The "Natural" Medium

To explore the historicism of legal theory further, we turn now to the aesthetic dimensions of Shaftesbury's work, a turn that ought not to surprise us because aesthetics was, in crucial ways, inextricable from legal theory in the early eighteenth century. Most famously, Henry Home, Lord Kames advanced both legal and aesthetic theory while sitting on the bench in Scotland.[29] But decades before Kames's contributions, Shaftesbury's meditations on the Camisard trials reflect the imbrication of aesthetic value and enthusiastic rapture with the problem of jurisdiction. This aesthetic-juridical dyad becomes easier to recognize as we investigate the form and logic of "Sensus Communis," a rejoinder to the numerous engagements with and refutations of the "Letter." In what follows, I will subject "Sensus Communis" to an analysis designed to demonstrate the legal logic that structures the essay. I will show that, not only does Shaftesbury's witty enthusiasm function as an ideal of self-regulation, but that this wit orchestrates the legal transformations that we have been outlined earlier. It does so by generalizing the question of regulation itself.

Nearly all interlocutors objected to Shaftesbury's proposition that enthusiasm self-regulates, and in response, "Sensus Communis" brought to the foreground the specifically jurisdictional stakes of the Camisard trial. The essay begins with a legalistic anecdote structured by the neoclassical convention of an imagined conversation between two speakers. Shaftesbury opens by gesturing to an interlocutor who is posited as having impugned Shaftesbury's ability to withstand wit's critical pressure. "Were you not afraid," Shaftesbury wonders aloud, "I should not stand the trial, if you put me to it, by making the experiment in *my own case*?"[30] Placing himself in the position of the defendant, Shaftesbury suggests that only a true "zealot" would fear the application of wit to his arguments, because only a zealot makes, and thus seeks to protect, false claims to truth. In making a distinction between zealotry and enthusiasm, Shaftesbury returns to his claims in the "Letter" by reminding the reader that wit assists the subject in discriminating between true and false enthusiasms: wit breaks with custom and received opinion, and serves to expose truths taken on the authority of others.

More than this, in framing his own essay as a kind of trial, Shaftesbury explicitly counterposes enthusiastic wit to the common-law tradition of custom. Here, the freedom of raillery is compared to the terrors of theocracy in general, and to the codification of superstition in the law more specifically. For Shaftesbury, custom *is* a kind of superstition: as opinion received on the authority of convention or force, rather than through self-regulation and inquiry, the custom underpinning common law becomes both tyrannical and ghostly, or monstrous:

> The question is ... whether it be not just and reasonable to make as free with our own opinions as with those of other people. For to be sparing in this case may be looked upon as a piece of selfishness. We may be charged perhaps with willful ignorance and blind idolatry for having taken opinions upon trust and consecrated in ourselves certain idol-notions, which we will never suffer to be unveiled or seen in open light. They may perhaps be monsters, and not divinities or sacred truths, which are kept thus choicely in some dark corner of our minds. The specters may impose on us, while we refuse to turn them every way and view their shapes and complexions in every light. For that which can be shown only in a certain light is questionable. Truth, it is supposed, may bear *all* lights, and one of those principal lights, or natural mediums, by which things are to be viewed, in order to a thorough recognition, is ridicule itself, or that manner of proof by which we discern whatever is liable to just raillery on any subject.[31]

"The specters may impose on us," Shaftesbury warns. Here, common law's reliance on trial and testimony—a tradition that Shaftesbury associates not just with the "Norman Yoke," but also with the "barbarism" of contemporary France—makes common law dependent on "monsters," or the lurking presence of things unseen. This critique of the common law courts at which the Camisards were tried anticipates Geoffrey Gilbert's argument, in 1724, that the trial format is fundamentally flawed since it relies on evidence that exists either in memory or on the ability to convince the juror of evidence that can never be verified through direct experience.[32] Indeed, the fundamental assumption of a common-law trial is that it is possible to recollect and to communicate with accuracy acts that have taken place at a prior time, so to gain "perfect knowledge of events that cannot be seen."[33] As such, the law, Gilbert argued, dealt with "transient things of no constant being." Against the unverifiable structures of trial law, Shaftesburian wit is posited as both judge and instance of enthusiasm—a passionate comportment that does the impossible double duty of regulating its own excesses, a "lawfulness without a law,"[34] we might say, *avant la lettre*.

Shaftesbury's lawfulness without law predates Kant's leap from self-regulation to "true autonomy." But philosophizing on the far side of the Kantian leap has its advantages—or at least its particularly acute symptomaticity. Lacking a theory of the psyche that would take him from instinctive self-regulation to reasoned transcendence, Shaftesbury conceives enthusiastic wit as a kind of mediator, or "natural medium," that grounds itself in the subject's "thorough recognition" of his or her own situatedness in the context of the larger social order. That this "natural medium" is both an aesthetic frame—"by which things are to be viewed"—and a proposition about the larger social field, recalls John Guillory's account of the emergence of civil society as a sector of economic competition but also of cultural production, a process that necessitated new discourses and apparati of social regulation. For Guillory, this entailed a "massive rethinking of the nature of that [social] order, indeed a new formulation of the question of 'society.'"[35] Such rethinking is made urgent by the foreclosure of monarchical or theological authority on questions of public policy. The questions that haunted public policy were ones for which traditional discourses—and traditional jurisprudence—did not have adequate answers, particularly those issues to do with the state's imbrication with expanding channels of commerce. Without recourse to customary sources of authority, moral philosophy took up the mantle of "constructing a theoretical basis for such policies as taxation".[36] We might see Shaftesbury's denigration of custom in this frame: as part of a discourse that ranged around the valorization of statute, which argued policy in general rather than on common law's case-by-case basis. Such abstraction was necessary, furthermore, because moral philosophy operated without the kinds of discursive distinctions with which we are familiar today. As Guillory argues, questions of law and economic policy were not always debated within the respective discourses that these fields now occupy; accordingly, such questions "could also be posed (and had to be posed) at a level of philosophical abstraction, as questions belonging to the field of moral philosophy, the discourse whose largest project was to relate 'private interest' to 'public good'".[37]

Wit registers the pressures of economic transformation and the legitimation of a centralized state power in the form of the law, and it does so in language that aestheticizes this dialectic of regulation and "freedom." As that aesthetic frame that represents the world of "things" to the viewer, wit also regulates them—it is the medium through which things are viewed, and one that structures, as well, the subject's critical capacity to order these things. In constructing this self-authorizing, self-regulating wit, Shaftesbury overturns the traditional distinction between wit and judgment, a distinction hewed to by virtually all commentators and, most famously, by Hobbes, Locke, and Dryden. The latter's definition will serve to mark the place of this contrast:

> Those that observe their similitudes, in case they be such as are but rarely observed by others, are said to have a *good wit*; by which in this occasion is meant a *good fancy*. But they that observe their differences, and disimilitudes; which is called *distinguishing*, and *discerning*, and *judging* between thing and thing; in case such *discerning* be not easy, are said to have good *judgement* . . . The former, that is fancy, without the help of judgement is not commended as a virtue, but the latter, which is judgement, and discretion, is commended for itself, without the help of fancy.[38]

The neoclassical tradition of parsing the interrelation of wit with judgment finds its terminus in Shaftesbury, for whom the enthusiasm of wit makes it its own judge. Such enthusiastic wit, is, moreover, the very cause of reason since, according to Shaftesbury, it is the pleasure of wit alone that makes the subject want to exercise the regulatory mechanism of reason in the first place: "It is the habit alone of reasoning which can make a reasoner. And men can never be better invited to the habit than when they find pleasure in it".[39] This canny disruption of the concept of habit, so critical to the customary claims of common law, asks the reader to consider more explicitly the structures of reasonable thought. The self-sufficiency of the "habit of reasoning *alone*," is wittily upended as Shaftesbury shows that habits are not instinctual but "invited" or negotiated: the subject forms a habit because it is pleasurable. Such a reading distinctly complicates both the presumptions of custom as well as the longstanding reception of Shaftesbury as a theorist of the aesthetics of instinctual pleasure.

The Ethical Aesthetics of Wit: The Extant Critical Tradition

In John Barrell's well-known formulation, Shaftesbury conceives a disinterested, desire-free pleasure that functions as an allegory for relief from material constraint: "The discourse of civic humanism . . . represented civic freedom not only as an emancipation from servility and dependence, but an emancipation from desire. [T]he vocabulary of the civic discourse, which could describe acquisitive and especially commercial activity in the same terms as it described sexual indulgence [i.e., interested desire or pleasure] . . . enabled emancipation from sexual desire to stand as a mark for emancipation from material desire and vice versa."[40] For Barrell, the subject invested with this aesthetic instinct is, by implication, aristocratic: his idealized independence from material constraint purifies his moral perspective: "only the true citizen is capable of being polished and not corrupted by the purely aesthetic characteristics of works of art. Those who are not citizens are excluded as firmly from participation in the republic of taste as they are from the political republic."[41]

For Lawrence Klein, by some contrast, the possibilities for "moral improvement" offered by Shaftesbury's ethical aesthetics are opened up to the bourgeois and accompany the transition out of a rank-based social hierarchy. We do not need to side with either critic, however, to recognize that although the formal relation of pleasure to reason grounds wit's democratic capacity for self-regulation, the potential dangers of a social order regulated by this pleasure drive "Sensus Communis" further and further into a number of intractable contradictions. The most immediate of these contradictions is the untenable democracy of wit itself. If pleasure is the measure of reasonable thought, what will regulate pleasure itself? Indeed, the pleasures of wit can be exercised by anyone, with unpredictable results and a potentially unchecked tastelessness: "when one considers what use is sometimes made of this species of wit and to what an excess it has risen of late in some characters of the age," Shaftesbury worries, "one may be startled a little and in doubt what to think of the practice or whither this rallying humour will at length carry us."[42] Wit, admits Shaftesbury, inherently produces vertiginous oscillations between its legitimate and illegitimate, excessive aspects. How to manage this "excess," the naturally pleasurable lure of raillery?

This question had traditionally been answered with "judgment." But Shaftesbury, having elided wit with judgment under the aegis of enthusiastic self-regulation, requires a new solution to the question of excess. Indeed, without such a solution, the democratic potential of pleasure poses more problems than it solves. As Shaftesbury points out, the problem with wit is that it is the language of the state, and the rabble too: wit has grown excessive and has "passed from men of pleasure to men of business. Politicians have been infected with it, and the gravest affairs of state have been treated with an air of irony and banter. The ablest negotiators have been known the notablest buffoons, the most celebrated authors, the greatest masters of burlesque."[43] Against the universally confounding wit of *both* the common man and the state under the Tory ministry—which "amuses all alike and leaves the most sensible man and even a friend equally in doubt and at a loss to understand what one's real mind is upon any subject"—Shaftesbury seeks another agent of regulation.

Shaftesbury's "Something Which Thinks"

In the scholarship on Shaftesbury, it has been generally agreed that culture functions as a regulatory zone defined by the constraints of politeness; this zone is, furthermore, strictly self-policing. Shaftesbury's prescription for wit's threatening excesses appears to model such self-regulation. Wit, he argues,

> . . . will mend upon our hands and humour will refine itself, if we take care not to tamper with it and bring it under constraint by severe usage and rigorous prescriptions. All politeness is owing to liberty. We polish one another and rub off our corners and rough sides by a sort of amicable collision. To restrain this is inevitably to bring a rust upon men's understandings. It is a destroying of civility, good breeding and even charity itself, under pretence of maintaining it[44]

In the absence of another regulatory power, it falls to "good breeding" to organize and standardize cultural expression. Such a formula conforms to Klein's definition of politenes as a mode of cultural and discursive conduct attendant on the rise of a commercial culture that produces its own ethical lexicon. Here, Shaftesburian enthusiasm exemplifies the distension of a Whig culture of market expansion into its discursive dimension: a language of distinction that accords with the theory of a market free of state and monarchical control. Against its classical connotation as the sheer exteriority of manners, Shaftesburian politeness, Klein argues,

> provoked moral tensions, evident in major writers of the early eighteenth century. Shaftesbury and the writers of the *Spectator* distrusted 'politeness' either as a cant term for social license or as a notion of amoral social strategy. However, they were interested not in aspersing "politeness," but in absorbing it into a moral framework. While they continued, in a general way, the moral concerns of the native moralist tradition, they also esteemed more highly the claims of politeness whose prestige they, in turn, did much to enhance.[45]

For Klein, suturing politeness to philosophy severs the practice of critique from the philological and the antiquarian traditions and transforms critique for the new public sphere:

Thus, Shaftesbury embraced the word 'politeness' and the concern with sociability it raised, but he sought to avoid its moral turbidity by anchoring it in philosophy. The philosophical grounding of "politeness" presupposed an expansion of the term's meaning. In one formulation, Shaftesbury wrote: "To philosophise, in a just Signi-ication, is but to carry good-breeding a step higher. For the accomplishment of breeding is, to learn whatever is decent in company, or beautiful in arts: and the sum of philosophy is, to learn what is just in society, and beautiful in nature, and the order of the world."[46]

For Klein, the marriage of politeness with philosophy represents Shaftesbury's broader aspiration for politeness to "rule areas of discourse beyond social behavior." By bridging the rhetoric/philosophic divide—"[w]here 'polite learning' was 'ornamental,' 'philosophy' was 'solid' and 'useful'"—Shaftesbury reclassifies politeness to "designat[e] a [new] social elite."[47] In borrowing from the culture of ancient public spaces and urbane liberty, Shaftesbury, Klein concludes, formulates politeness as the discursive manifestation of

> a vibrant and free public, a site of endless, intermingled political and philosophical discourse . . . The ideal of 'politeness' registered an aspiration toward a profound discursivity in cultural forms. Thus in Shaftesbury, 'politeness' reformulated commerce on a high cultural plane and secured virtue to it.[48]

But is the securing of virtue to commercial culture as certain as it appears here? Indeed, even Shaftesbury has to admit that the basis of "good breeding" is largely up for debate: "[t]o describe true raillery," he admits, "would be as hard a matter, and perhaps as little to the purpose, as to define good breeding. None can understand the speculation beside those who have the practice. Yet everyone thinks himself well-bred. . . ."[49] By the Kleinian reading, Shaftesbury's claim that "everyone thinks himself well-bred" reflects the rise of a bourgeois order in which, by opening the category of value to the qualifications of taste, "everyone" may begin to think himself well-bred. I wish to argue, however, that this delinking of value from peerage does not necessarily result in a new suture. For, when Shaftesbury tells us that "none can understand the speculation beside those who have the practice," landed wealth is not replaced with the fullness of a subjectivity aligned with market culture. It would be more accurate to say, rather, that although the terms of the production of value have shifted, the subject is not secured to this value in any meaningful way, but instead appears as an emphatically empty bearer of this value.

Shaftesbury's contemplation of the content of virtuous subjectivity places his work within an epistemological movement that defined eighteenth-century philosophy, and one by which the Cartesian *cogito* was continually radicalized in Enlightenment theories of the subject. Indeed, as Shaftesbury's "breeding" loses its empirical signification as a marker of rank, it becomes a movement of self-reflection: "everyone *thinks himself* well-bred." Unlike the Cartesian "I think," which fantasizes that in "every representation of an object, we get hold of a positive phenomenal entity . . . which thinks and is transparent to itself in its capacity to think,"[50] Shaftesbury offers us a subject empty of content, and a conception of value without a secure referent.

This movement is explored further in *Miscellany IV*, in which Shaftesbury objects to the mechanical nature of the Cartesian *cogito*. Shaftesbury's eloquent grasp of the contingent nature of subjectivity is remarkable and merits citation at length:

> That there is something undoubtedly which thinks, our very doubt itself and scrupulous thought evinces. But in what subject that thought resides . . . this is not a matter so easily or hastily decided . . . It will not, in this respect, be sufficient for us to use the seeming logic of a famous modern and say, "We think; therefore we are" . . . For the Ego or I, being established in the first part of the proposition, the *ergo*, no doubt, must hold it good in the latter. But the question is, "What constitutes the 'we' or 'I'?" . . . we may be conscious of that as truth which perhaps was no more than dream, and we may be conscious of that as a past dream, which perhaps was never before so much as dreamt of. This is what metaphysicians mean when they say "that identity can be proved only by consciousness, but that consciousness, withal, may be as well false as real in respect of what is past." . . . To the force of this reasoning, I confess, I must so far submit as to declare that, for my own part, I take my being upon trust . . . This to me appears sufficient ground for a moralist. Nor do I ask more when I undertake to prove the reality of virtue and morals . . . The affections of which I am conscious are either grief or joy, desire or aversion. For whatever mere sensation I may experience, if it amounts to neither of these, it is indifferent and no way affects me.[51]

Shaftesbury's punning acknowledgment of the transitive properties of "Ego" and "*ergo*" makes Descartes' "therefore I am," sheerly repetitive. Indeed, the Cartesian' "I think" presupposes an "I," which Shaftesbury cannot credit quite so easily: "'What constitutes the 'we' or 'I'?" he asks, in a flurry of quotation marks that structurally reinforce the contingent nature of subjectivity. Here, the Shaftesburian "something which thinks" nears the artefactual logic of the Kantian *I*, for which the dreamlike, unverifiable quality of memory confirms at once the melancholic structure of self-consciousness (with its eternally receding Real), and the specifically human capacity for abstraction—the subjectivization of the subject in the irreducible gap between what Slavoj Zizek calls "the analytical proposition on the identity of the logical subject of thought, contained in 'I think,' and the synthetic proposition on the identity of a *person* qua thinking thing-substance"[52]

Here, Shaftesbury intervenes in the Lockean debate over the reliability of memory and the consistency of the subject over time. If for Locke the ultimately undecidable truth of memories—particularly memories of dreams, which for Locke have no empirical authorization outside of the subject's own testimony—makes the subject's confirmation of his own self-identity a matter of some vertigo, Shaftesbury resolves this problem by sidelining the question of the truth of memory itself. To be "conscious of that as truth which perhaps was no more than dream," is not a matter of particular anxiety for Shaftesbury. Indeed, ethical action does not depend on the truth or consistency of the subject—matters that are of some "indifference" to Shaftesbury—but rather on the act of self-reflection. As opposed to the Cartesian cogito, the moralist does not need to prove his own existence in order to "prove the reality" of morals. The "something which thinks," accesses judgment precisely in suspending the empirical confirmation of subjective reality.

I have placed Shaftesbury's reflections on subjectivity in relation to a number of truisms about the Kantian subject in order to intervene in the standard account of pre-Kantian ethics, which tends to dismiss the theorization of pre-Kantian subjectivity as one-dimensional. What I have attempted to briefly illuminate is that, although Shaftesbury does not conceive a particularly dimensional subject, he does conceptualize the location of this subject in relation to the social field in ways that are critical to our understanding of how early Enlightenment culture thought through the relationships between subjects and social order. With this in mind, we may acknowledge without lament that the Shaftesburian subject may not be particularly complex. It contains none of the Kantian acrobatics of deduction, nor does it present an articulate Lockean extrapolation on the subject's existence. Shaftesburian judgment, rather, hinges on the direct action of the senses (or, at least, those senses that are affecting), and on the moralist's "disinterested" relation to this sensory data. And although this sensory foundation for ethical thought does condemn Shaftesbury to a rather untranscendental and possibly even mundane conception of the subject as enchained to the simple data of daily stimuli, what is most interesting is not to weigh Shaftesburian ethics against the Kantian successor, but rather to consider what the "something which thinks" forces into view.

Ultimately, Shaftesbury's "something which thinks" does not showcase the subject's self-consciousness as such. Indeed, the analysis of subjectivity results only in its progressive enmurkment, its eventual consignment to the realm of "trust." What becomes more significant, however, is the process of proving the reality, not of the self, but of the process of moral self-regulation. Value does not easily or inevitably stitch itself to a new object, and the language of politeness, freed from its referent in peerage, is less the provision of a language for burgeoning bourgeois culture, and rather more an act of sublimely receding self-reflection that generalizes the problem of value itself.[53]

For some, the fact that Shaftesbury takes his being "on trust" appears at first as a simple and even clumsy negation of Locke's insistence that reason must be proportionate to evidence, and that only on the basis of this can we reckon the existence of ourselves, over time, as subjects.[54] This, in any case, is Klein's interpretation of Shaftesbury's position on innate ideas and on instinct. As Klein argues, in "The Moralists," Shaftesbury stages a debate between two interlocutors, and has them put it thusly: " . . . if you dislike the word 'innate,' let us change it, if you will, for 'instinct,' and call that instinct that which nature teaches, exclusive of art, culture or discipline.'" Klein's annotation remarks that, of the Lockean notion of innate ideas, "[i]n characteristic fashion, Shaftesbury was dismissive of the technical side of this debate."[55] And yet, the elision of the "technical" specifics of subjectivity is precisely the point. Indeed, this elision is not a simple negation, but rather puts in place a set of claims obscured beneath the seemingly minute "dismissals" strewn throughout the *Characteristics*. By bracketing the substance of subjectivity, Shaftesbury produces an argument for moral social regulation, not by precedent, but by general principle. Against the common-law logic of cases and specifics, Shaftesbury articulates the universalizing logic of analogy. Indeed, it is here, in the universal logic of analogy by which anyone could be a "something which thinks," that Shaftesbury's schema of harmonious social order is most fully articulated. It is, however, also here that this logic will fail most spectacularly.

Sovereignty and Statistics: The Mandevillian Shaftesbury

Just after the appeal to "good breeding" dissolves in the ambiguities of social station, Shaftesbury addresses the fissures in a dangerously democratic wit by seizing on an economic analogue. To wit's vertiginous spirals, Shaftesbury offers another arena of self-regulation: the free market. Like wit, both run on credit. Just as there must be a distinguishable difference between true and false enthusiasms, Shaftesbury argues, so there must be a difference between appropriate and inappropriate forms of raillery: "there is as much difference between one sort [of raillery] and another as between fair dealing and hypocrisy, or between the genteelest wit and the most scurrilous buffoonery."[56] Shaftesbury follows this assertion with a "But." "But," he says, "by freedom of conversation this illiberal kind of wit will lose its credit."

"But" reads as the rejoinder to an unposed question: "But of course," this interlocutor is posited as having interjected, even the "illiberal" forms of wit will find their audience and will move through the social field as a kind of imposter-wit, one indistinguishable (to the common ear) from wit's more "legitimate" forms. The presumption here—one that Shaftesbury conjures while performatively warding off—is that wit replicates the very problem associated with enthusiasm: its "true" and "false" forms are indistinguishable because both are severed from exterior forces of authorization. More than this, like wit, the market shores up its own potentially boundless powers by a delicate balancing act of exchange and circulation:

> For wit is its own remedy. Liberty and commerce bring it to its true standard. The only danger is the laying an embargo. The same thing happens here, as in the case of trade. Impositions and restrictions reduce it to a low ebb. Nothing is so advantageous to it as a free port.[57]

Through the image of the free market, Shaftesbury posits a model for a proto-enlightenment critical subject that regulates itself, not through the exercise of transcendental reason and not through the exercise of empirical reason, but rather—in an analogical generalization of regulation—as the market regulates itself.

At least some of Shaftesbury's contemporaries regarded his vision of a friction-free, harmonious social whole just as skeptically as his idealistic model of sociality is regarded today. Shaftesbury's most famous critic was of course Bernard Mandeville, whose *Fable of the Bees* advanced a theory of vice and self-interest as the motor of social regulation. The Mandeville-Shaftesbury debate has been well researched and redacted, and does not require review here.[58] What may be instructive, however, is to briefly revisit Mandeville's conception of market practice in order to refine our sense of the terms in which market practice was conceived in this period. This debate largely hinged on the distinction between a spontaneous Shaftesburian social cohesion and Mandeville's rather more regimented insistence on the necessary forces undergirding social order, specifically those that organize the division of labor.

Mandeville's enthusiasm for the division of labor comes across most richly in his description of watch production: "The truth of what you say [about the natural efficiency of the division of labor] is in nothing so conspicuous, as it is in Watch-making, which is come to a higher degree of Perfection, than if the whole had always remain'd the Employment of one Person; and I am persuaded, that even the Plenty we have of Clocks and Watches, as well as the Exactness and Beauty they may be made of, are chiefly owing to the Division that has been made of that Art into many Branches."[59] Mandeville, it is well known, held that social order did not cohere due to enthusiastic, spontaneous virtue, but rather was defined as

> a body politic, in which man is either subdued by superior force, or by persuasion drawn from his savage state . . . [to] become a disciplined creature, that can find his own ends in laboring for others, and where under one head or other form of government each member is rendered subservient to the whole, and all of them by cunning management are made to act as one.[60]

In describing the division of labor, Mandeville asserts that only through force or persuasion could a society sustain the inequalities that result from a division that leads some to prosperity and others to impoverishment. Such is the tenor of Mandeville's attacks on Shaftesburian social order, and on that spontaneous, social cohesiveness that Mandeville diagnoses as itself an inspirational "enthusiasm," believed only by those under the influence of its appeal.[61] Against Shaftesburian enthusiasm, Mandeville offers the forces that organize the division of labor. The result is a "plenty" that serves to illustrate the historicization of the English present in terms of other possible English presents. For if the division of labor had not come to pass, the "plenty" of Watches, with their gorgeous exactitude, would not now exist.

This speculation on a possible future present anticipates what Mary Poovey describes as the turn to "conjectural history" in the Scottish Enlightenment in the second half of the eighteenth century. A short excursus on Poovey's argument will serve us well in interpreting the Mandeville-Shaftesbury debate here. Briefly, Poovey argues that moral philosophers and political economists authorized conjecture as a way of augmenting their claims about histories that they could not possibly empirically document because they had already past. Conjecture was perhaps counterintuitively bound up with the "political arithmetic" founded by Petty's Irish surveys.[62] The statistical, systematizing drive exemplified in Petty's work was supplemented by historiographical conjecture in order to produce wider-ranging systematic knowledges about British history and historical transformation. Mandeville adumbrates this logic in his description of the division of labor; indeed the subject of watchmaking is particularly opportune, as Mandeville enjoins the reader in an aestheticization of watch precision that entails an appreciation for the historical present as differentiated from its possible alternate present—a present in which one single individual would have had to complete the production of watches from start to finish. In such an alternate present, Mandeville posits, the accumulation of watches would have been delayed, if not impossible. This present, in other words, would have been always in a sense *past*, the specter of a present that is always behind in time, irremediably delayed and productively handicapped.

Here, the technologies of production map onto a historicization of time and its differential rates of progress, and they do so not only in the production of a conjectured past, but in conjuring the possibility of an alternate present. The singular chronologies of individual production are replaced by the proliferative chronologies of the division of labor and its temporal logic: the infinitely expansive possible histories of the present. It is worth noting, finally, that Mandeville's appreciation for the division of labor was, in 1732, itself a conjectured history of the present because such division was, by all accounts, not fully institutionalized until the later eighteenth century. In this way, Mandeville's assertion of a present distinguished by a highly efficient division of labor was, not an empirical account of that present, but rather a conjecture about a possible future characterized by the institutionalization of a division of labor systemwide.

Conjectural Geographies, Execution, Inquisition

Mandeville's vision of the division of labor reminds us that theories of market practice—particularly in the early eighteenth century as the abstraction of the market itself was only just beginning to be articulated as such—were, at one and the same time, theories of temporality and of history. Although Mandeville has been regarded as Shaftesbury's staunchest opponent, the thinkers shared a conception of historical time that not only created conjectures regarding the historical past but, in doing so, naturalized new concepts of social regulation on a large scale. Consider that the Shaftesburian figure of the free market—one that putatively regulates itself in a harmonious syncopation at all levels of social order—introduces a set of preoccupying anxieties. Indeed, wit may be "its own remedy," but, the reader is tempted to ask, why should it need a remedy in the first place? The reference to a free market becomes, in this way, an ultimately contradictory commonplace for self-regulation, and the subject's ability to manage his or her wayward enthusiasm is, like free trade, always in danger of running to "excess." If Shaftesbury doesn't explicitly detail the regulatory forces that must constrain such excess, he suggests their enforcement by a return to wit as the protagonist in an epic history of sorts:

> We have seen in our own time the decline and ruin of a false sort of wit, which so much delighted our ancestors that their poems and plays as well as sermons were full of it. All humour had something of the quibble. The very language of the Court was punning. But it is now banished the Town and all good company, there are only some few footsteps of it in the Country, and it seems at last confined to the nurseries of youth as the chief entertainment of pedants and their pupils.[63]

Shaftesbury's long view of the English landscape past and present, borrows something of the conjectural, systematizing logic of Petty and Mandeville, if unwittingly so. In tracking wit, Shaftesbury tracks the differential development of town and country, with the latter posed as delayed and childish. If here Shaftesbury only appears to be reveling in the refinements of the town, the formal structure of this passage—its movement from town, to country, to the nursery—demands a more exacting analysis. Indeed, his aerial view of the English counties suggests there is something quite a bit closer to the systematizing, economic logics of the Mandevillian perspective than the holistic harmonies for which Shaftesbury has been celebrated. Such mapping, charting the progress of culture by region, resounds with the statistical logic that regards regional development by production capacities and the division of labor. That this section serves to reinforce the weakly bolstered regulatory potentials of the market only affirms further the conjectural logic of this apparent paean to self-regulation. The "free" market is then a myth, we must conclude, of a possible present.

It has not, moreover, escaped our notice that the purging of false wit from the town takes place via a "banishment" that returns us to the problem of evidence and of the legal arm of state sovereignty. Here, Shaftesbury cannily connects the figure of the cogito with the logic of the trial, particularly as it applies to the problematic nature of faith. As we know from the "Letter," in charging the Camisards with guilt, Shaftesbury argued that the courts ruled on something that was ultimately undecidable: the truth of enthusiastic claims.[64] By putting the Camisards on trial, in other words, the courts unwittingly confirmed that which they sought to deny: that the Prophets' enthusiastic visions were substantial and thus a threat. In "Sensus Communis," Shaftesbury proposes an alternative to the inquisitorial approach. A far better method would be to treat these enthusiastic claims as "unaffecting"; to do otherwise is a form of what he calls "zealotry":

> I have known some of those grave gentlemen undertake to correct an author for defending the use of raillery and at the same time have upon every turn made use of that weapon, though they were naturally so awkward at it. And this I believe may be observed in the case of many zealots who have taken upon them to answer our modern free-writers. The tragical gentlemen, with the grim aspect and mien of true inquisitors, have but an ill grace when they vouchsafe to quit their austerity and be jocose and pleasant with an adversary.[65]

Shaftesbury weaves the language of the law together with the concerns of oratory and argument. By casting into question both the critique of Deists and Dissenters ("free-thinkers"), and the continental system of inquisitorial law that invests the ecclesiastical courts with unassailable power, Shaftesbury broadens the category of "zealous" inquisitors to include anti-Deist writers as well as those judges who believe that religious faith can be made legible by a confession. The inquisitorial method determines the authenticity of belief via a legal system that marries court and church power in interrogating individuals directly about their faith. This is a "graceless" hermeneutic, according to Shaftesbury, who prefers the imminent self-critique of raillery which, in the wrong hands, should reveal itself by the "awkwardness" with which it is articulated. Inquisitors read for content, believing that they can produce truth through confession. But the act of inquisition, which relies on the ability to rout out false belief through force, produces a "Janus-faced" writing that does not require the function of active judgement: wit, in the wrong hands, always exposes itself as ridiculous:

> ... [T]o do them [the inquisitioners] justice, had they their wills, I doubt not but their conduct and mien would be pretty much of a piece. They would in all probability quit their farce and make a thorough tragedy. But at present there is nothing so ridiculous as this Janus-face of writers, who with one countenance force a smile and with another show nothing beside rage and fury.[66]

The imprecision of intention—the "Janus-faced" contradictions of speech—suggests that inquisition cannot determine ethical truth because claims cannot be searched for their intended meanings. However, although the content of meaning cannot be located through inquisition, the "ridiculous" *form* of "Janus-faced" speech signals a truth—that of the weakness of the zealots' approach—otherwise unavailable to the logic of common law, which relies on the ability of the courts to infer the meaning of any particular precedent. Whereas common law depends on "deduction" to arrive at a ruling, statute promotes a foundation of positive law as "legislative sovereignty."[67] Shaftesbury's suspension of the question of intention from the scene, both of reading and of legislation, is a quite direct reference to this legal relationship. The implications of this argument come to the fore in a seemingly incidental reference to the scene of execution, as Shaftesbury expands his argument.

> There cannot be a more preposterous sight than an executioner and a merry Andrew acting their part upon the same stage. Yet I am persuaded anyone will find this to be

the real picture of certain modern zealots in their controversial writings. They are no more masters of gravity than they are of good humour. The first always runs into harsh severity and the latter into an awkward buffoonery. And thus between anger and pleasure, zeal and drollery, their writing has much such a grace as the play of humoursome children, who, at the same instant, are both peevish and wanton and can laugh and cry almost in one and the same breath.[68]

Surely a Merry Andrew (or, clown) and an executioner together would have been a preposterous sight. But this pairing was a familiar one to eighteenth century subjects, at least conceptually. In depicting the carnivalesque nature of public executions, Shaftesbury links the spectacular display of state power (in the form of an execution) with an anti-enthusiastic argument and writing style. Such writing is allegorized as a clownish display of state sovereignty. Much more preferable, for Shaftesbury, is the quiet exercise of self-correction.

In raising the specter of public execution, Shaftesbury engages in a debate that preoccupied early eighteenth-century political philosophers, and in particular he disputes the Lockean notion that the sovereignty of the state is showcased in its power to mete out death. As Locke had argued,

Political power, then, I take to be a right of making laws with penalties of death, and, consequently, all less penalties for the regulating and preserving of property, and of employing the force of the community in the execution of such laws.[69]

For Locke, the right to legally regulate economic transactions and the fiscal life of the nation hinged on—indeed was "consequent" to—the institution of the death penalty as the signifier of state sovereignty. We shall see this conjuncture illuminated in Shaftesbury's apparently tangential remarks on capital punishment in the following section.

The Bureaucratization of Capital Punishment

Recent scholarship on early modern executions has been generally divided. On the one hand, we have that scholarship that finds early modern execution to have functioned as "titillat[ing]" "light entertainment," which, despite its design to showcase the power of the crown, inevitably subverted it. On the other hand, scholarship has regarded the phenomenon of execution as a crucible of class struggle, an "earnest battle" which pitted the criminalized poor against the agents of the state.[70] The debate, in other words, ranges precisely around those terms with which Shaftesbury also engages: the question of the comical or earnest nature of the execution. Indeed, even in the eighteenth century, execution was framed as tilting between an irreverent and profound signification. But, as Peter Linebaugh has argued, if we regard eighteenth century executions as largely a ludic spectacle, we may be missing the ways in which these events engaged the increasingly troublesome class divisions of the period.

Eighteenth-century representations of executions underscore both their spectacular nature and the ways in which such spectacles consolidated the laboring poor into collective, resurgent public groupings. If we turn to Mandeville, whose work on executions was well known within the eighteenth century, we get a feel for the ways in which the tragic-comic aspect of the figure of the execution tends to bleed into an anxiety about the troublesome forces of the crowd—the potential coherence of a resistant body of the poor in the face of the state's monopoly on violence. It is worth citing Mandeville at length to establish the terms of the debate in which Shaftesbury participated.

Mandeville's polemic on executions is the early eighteenth century's most enduring example of liberal exegesis on the reformation of capital punishment, and as the most detailed, vivid narrative description of the public scene of executions, the *Enquiry* was the source for many later literary representations of capital punishment. On the day of execution, Mandeville mused, "one would expect a deep Sense of Sorrow . . . and that all, who had any Business there, should be grave and serious, and behave themselves, at least, with common Decency."[71] Not so, he reports,

> [T]he very Reverse is true. The horrid aspects of Turnkeys and Gaolers, in Discontent and Hurry; the sharp and dreadful Looks of Rogues . . . the Bellowings of half a dozen Names at a time . . . the Variety of strong Voices, that are heard, of howling in one Place, scolding and quarrelling in another, and loud Laughter in the third; the substantial Breakfasts that are made in the midst of all this; the Seas of Beer that are swill'd; the never-ceasing Outcries for more; and the Bawling Answers of the Tapsters as continual; the Quantity and Varieties of more entoxicating Liquors . . . the Impudence, and unseasonable Jests . . . all these, joined together, are astonishing and terrible, without mentioning the Oaths and Imprecations, that from every Corner are echo'd about . . . or the little, light, and general Squallor of the Gaol itself, accompany'd with the melancholy Noise of Fetters, differently sounding, according to their Weight: But what is most shocking to a thinking Man, is, the Behavior of the Condemn'd, whom . . . you'll find, either drinking madly, or uttering the vilest Ribaldry, and jeering others . . . At last, out they set; and with them a Torrent of Mob bursts through the Gate. Amongst the lower Rank, and working People, the idlest, and such as are most fond of marking Holidays, with Prentices and Journeymen to the meanest Trades, are the most honourable Part of these floating Multitudes. All the rest are worse. The Days being known beforehand, they are a Summons to all Thieves and Pickpockets, of both Sexes, to meet. Great Mobs are a Safeguard to one another, which makes these Days Jubilees, on which old Offenders, and all who dare not shew their Heads on any other, venture out of their Holes; and they resemble Free Marts, where there is an Amnesty for all Outlaws. All the Way, from Newgate to Tyburn, is one continued Fair, for Whores and Rogues of the Meaner Sort.[72]

Mandeville's argument is classically reformist in that he does not advocate doing away with capital punishment altogether—just its public nature. Mandeville argued for private executions or solitary confinement as expeditious measures to obviate riling the "mob."[73] Here his argument adumbrates Henry Fielding's recommendation that executions be enacted privately—the fear generated by the imagination being much more potent than the evidence available to the eye: "Instead of making the gallows an object of terror, our Executions contribute to make it an Object of Contempt in the Eye of the Malefactor; and we sacrifice the Lives of men, not for the Reformation, but for the Diversion of the Populace."[74] As an anticipatory illustration of Fielding's imaginative objects, Mandeville's narrative litanizes, unscrolling inexorably in its broad view of the event. In doing so, perhaps unwittingly, Mandeville depicts the mob—not the execution—as the object of terror, even as, in comparing the execution to a "Free Mart," Mandeville establishes the kind of connection upon which has rested our scholarly assessments of executions as spectacle.

In the customary Free Mart, inaugurated in 1194, the hanging of a golden glove on the jail door announced fifteen days of general immunity, during which subjects were purportedly free to convene, exchange goods, and enjoy performances at the Free Mart Fair without fear of being arrested for debt or other infractions. Scholars have read Mandeville's comparison as evidence for the comical nature of executions, but the irony of comparing execution day—a day of purportedly exemplary justice—to the Free Mart—a day of immunity for all offenders suggests not just the comical nature of execution day, but Mandeville's desire to periodize both the spectacular nature of the executions and the convened "mob" themselves as the residua of a prior social order. Indeed, against the antiquated format of the public execution, Mandeville advises what he regards as the more modern Dutch method of correction: the workhouse—"the great Cities [of Holland] . . . have all Work-houses for Criminals," where the state can "make use of Malefactors in their Gallies"[75] For Mandeville, a public execution amounts to a Free Mart; it gives the Mob the opportunity to convene and conduct offenses.

In drawing on the Dutch case, Mandeville demonstrates that his objection to the public death penalty revolves largely around the English system's dearth of productivity. Not only did the extant laws around capital punishment fail to fully exploit the living labor embodied in the criminal person while incarcerated, but because they had not yet fully institutionalized the dissection of the bodies of the condemned for scientific use, the laws did not fully extract the value of the body after death either. Here, too, Mandeville looked to Holland as an exemplar of national productivity:

> The University of Leyden in Holland have a Power given them by the Legislature to demand, for this [scientific] Purpose, the Bodies of ordinary Rogues executed within that Province; but with us, it is the general Complaint of all Professors of Anatomy, that they can get none to dissect: Where than shall we find a readier Supply; and what Degree of People are fitter for it than those I have named? When Persons of no Possessions of their own . . . die without Restitutions, indebted to the Public, ought not he injur'd Publick to have a Title to, and Disposal of, what the others have left?[76]

For Mandeville, the debate around public execution was not a debate around the limits of state sovereignty so much as it was a debate around the most *productive* uses of this sovereignty. Such an argument, of course, returns us to Mandeville's position on the division of labor and its necessary enforcement; by contrast to the Dutch, English public capital punishments were an inefficient use of the state's sovereign powers.

It is here, in the conjunction of British productivity and the transformation of the law, that Shaftesbury and Mandeville's positions come nearer to one another than scholars have previously imagined. Neither Mandeville nor Shaftesbury argues explicitly against the death penalty. Rather, both draw on—and exacerbate—the literary convention of the clownish nature of executions. In Mandeville's case, he does so in order to demonstrate the reasonableness and productiveness of private punishments: the Free Mart is a relic of English national backwardness and nonproductivity; the masses who attend the executions, by extension, are similarly nonproductive, holiday-making subjects who could be put to better use. For Shaftesbury, the convention of spectacular executions allows him to begin to elide the differences between writers and judges: poor writers are afflicted by the awkwardness of an inquisitorial approach that creates clownish writing more appropriate to a "Merry Andrew." Both inquisitors and poor writers would be more effective if they properly practiced a self-regulating wit. In critiquing inquisitors as poor writers, Shaftesbury effects a subtle shift, but one that is worth noting, weaving together the agent of the law with the formal function of the author. As such, Shaftesbury makes an implicit argument for a legal system that would begin to favor the letter of the law—the written law, or, as Hale had put it, the *legis scriptae*—over the sovereign power of the courts.

The Legis Scriptae

This statute-based legal system, of course, was not any less ruthless than the common-law dominated state system. In fact, the increase in statutes increased the number of capital crimes considerably.[77] In advocating for the written law over the inquisitorial approach, Shaftesbury did not make any great interventions against the violent deployment of state power. But, in light of the fact that the majority of the statutes passed by Parliamentary Act had to do with the minutiae of exchange, circulation, property crime, and the like, such a shift between written law and inquisition reflected in critical ways the legal transformations enacted in the development of the modern British state. As the nineteenth-century legal theorist, James Fitzjames Stephens, recognized, the increase in statute was particularly vigorous in addressing crimes of an economic nature.

> In particular as the paper currency developed itself, provisions of extreme elaboration and minuteness were passed, punishing not only the forgery of bank notes and everything of the nature of a bank note; and the uttering of forged bank notes; but the making and possession of paper suitable for forgery, and of instruments suitable for its manufacture.[78]

By the late eighteenth century, this wealth of statute laws around property had fundamentally altered the British legal system: "No part of the criminal law," Stephens argued, "of the latter part of the eighteenth century was more severe in itself, or was executed with greater severity than this"[79] Benno Teschke has recently expanded on these claims, clarifying the relationship between property and statute: "After the establishment of an agrarian capitalist property regime and the transformation of the militarized, landholding feudal nobility into a demilitarized landed capitalist class, with full and exclusive property rights in late-seventeenth-century England, political authority was redefined in terms of Parliamentary sovereignty."[80] It is this context within which we can most profitably understand Shaftesbury's exegesis on Merry Andrews and executioners. In eschewing what he represents as the carnivalesque nature of executions, Shaftesbury contributes not only to a debate over religious enthusiasm, but simultaneously to one of the defining debates of the time: that over legal practice and the seemingly endlessly new provisions of statute. In defending the basis of such provisions—the law as the *letter* of the law, as an authored Act of writing, rather than a singular string of court enactments—Shaftesbury's "freedom of wit and raillery" not only reveals the interwined histories of economic circulation and the development of the juridical arm of the state, but recodes the traditional problem of enthusiasm. If enthusiasm had long been a problem of interpretation, and had ranged around the problem of whether or not one could reliably decipher its "true" or "false" nature, Shaftesbury redefines enthusiasm as a general principle of sovereign self-management, one exemplified in the *legis scriptae*.

In Shaftesbury, it is the interpreters and inquisitors who are "buffoons" for believing in the possibility of reading legal language for the "spirit" with which this language is issued. What is buffoonish about the zealot inquisitors is that they attempt to elicit *confessions* or, put another way, to co-ordinate the profession of faith with the "truth" of belief. Here, Shaftesbury turns the claims of the enthusiasts that the spirit speaks through them into an accusation leveled at the inquisitors themselves. If we compare Dr. Edmund Calamy's account of John Lacy's enthusiastic fits with "Sensus Communis"'s description of the inquisitors, the rhetorical inversion Shaftesbury effects will become clearer:

> I went into the room where he [John Lacy] sat, and walked up to him, and asked him how he did, and took him by the hand, and lifted it up, and it fell down flat upon his knees, as it lay before. He took no notice of me, nor made me any answer; but I observed the humming noise grew louder and louder by degrees, and the heaving in his breast increased, till it came up to his throat, as if it would have suffocated him, and then he at last proceeded to speak, or as he would have it taken, the spirit spake in him.[81]

In response to the anti-enthusiastic writers, Shaftesbury literalizes the enthusiast's claim—that the spirit speaks in him—but diagnoses the zealot inquisitors with precisely this condition. The inquisitors take on the enthusiastic qualities by which the spirit speaks through the body for they are "at the same instant ... both peevish and wanton and can laugh and cry almost in one and the same breath." The inquisitors exhale a delirium of contradictory sentiments simultaneously and, in identifying this doublespeak, Shaftesbury raises to the reader's view the problem of intention. If the zealotry of simultaneous laughter and tears recalls the enthusiastic spirit speaking through the body, against this endless regress of interpretation, Shaftesbury outlines a legal solution to the illegibility of intention: the legal principle of positive law as the rejection of deductive reasoning.

Enthusiasm: The Vanishing Mediator

Although Shaftesbury explicitly argues against state control of economic practices, and insists instead that an "embargo" is the greatest danger to the market, his argument opens a question about state regulation that it does not answer explicitly, but rather in its structure and movement. On the one hand, "enthusiasm" is a fantasy of the self-regulating nature of the subject and of the subject's harmonious reflection of universal order. On the other hand, "enthusiasm" is the formal structure by which a host of material relationships—between legislative power and economic growth, between religious freedom and the containment of religious passion, between capital punishment and state sovereignty—reveal their simultaneously contradictory and mutually sustaining architectures.

Let us, in closing, take stock of this intersection of the law with Shaftesbury's figurative appeal to the market, and let us do so in terms of the long arc of Shaftesbury's argument about enthusiasm. This will allow us to contextualize the findings of our current chapter with those of the previous one and, in combining them, to move on to the second half of this book. As we saw in the "Letter," in counterposing the Mosaic prohibition on enthusiasm to the civilizing influence of English mimicry, Shaftesbury invokes the specter of the ungainly forces of theocratic accumulation as a foil for the putative equilibrium of the English social order. In "Sensus Communis," Shaftesbury specifies this equilibrium further with the figure of the market, which mirrors the self-regulating qualities of enthusiastic passion. But when even this model of market equivalence spins toward doubt, the threat of market accumulation redoubles the reader's concern about the dubious possibilities of denaturing enthusiasm, too. Here, the question of state regulation returns not at the level of content, but in the form of an implied but unasked question: What will regulate the self-regulator?

In generating this question, Shaftesbury invests enthusiasm with the contradictions by which ideals of the state and the market were woven together at just this historical moment. Indeed, the threat of theocracy that functions in Shaftesbury as a historical cipher—one by which the accumulative tendencies of the present are cast as a property of the past—now has the perhaps surprising effect of introducing the prospect of state-regulated accumulation into the ambit of enthusiastic autonomy. In doing so, the figure of theocracy works as a narrative device to provisionally link the problematic of accumulation—associated at first, for Shaftesbury, with ancient priestcraft—with that of the modern state. The most appropriate name for this provisional linkage is the "vanishing mediator," that catalytic agent that, as Fredric Jameson has argued, "permits an exchange of energies between two otherwise mutually exclusive terms."[82] In conceptualizing the vanishing mediator, Jameson describes the discursive textures surrounding moments of great historical transition: the vanishing mediator naturalizes new cultural forces, vanishing once they have become dominant.[83] Enthusiastic prophesy, for Shaftesbury, is just such a narrative device: a vanishing mediator that sutures the ancient to the modern state, permitting the exchange of accumulative energies between the two—an exchange that takes place even as the "freedom" of the modern state appears to be, by definition, incompatible with the violence and imbalance of the ancient one.[84]

As we close this chapter, we may find that *vanishing* is an ultimately more useful concept for us than *secularization*. If Shaftesbury broadens enthusiasm to apply to a number of other self-regulations such as the subject and the market, enthusiasm's specificity as a marker of prophetic fervor has indeed vanished to some extent. This vanishing, however, is not by any means a wholesale secularization, but rather a narrative movement by which the apparent autonomies of Enlightenment culture are brought into relation with the accumulations of a state structure imagined as irretrievably past. For Jameson, too, the vanishing mediator is conceptualized in terms of the status of Enlightenment prophesy and the Weberian formula. In *The Protestant Ethic*, Jameson argues, the prophet is a transitional figure who mediates historical change by "debracketing" the "charismatic authority implicit in the traditional institution of the magician."[85] Although both are charismatic, the difference between the magician and the prophet is that the former is associated with a traditional institution of monetary compensation, while the latter is not. In this way, the figure of the prophet establishes a linkage between the charismatic sway of priestcraft and the rationalized religious structures of Protestantism, which are fantasized as delinked from state power, corruption, and force. As critics have persuasively shown, however, Protestantism is not at all autonomous from the state.[86] Prophesy is, then, that vanishing mediator that briefly articulates key attributes of two different historical formations—enchantment and rationalized religious organization—holding these attributes together in a discursive suture that naturalizes a new order and vanishes once that order has become dominant.

The hermeneutic of the vanishing mediator gives us a framework within which to understand Shaftesbury's conception of enthusiastic prophesy. It allows us to see that, while Shaftesbury imagines enthusiasm as a self-regulating force that obviates the need for state control, the very logic of his argument posits a third term. This third term is the state itself, which is coming into focus in its modern bureaucratic sense. Via a hermeneutics of accumulation, then, we see that Shaftesbury's series of negations drawing on the threatening figure of theocracy, in fact mirror the logic of the state's transition to rule and regulate its population increasingly through statute. This transition, furthermore, supports the kinds of accumulation, imbalance, and violence figuratively associated with the theocratic past. Shaftesbury's appeals to Hermeticism and primitive Christianity on the one hand, and his idealizations of market, moral, and individual sovereignty on the other, are thus two dynamic, though seemingly oppositional, components of his text's larger formal structure: a structure by which the emergent logic of capitalism is encoded in the paradoxical intensification of that logic's seemingly archaic past. In naturalizing a more "rational" religious order, then, enthusiastic prophesy functions as a vanishing mediator that narratively embeds, within secularization's claims to self-regulation and subjective sovereignty, the problem of the state in general, and its relationship to the accumulation of wealth more specifically. We see this motion exposed in its most heightened form when Shaftesbury posits the autonomy of both the citizen and the market, a movement that derails into a meditation on capital punishment. It is in this derailment, as "Sensus Communis" struggles to articulate in aesthetic terms the perfectly non-accumulative practices of this system of civic and economic self-regulation, that the essay reveals what the equivalence and autonomy of enthusiasm conceals at its core: the violent forces that organize and regulate accumulation.

Section Two

Space

Chapter 3

Social Regulation and Transatlantic Accumulation

Thus far, our study has established two interrelated argumentative threads. The first is that enthusiasm informs a historicist sensibility expressed in a number of early Enlightenment discourses. From Lockean individualism to accounts of comparative monotheisms, enthusiasm fosters a model of historical transformation and a revalued conception of religious history. In these comparative accounts, enthusiastic discourse becomes bound up with theories of statecraft, and with the legislative transformations of the early eighteenth century. This latter claim introduces the second argumentative thread: that enthusiastic historicism is bound up with the transformation of the law and, by extension, with naturalizing the implementation of capital accumulation on a large scale. As such, enthusiasm is incorporated into a dialectical movement that at once expresses and conceals early modern legal transformations. This movement may be further understood in terms of Marx's concept of primitive accumulation the encoding, in narrative form, of processes of economic transition.

As I have shown, narratives of primitive accumulation accomplish a number of things simultaneously; first, they strive to resolve discursively the contradiction between ideals of self-management and England's violent, systemic accumulative practices. Next, they furnish the backbone for a conception of subjective and Parliamentary sovereignty. In what follows, I begin with the nexus of concerns with which we left off in chapter 2: the mutually-constitutive, and yet seemingly contradictory relationship between Enlightenment ideals of self-regulation and the implementation of extensive new forms of legal control in early eighteenth-century England. This contradictory dyad is not unfamiliar to scholars of the period, particularly those who locate the birth of liberal ideals of self-management within the complex matrix of Parliamentary and Constitutional Law.[1] What I will add to the extant literature on the subject, however, is a discussion of the ways in which enthusiastic discourse iterates the spatial and geographic dimensions of this contradictory dyad. More specifically, I will show that the Camisard emigration and the debate that it occasioned around enthusiasm was not only about the legitimacy of sudden or seemingly spontaneous religious visions, but also—and crucially—about the sudden or seemingly spontaneous appearance of the Camisards themselves in London.

The Camisard emigration functioned as a dynamic cipher for a number of very real developments underpinning the political geographies of the early eighteenth century. Indeed, the debate around the Camisards channeled a two-pronged geographical project that might be said to define the period: the yoking of the English countryside into a productive and yet devastating relationship with rapidly developing urban spaces, and the unleashing of colonial and commercial depredation in a transatlantic circuit. I focus on the Camisard debate, in other words, as the mediation of another, perhaps larger, set of geographical concerns. Within the figure of the Camisards, the urban landscape of London met the rural Cévennes, in so doing, the Camisard controversy tapped into a set of problems central to early-eighteenth-century life: the relationship of the country to the city, and of the peripheries of empire to the metropole.

These concerns are fundamental to the contradictions of Enlightenment ideology. The legal transformations experienced in England relied upon the massive and unprecedented transformation of the land, and on the overlapping and constantly changing relationships between, on the one hand, rural and metropolitan England, and, on the other, between this vexed matrix itself and the transatlantic expansion of English trade and colonization. This process was well articulated by the eighteenth century, not only in terms of urbanization, but also in terms of the reproduction of the countryside and of nature as a *new* nature, one much more complexly interwoven with the life of the city. Indeed, as the French scientist Buffon argued, "a new nature can come forth from our hands"—a "seconding of nature."[2] This "seconding" of nature was not the urbanization of the landscape per se, but the recoding and reforming of both the concept and the physical contours of nature itself within the new matrix of early capitalism—the reconfiguring of the rural landscape to function in a complex syncopation with urban development. Neil Smith explicates this process in terms of the intense economic and social transfiguration of the Atlantic circuit. In this circuit, he argues, the natural landscape came to be comprised not only of the physical terrain—trees, water, earth, and crops—but also of "the institutions, legal, economic and political rules according to which society operated."[3] The matrix Smith describes is not a simple interchange between country and city or between periphery and metropole; rather, it is the production, anew, of nature itself. The production, that is, of the countryside and the peripheries in a complex dialectical bond with the city:

Elements of the first nature, previously unaltered by human activity, are subjected to the labor process and re-emerge to be social matter of the second nature. There, though their form has been altered by human activity, they do not cease to be natural . . . .—gravity, physical pressure, chemical transformation, biological interaction. But they also become subject to a new set of forces and pressures that are social in origin. Thus the relation with nature develops along with the development of social relations, and insofar as the latter are contradictory, so too is the relation with nature.[4]

Enthusiastic discourse provides us with a unique window onto the contradictory constitution of this "seconding" of space. As it unfolded around the Camisard trials and the emigration of the Prophets to London, enthusiasm registered the intricate interweaving of rural with urban—the seconding of nature in a new, aggressively social order, and the reinscription of the paradoxes of development into the language of religious relationality. More than this, enthusiasm had traditionally committed itself to the theorization of both terrestrial and supernatural spaces. Although I will discuss the representation of supernatural space at greater length in chapter 4, let us note here that it is this commitment that makes enthusiasm such a productive critical lever for us. Because enthusiastic discourse was often in conflict with empiricist theories of scientific space and of statistics, the tensions between enthusiastic space and the technical drive of early modernity can open up and expose the contradictory course of England's geographical transformation, and the linkages between this transformation and those ideologies of self-management and self-regulation so crucial to the legal constitution of Parliamentary governance and of national sovereignty.

Despite our shift in concern from time, broadly speaking, to space, our exploration of the geographical dimensions of enthusiastic discourse is not a departure from the set of claims we have been extrapolating. Rather, it is their extension. The historicisms of the early eighteenth century were ideologies of social development that were conceived as geographical in character. Such a claim, of course, is nothing new. The characterization of peripheries as temporally backward was a key ideological component of English colonial projects, and such chronotopes of colonial development are familiar to scholars of the period, particularly scholars of the Atlantic World.[5] What we can add to the chronotopic study of the Atlantic World is this: if the debate around enthusiasm was vital to the conceptualization of historical time—particularly insofar as enthusiasm had traditionally fostered a long view of time, stretching from the inception of man to his apocalyptic end, and then beyond—this knottily nonsecular historicism was inextricable from a sense of geographical space as well, and particularly from the changing nature of land use and the politicization of that land in the period of intense capital accumulation with which we are concerned. The spatial dimension of enthusiasm thus constitutes the third lobe in our hermeneutic of accumulation. This analytic of spatiality allows us to bring together questions of historicism and legal transformation with large-scale changes to the early modern landscape. I will argue in what follows that, in recovering a nonsecular enthusiastic conception of spatiality, we uncover as well the ways in which the spatial dynamics of transatlantic capital accumulation were encoded in the ideals of enthusiastic self-management that informed conceptions of the sovereignty of both the state and the subject.

This chapter is divided into two sections, each taking up a different deployment of enthusiasm as a spatial metaphorics. In both, I continue to hew to the Camisard controversy as a historical reference point. The first section of this chapter continues our inquiry into Shaftesburian enthusiasm's negotiation of the untenable contradiction between ideals of sovereign self-management and an increasingly market-driven, unstable, and accumulative England. Here and in the second section, the chapter builds on critical accounts of race and capitalism to argue for the influential force of the colonial context on British moral philosophy. Though much transatlantic work has tracked the impression that British political theory and philosophy made on colonial and Early American ideals, I invert this relation. In what follows, I show that the racial dynamics of the colonies influenced the conceptualization of sovereignty in striking ways, and I demonstrate the transatlantic, colonial, and racialized conditions of moral philosophy's core concepts. Building on historian Robin Blackburn's account of the role of plantation slavery in the development of capital accumulation in Britain, as well as on histories of labor alliances in the colonies, I show how moral philosophy reflects the role of New World slave and indentured labor in the processes of accumulation that laid the basis for the Industrial Revolution.

For eighteenth-century moral philosophy, the tension between social regulation and market freedom is addressed through the intensification of two ideological and material apparati: that of institutionalized racism and the development of the law to establish and protect private property. Where chapter 2 explored the legal dimensions of market ideology, sections two and three of this chapter concentrate on the organization of theories of racial difference in relation to the seemingly "democratic" freedoms of the market and of enthusiastic subjectivity. In what follows, I read Locke's *Fundamental Constitutions of Carolina*, Shaftesbury's letters concerning the management of both his estate in Dorset and the Carolina Colony, and metaphors of market regulation in *Characteristics* to show how racialized blackness functions in the period to secure an ideology of market self-regulation. I focus in particular on the Carolina Colony as the critical theater for a number of conflicts and combinations: the ideals of the *Fundamental Constitution* and the material constraints of Indian policy and wars; the ideal of freedom and the ongoing realities of the slave trade and indentured labor; and religious discourse and local, colonial competition for resources and profit. I show further the ways in which the institutionalization of racial oppression as a transatlantic form of social control served to intensify capital accumulation. Ultimately, I show that racial difference operated as both the material precondition for and the ideological limit to the enthusiastic self-regulation that the moral philosophers sought to ascribe to market practice. To make this argument, I offer a concluding reading of Shaftesbury's "Sensus Communis," in which I combine James Chandler's elucidation of the literary dynamics of capitalism's uneven development with David Harvey's concept of "spatio-temporal fix." The fruits of this combination are an analytic I describe as the "spatio-temporal secular fix." The spatio-temporal secular fix is, I argue, the historicization, narrativization, and aestheticization of enthusiastic sovereignty as a model for market freedom and the ethical autonomy of the citizen-subject. This fix both obscures and encodes the racialized conditions of labor upon which ideologies of sovereignty are based, and thus becomes a hermeneutic for our understanding of the spatial and discursive dimensions of capital accumulation.

Primitive Accumulation: "The Bolder Husbandry"

I want to begin by exploring the relationship between English sovereignty and the expansion of the early Atlantic circuit. Here, spatiality—as a hermeneutic that binds the transformation of the land to the institutional administration of territory, and to the discursive mediation of these relationships as well—enables us to grasp the political geographies of national wealth. These geographies included the transformation of the English countryside and the concomitant colonization of the New World. As it happens, Shaftesbury was an architect of both such territories. Indeed, although not ordinarily discussed in the Shaftesbury scholarship, the Third Earl inherited a proprietorship in the Carolina Colony and took an active role in debates over how to manage the land both in the colonies and at his estate in England. In turning to the question of spatiality, we thus return the discourse of enthusiasm more emphatically to the context of the transatlantic designs increasingly put into practice during the early eighteenth century. I consider Shaftesbury's letters concerning the management of both his estate in Dorset and the Carolina Colony, not to insist on integrating the biographical details of Shaftesbury's life into our account of his work, but because these particular details go some way in illustrating the material underpinnings of the contradictory ideological juncture of the early eighteenth century. Indeed, the letters provide a striking illustration of the dialectics of residual and emergent economic and cultural modes in the Atlantic circuit.

As we know from Shaftesbury's biographer, when he took over the estate in Dorset, he set about not only making and encouraging all sorts of changes on his land—eliminating rabbit warrens; draining bogs, enclosing land—but also converting rack-rented properties on his estate to copyhold.[6] These changes represent the heart of not only land enclosure and primitive accumulation in general, but the commodification of land under early capitalism more specifically. Indeed, in converting his feudal tenures to copyhold, Shaftesbury reconfigured his relationship to his tenants in a manner consistent with the transformation of landed property in this period. The hallmark of this transformation, according to Harvey, is "a thorough dissolution of 'the connection between landownership and the land' that the landlord, in return for a straight monetary payment, confers all rights to the land as both instrument and condition of production upon capital. The landlord thereby assumes a passive role in relation to the domination of labor (which control of the land allows) and to the subsequent progress of accumulation."[7] By converting his rents to copyhold, Shaftesbury set into motion the transformation of his land into an abstractable commodity—something subject to "the law of value, [which] begins to regulate prices through market exchange."[8]

In converting to rents, landlords no longer controlled the usage of their land directly. Shaftesbury's letters evince a frustration with the contingencies of this process. Here, he recounts an exchange with one Farmer Hiscock that ranges around the landlord's anxieties about the demands of productivity at the brink of new agricultural technologies:

> Note that tho' farmer Hiscock be a Laboriouse Man, yet but a Sloven as to Husbandry & tho' his ground be but Poor . . . yet he having been ever poor himself & not having the new way of Husbandry, this Farm is much wors in his Hands. He hardly clovers any: and French-grass he is frighted at because of the Charg of Seed & length of time loosing the first years profit: and this notwithstanding the plain advantage of it before his Eyes . . . Note also that He lets his Clover remain but a year whereas Biggs of Rockborn, Harris of Marti, & others have of late let theirs lye 3 years. . . . & thus the sheep & feedng & so the penning and foddering more & the Labour of the Arable Seed & the less . . . This I call the *Bolder Husbandry* newly on foot amongst us which the older Selfwilled Farmers or Shallow Men that have no Genius or mettle in their way, many of them, will not be brought to. Of this kind I look upon this Hiscock tho' tyed to him as he is an Old Tenant & had my Grandfather's favour, & promise of good usage when brought (tho' then poor) to rent this.[9]

Plainly put, Shaftesbury wishes to convert Hiscock's land to French grass seed in order to function as pasturage for sheep, rather than as arable land for growing wheat or legumes. This is the process he refers to as "the Bolder Husbandry." As a landlord, Shaftesbury sought these changes to keep pace with the economic demands of early capitalism, which began to focus profit-return on the commodification of pasturage. As Theodore Allen explains, due to the central role of cloth making in England's economic life, "[t]he price of wool rose faster than the price of grain, and the rent on pasture rose to several times the rent on crop land. The owners increased the proportion of pasture at the expense of arable land."[10] The painstaking transformation of arable land to pasturage, and the commercialization of land, are well-documented features of early modern enclosures.[11] Marx describes this process as the "conver[sion of] the land into a merely commercial commodity, extending the area of large-scale agricultural production, and increasing the supply of free and rightless proletarians driven from their land."[12] Such commercialization was key to the processes of primitive accumulation and the removal of the peasantry from subsistence farming. We must interpret Hiscock's resistance to Shaftesbury's pressures in terms of this process—a resistance Shaftesbury describes as characteristic of an "older Selfwilled" contingent. In the face of such resistance, Shaftesbury reports a hesitation in the process of treating his land as an abstractable commodity. His letters state that he intervenes, and buys the preferable French grass seed himself to "persuade his farmers to use it."[13]

In supplementing the labor and raw materials of his tenants himself, Shaftesbury both materially and discursively positions himself as responsible for his tenants. For Voitle, this relationship reflects Shaftesbury's obligation to those in his parish, specifically the nonproductive workers. Rather than a felt relation of sympathy, however, this responsibility reflects the ways in which Shaftesbury maintained some residual forms of control over his manor. More than this, such obligation is deployed to rhetorically authorize Shaftesbury's proposition for building a workhouse on his estate:

> [I have] propos'd a workhouse that the Children of Idle Familyes might work with the more industriouse, having a Matron over them, & I delivering them Materials, & buying again of them when wrought, in case of Wool & Flax dealers refus'd, or slacken'd sometimes, either through deadness of trade or as imposing on the people & beating down the price of their Labour . . . and [thus] the Parish [would be] multiply'd, thieving and Vice suppress'd & Order establish'd.[14]

Shaftesbury's characterization of his tenants as "Idle" highlights an irony: this "idleness" is the very result of Shaftesbury's own conversion of the land to pasturage through the "Bolder Husbandry" that provides no sustenance for the farmers working that land. As Theodore Allen explains, "one shepherd and his flock occupied as much land as a dozen or score of peasants could cultivate with the plough."[15] Voitle's bizarre redaction of this letter stresses Shaftesbury's "concern" for the "children on the estates," but it is worth noting, in fact, that in his enthusiasm for the workhouse, Shaftesbury was so far from concerned that we might see here a rather direct indebtedness to Locke's tutelage on the matter. The "true and proper relief of the poor," argued Locke, "consists in finding work for them, and taking care that they do not live like drones on the labour of others."[16] More than this, Shaftesbury appears to have hoped, *avant* Adam Smith, that through a sort of modified patriarchalism he could increase the numbers of workers on his land, and in so doing increase his manor's profitability: "thus the Parish would be," as Shaftesbury puts it, "multiply'd." In this way, Shaftesbury treats his own land as a miniature nation of the Mandevillian sort, a "free nation where slaves are not allowed of," in which "the surest wealth consists in a multitude of laborious poor".[17]

Shaftesbury's estate, however, is not a miniature nation, and in large part what is sensed to be missing is a nation's judicial arm, which was beginning to legislate in a general sense against, for example, the incipient formation of collective actions and early trade unionism on the part of the laborers—the very kinds of "SelfWilled" resistance encountered in Hiscock.[18] It is for this reason, we might imagine, that Shaftesbury reports hiring a spy to determine what sorts of alliances are forming on the manor: "I thus engaged Bishop as an *Explorer* & spake to him thus & with these Instructions 'That being confederated against by

Tenants, Servants & all, as he saw . . . having not the way of conversing with them & being on the square, drinking in their Companyes, & entering into their Caballs . . . therefore I recommended to him *Intelligence* . . .'"[19]

The capacities of the "intelligencer," however, appear not to have been able to stave off incipient unrest on the manor. Ultimately, in answer to the dual problem of intramanorial, low-profit circulation, and the threat of labor ferment, Shaftesbury finally settled on transporting his tenants to the Carolina Colony, a "solution" that accords perfectly with what Allen describes as England's approach to the effects of primitive accumulation. As the severing of persons from the means of production unleashes vagrants upon the land, these masses of the poor—with their always-looming potential for proletarian unrest—are countered by their removal from the national space.[20] In England, as Allen explains, what we popularly understand as "secularization"—the process of the dissolution of the monasteries and the casting adrift of this population, along with the massive uprooting of the peasantry from the land—produced enormous unemployment and a threat of rebellion so imminent that "[t]he English case for colonization came thus to be distinguished from those of Spain, Portugal, France, and Holland in its advocacy of colonization as a means of 'venting' the nation's surplus of 'necessitous people.'"[21] Indeed, secularization so-called concatenates, among other things, this phenomenon of transportation and the dissolution of specific, traditional, land-based religious institutions. Shaftesbury's determination to vent his land of its laborers—laborers that as Voitle notes, had at one time been the responsibility of the parsonage—demonstrates as much: "Much of the land Shaftesbury owned naturally had some sort of ecclesiastical background. A number of estates have tithe farms, and in some cases great tithe farms; part of the proceeds once went to the local priest . . . The decline of religion in the recent past, rather than the dissolution of the monasteries, is responsible for the shift from religious to secular uses. All of these properties, whatever their origin, became the daily business of Shaftesbury whenever he lived at St. Giles's House"[22]

Voitle's reading, whereby the "decline of religion" directly inflicts a shift in the usage of land, is not sufficiently explanatory and thus does not bear analysis. What is of greater interest, however, is the way in which Voitle's *narration* of this process takes the form of a secularization thesis about the decline of religion, and, in doing so, obscures a larger historical phenomenon, namely, that the availability of labor as a result of forms of primitive accumulation underwrote perceived shifts in religious comportment. The "freeing" of the laborer from the land through the divesting of land from the monasteries is, in Voitle's account, the consequence of a shift in the status of religious ideology. But we ought to reverse this process: our reading of Shaftesbury's letters suggests that one way we may understand secularization is as the narrative mediation of another set of linked transformations to the system of English agriculture, and to the institutionalization of an Atlantic, plantation-based circuit that served to uptake those individuals previously cared for by the ecclesiastical system. Such, in any case, are the historical variables that created the conditions for Shaftesbury's peculiar relationship to his tenantry. Here we are reminded of Hans Blumenberg's pointed question regarding the secularization thesis:

> Is it not enough to admit that quantitative statement about the lessening of an influence, the disappearance of an imprint, the subsidence of an intensity, in order to grasp the limiting case to which the formulation that describes worldliness as the signature of the modern age refers?[23]

To this we answer, along with Blumenberg, no. No, because, as Blumenberg shows us, truisms about the "lessening of an influence" have simply institutionalized the thesis that modernity's "progress" is the secularization of the eschatological impulse of theology.

This metaphysics of secularization is rejected by Blumenberg in favor of a more material analysis rooted in "the decline of obligations owed by village communities to the church."[24] Such an analysis allows us to see that the transition of responsibility from the church to the aristocratic landlords allowed for a supply of indentured labor that was both exploited at home (although this increases what Shaftesbury sees as the problematic "Caballs"), and utilized to populate the colonial territories. Indeed, in one telling instance, Shaftesbury "purchases" one of the young women on his estate to send to Carolina, threatening to her mother that "she should be us'd with the greatest severity if she refus'd to go to Carolina as propos'd I offering . . . to pay $5 for her passage."[25]

Encounters such as this one suggest that Shaftesbury's "responsibility" to his tenants has nothing to do with doing well by his grandfather's word, though he poses himself as upholding a longstanding "promise of good usage." Instead, Shaftesbury's framing his relationship to his tenants as one of responsibility reflects the ways in which, through interstitial types of direct control of his land in England, Shaftesbury contributed to the generation of profits in the colonies through the plantation system's more fully abstracted relation to the land. More simply put, Shaftesbury was able to collect exploitative rents from his tenants in England while maintaining enough direct control over his manor to not infrequently send his tenants as laborers to the Carolina Colony; in this way, the drag on the full commercialization of English land was tied directly to the promotion of forms of capital accumulation on the Atlantic circuit.

The Carolina Colony and Social Control

The Carolina Colony stretched from the southern border of the Virginia colony to Spanish Florida, and from the Atlantic Ocean to the "South Seas." The Fundamental Constitutions of the Carolina Colony were written by John Locke, and title to the colony was granted to eight Lords Proprietors, including the first Earl, by Charles II. The Carolina Colony was a county palatine, semi-autonomous from the monarch. Granting palatine status had a longstanding, and practical (from the standpoint of the king) feudal history: palatines were set up along the nation's borders in order to defend the outlying territories and exercise state control in areas that were geographically remote from the center of power. In those areas where it would be difficult to achieve royal assent on a matter in a timely manner, the territory was granted semisovereign, palatine status.

In 1663, the Carolina colony was established with the hopes that it, too, would function as this kind of a feudal extension of England. The Fundamental Constitutions "mandat[ed] that land be divided into counties of 480,000 acres. Each county would contain eight 12,000-acre seigniories belonging to the eight proprietors, eight 12,000-acre baronies granted to a hereditary nobility, and four precincts (each with six 12,000-acre colonies) to be planted by freemen."[26] As one of the Lords Proprietors, the Shaftesbury family transported both Huguenots and indentured laborers to the colony. The family also aided in the resettling of Barbardian plantation owners and plantation slaves, who moved in large numbers from the islands in the 1670s and 1680s.[27]

Promotional literature, printed by the Lords Proprietors in French, appealed to the exiled Huguenots as aristocrats-to-be, complete with manor and title:

> Wealthy Huguenots had been lured to Carolina by the hope of gaining large estates and recovering their social status. Promotional literature produced in French by the Lords Proprietors of Carolina advertised the possibility of acquiring manorial estates with judicial privileges at low prices or even as a gift. The *Nouvelle relation de la Caroline*, printed in The Hague around 1686, described how land could be acquired by headright, grant, or direct purchase. The pamphlet dwelled on the advantages of English law, local self-government, and easy naturalization, and it implied that prosperity might lead to the acquisition of a barony. It even assured its readers that newcomers would find houses to rent. Glowing accounts of the colony's mild climate, fertile soil, and peaceful natives appeared in pamphlets such as *Suite de la description de la Carolline and Plan pour former un éstablissement en Caroline*.[28]

For the Huguenots, the lure of the New World was significant. Of the greatest appeal was the fact that they would be naturalized in the Carolinas while they could only be denizened in England. This meant that, in the Carolina colony, Huguenots could buy and sell slaves as well as inherit property. This relative freedom was touted as "religious freedom," but we can see that it had much larger stakes, especially for the Huguenots' aristocratic sponsors in England, who relied on the Huguenot "freedom" to make inroads in the Indian slave trade and in the trade in goods—largely rice and naval stores—in the New World.[29]

Labor on the Huguenot manors was comprised of a mixture of indentured and slave labor. The anticipation of not only attrition, but also rebellion, is evinced in the Fundamental Constitutions' explicit provision vesting the Lords Proprietors with the privileges of commanding martial law to secure the territory against, not only incursions from without, but also "loiterers and stragglers" within. As Locke explained in the *Fundamental Constitutions*:

> Also our will and pleasure is, and by this our charter we give unto the said [Proprietors] . . . full power, liberty and authority, in case of rebellion, tumult or sedition, (if any should happen,) which God forbid . . . to exercise martial law against mutinous and seditious persons of those parts, such as shall refuse to submit themselves to their government, or shall refuse to serve in the wars, or shall fly to the enemy, or forsake their colours or ensigns, or be loyterers or straglers, or otherwise howsoever offending against law, custom or discipline military, as freely and in as ample manner and form as any captain general of an army by vertue of his office, might or hath accustomed to use the same.[30]

The Fundamental Constitutions outline a joint provision to exercise martial law against attacks from the many indigenous tribes that encircled the Carolina coastline, and simultaneously to use this martial law against indentured laborers on the plantations. The semisovereign status of the colony, as reflected in the granting of martial law, thus seeks to solve at once the problem of insurrection and the contingencies of colonial productivity. Simply put, laborers were deployed to defend and establish the colony; but the sheer number of these laborers continually presented the problem of forms of solidarity among them that, the Lords Proprietors anticipated at the outset, would require the exercise of martial law. More than this, the Fundamental Constitutions sought to ideologically and legally encode a racial antipathy between whites and African slaves; as Locke prescribed, "Every Freeman of Carolina shall have absolute power and authority over Negro slaves of whatever opinion of Religion soever."[31] Blackburn makes the point that this effort to institutionalize racial antipathy was in many ways a response to Bacon's Rebellion, during which solidarities between European laborers and African slaves had sown deep unrest:

> The colonial authorities insisted on concessions to poorer freemen, replacing the hated poll levy with taxes on trade. The House of Burgesses sought to strengthen the racial barrier between English servants and African slaves. In 1680 it prescribed thirty lashes on the bare back "if any negroe or other slave shall presume to lift up his hand in opposition to any christian."[32]

As Theodore Allen has persuasively argued, the differentiation of African bond-laborers from European proletarians in the colonies functioned primarily to disrupt labor alliances and secure social order toward capital accumulation in the colonial Atlantic:

> the system of class relations and social control that emerged in the colonies in the seventeenth century rested on the rejection in fundamental respects of the pattern established in England in the sixteenth century. With few exceptions, historians of racial slavery have generally ignored, or inferentially denied, the significance of this oceanic disjunction in social patterns.[33]

The forced transportation of persons to the plantations produced such sheer numbers of laborers in the colonies that racialization was deployed as a wedge to stave off solidarities between these laborers, in part by promoting identification among whites of all classes. Such identification encouraged what Allen calls the "buffer stratum":

> The peculiarity of the system of social control which came to be established in continental Anglo-America lay in the following two characteristics: (1) all persons of any degree of non-European ancestry were excluded from the buffer social control stratum: and (2) a major, indispensable, and decisive factor of the buffer social control stratum maintained against the unfree proletarians was that it was itself made up of free proletarians and semi-proletarians.[34]

This buffer stratum of whites is "naturalized" in its alliance with the plantation bourgeoisie through the racialization of non-European laborers, and through the attempts, via Indian policy and the fomenting of wars, to enforce these alliances. In the interests of colonial productivity, the ideology of race-as-skin color was an effort to compel an ideological "recognition" and identification between proletarian and ruling class whites, and to neutralize the structural confrontation between laborers—slave, indentured, and "free"—and the colonial bourgeoisie.

In light of such historical evidence, Shaftesbury's letters not only reveal his struggle to maintain control over his manor at home and the Carolina Colony abroad; they also reveal the degree to which yoking the Carolinas into the development of capital ventures in the Atlantic circuit was staked on the implementation of ideologies of racial difference. We can see evidence of this immiserating conjunction in Shaftesbury's comments on Indian policy in the Carolinas. In a letter to Andrew Percivall, the manager to St. Giles plantation, Shaftesbury complains of the Carolinians' policy of fomenting wars between Indian tribes in order to trade with collaborating tribes for captives of those wars:[35]

> ... [T]here was an incursion made into theire [Yamassee or Savannah] Country whereby open Hostility has been Committed by which the Indians have been drawne together and drawn downe upon us. Whoever have been the Authors of this May the curse of God and Man, as they deserve, light upon them ... And may that greedy Pursuit of unjust spoil and Rapine, that thirst of Blood, of Murthering, enslaving of Torture and Inhumanity which they have showne and which they thus have taugh this Innocently Ignorant Poore and Harmlesse People; may it be all Acted and Executed upon Themselves ... Shall Wee call ourselves Civiliz'd People & those Barbarouse whom wee have been thus Learning and Teaching all this Treachery Barbarity, by acting it to such a degree on Them?[36]

Let us pause before we read this letter as a defense of the Indian tribes in the Carolinas. For, as was well known, it was through the fomenting of these wars and the increase in trade with the Indian tribes for supplies and slaves that the Carolinians began to extend the limits of their sovereignty from the Lords Proprietors. By posing the Indians as "Innocent" and "Harmlesse," Shaftesbury ventriloquizes the project of the Lords Proprietors to recruit the Indians as a buffer stratum against, not only those tribes affiliated with French or Spanish interests, but also the constant threat of solidarity between indentured servants and slaves. Indeed, in his anxiety over "draw[ing] together" the Indian tribes, Shaftesbury echoes the Lords Proprietors who, in their missive to governor Colleton in 1690, had instructed: "We hear that Indians are still being shipped away underhand... You will do your best to prevent this... Without them you cannot recover runaway Negroes."[37] The threat of Bacon's Rebellion hung heavy on the air of the colonies, and the Lords Proprietors attempted to establish Indian tribes as native caciques as a bulwark against slave mutiny and attrition.

In the Carolinas, Indian policy functioned, at least in part, as a way for the English aristocracy to retain control of their palatine outpost. The ideals of an Indian cacique class were written into Indian policy as early as 1646, and from that Virginian colony treaty through the early part of the eighteenth century, the return of runaway African slaves to their white masters was written into nearly every Indian treaty in the colonies.[38] In arguing against war with the Indians, then, Shaftesbury's letters are part of a broader effort to institutionalize the aims of the Fundamental Constitutions and of Indian policy as well; in other words, it was an effort to institutionalize a legal and conceptual apparatus for maintaining social control through the promotion of racial difference as skin color. The Carolina planters who rebelled against the Fundamental Constitutions did so, not on the basis of an ideological disagreement with the Constitution's racial politics, then, but on the basis of a drive to establish economic sovereignty from the English aristocrats. As the propertied class in Carolina gained wealth through plantation and trading economies, they sought to control their political and economic structures as well. By 1719, the Carolina elites had applied to the Royal government for province status, so to free the county from the governorship of the Lords Proprietors. Shaftesbury's letters provide a window into an early—and contested—moment during which English aristocrats engineered the legal provisions of institutionalized racism as a form of social control in the Atlantic circuit.

The combination of a colonial plantation system with English manorial structures produced a temporary circuit of capital accumulation in which emergent and residual economic formations were yoked together across the Atlantic. This process recalls Arrighi's caution that economic development can often in retrospect be illegible, particularly in moments at which the system appears to be moving "forward and backward at the same time." This simultaneous forward and backward movement is registered in Shaftesbury's highlighting traditional "bonds" to his tenants. Indeed, far from hindering Shaftesbury's aims, these bonds furnish the kind of proximities and forms of direct domination that enabled ventures in the Carolinas through the transportation of laborers directly to the colony. If, in forcing his tenants to transform their land from arable to pasturage—a process Shaftesbury represents in terms of traditional feudal bondages and patronage—Shaftesbury delays the full commercialization of his property, at the same time, this more direct relation to his land at home fosters more commercial ventures abroad. This simultaneously forward and backward movement is not at all contradictory when we consider that these residual and emergent economic practices are combined toward a single goal: capital accumulation within the Atlantic circuit. Finally, it is the mediation of this spatial matrix in the ideology of racial difference that becomes most strikingly visible in the record of Shaftesbury's estate management. It is this racial mediation to which we now turn more closely.

The Social Relations of Sovereignty: Enthusiasm and International Law

If Shaftesbury's letters on land management reveal some of the more acute contradictions of geopolitical spatiality in the early eighteenth century, the translation of these contradictions into the discourse of enthusiastic sovereignty heightens these contradictions further. Let us, therefore, return to the theater of moral philosophy, for which *Characteristics* has been serving as our touchstone.

For Shaftesbury, as we have noted, the figure of common law—with its reliance on inquisitorial techniques—serves as a foil for the sovereign capacities of enthusiastic self-regulation. However, in describing the polarities of inquisition and self-regulation, the *Characteristics* repeatedly undoes the distinctions it sets out to uphold and, instead, reveals the material relationships undergirding ideologies of sovereignty. In seizing on the Camisard trial as exemplary in exploring sovereignty, Shaftesburian enthusiasm indexes the inextricability of ideals of national sovereignty with the transnational dimensions of exile and of emigration. This conceptual collapse is mirrored by a formal transition. In arguing for the superior ethical potentials of enthusiastic self-regulation, "Sensus Communis" undergoes a stylistic or generic shift: from more or less straightforward interlocutory rhetoric, the essay metamorphoses into a series of speculative anecdotes. This shift, we will find, represents the moment at which contradictions that had been occupying a tense coexistence up to this point break down and, in breaking down, generate a number of narrative resolutions that reveal the material relationships upon which the fantasy of sovereignty relies.

Toward the conclusion of "Sensus Communis," Shaftesbury begins to give narrative form to his critique of inquisitorial law. Here, he imagines a scene of hypothetical debate over the relativity of "common sense." In this scene, a group of interlocutors discuss the subjects of morality, policy, and religion. Immediately chaotic, "Sensus Communis" lets loose a din of opinion in which recourse to common sense proves fruitless as the ground of judgment: "[A]mid the different opinions started and maintained by several of the parties with great life and ingenuity," Shaftesbury narrates, one or other would every now and then take the liberty to appeal to common sense. Everyone allowed the appeal and was willing to stand the trial. No one was but assured that common sense would justify him. But when issue was joined and the case examined at the bar, there could be no judgment given.[39]

Into this scene of general confusion, Shaftesbury scripts the character of a "gentleman" who demands that the group produce a definition of common sense:

> If, by the word 'sense', we were to understand opinion and judgment and, by the word 'common', the generality or any considerable part of mankind, it would be hard,' he said, 'to discover where the subject of common sense could lie. For that which was according to the sense of one part of mankind was against the sense of another. And if the majority were to determine common sense, it would change as often as men changed. That which was according to common sense today would be the contrary tomorrow, or soon after.[40]

Via a critique of Lockean naïve empiricism—which presumes the consistency of subjects over time—national difference serves to delimit subjective consistency. When it comes to "common sense," Shaftesbury admits, everyone has a different opinion: "As for policy, what sense, or whose, could be called 'common' was equally a question. If plain British or Dutch sense was right, Turkish and French sense must certainly be very wrong."[41] By inserting the question of individual changeability into a discussion of international relations, Shaftesbury demonstrates the ways in which Enlightenment disquisitions on subjectivity are, at the same time, meditations on geopolitical relations. Shaftesbury relies on the traditional concept of "natural allies" to make this point: in saying that British and Dutch senses are similar, Shaftesbury condenses the historical alliance of Dutch banking with British industry into a relation of likeness. And, in comparing British sense to Dutch, Shaftesbury cannily connects "sense"—that *je ne sais quoi* of subjective calibration with social order—with nationality.

It is important to note that, in organizing mercantilist policy in the early part of the eighteenth century, the British did not only seek to be *like* the Dutch but, more importantly, to supersede the Dutch. Thus, when Shaftesbury seems to name a friendship and a likeness—"British *or* Dutch"—he is marking not only the co-operation between Dutch finance and early British industrialization, but perhaps more importantly, naming the desire for an identificatory substitution at the heart of British mercantilist policy.[42] More than this, Shaftesbury's comparison of subjective changeability and national alliances replaces the prevailing wisdom that had guided international relations—"natural allies"—with a much more precarious concept of contracted coalition. As Benno Teschke points out, by the early eighteenth century, "British foreign policy no longer operated on the principle of 'natural allies'—the 'Old System', which allied England, the Dutch Republic, and Austria against France—but on the fluid principle of rapidly changing coalitions, earning her on the Continent the epithet 'Perfidious Albion.'"[43] As Britain's attention turned to the colonies as a source of capital accumulation, it readied itself for negotiations of diplomacy and "balance" with Continental powers. By comparing the subject's changeability to international relations, Shaftesbury does not just put the geopolitical determination of the subject in the foreground, he also demonstrates the changeability of the geopolitics of Parliamentary sovereignty with its unstable majorities and rapidly shifting alliances. If the old patterns of international relation begin to prove insufficient to sustain sovereignty in a consistent way over time, Shaftesbury links the question of individual changeability, the flux of individual development—the strange proximity of one subjective comportment to its seemingly alien neighbor-comportment—with a new, shifting map of early modern geopolitics.

International relations changed definitively after the Glorious Revolution and the rise of Parliamentary sovereignty, and this change had largely to do with the fact that the British state, which accumulated territory in order to accumulate capital, was in competition with states that did not primarily seek to accumulate capital but rather sought to accumulate territory for political power. As Teschke has argued, "[a]fter 1688, England started to employ new foreign policy techniques while remaining surrounded by territorially accumulating dynastic states."[44] As England became an international commercial force, the national status of its common law was slowly superseded by a law that transfigured the parallax of international "sense" into the "common" language of international relations. In this context, we may thus read Shaftesbury's anxiety about the relativity of "common sense" as an anxiety about the purely national applicability of common law, which was incapable of cementing the international balance of power.

In the gulf left by common law, however, neither market dominance nor Parliamentary legislation would be sufficient to steer the course of international relations in British favor. Shaftesbury's suggestion that a "common" language would balance powers, then, may be read as, not only a fantasy, but one that specifically conceals the forces that supplemented the field of political relations. As Marx put it so eloquently, market stimuli are "insufficient to explain the transition from one mode of production to the other."[45] Teschke expands, "Since commercial capitalism only mediates the exchange of surplus already extracted by commercial means, it does not fundamentally change the social relations of production. Trade does not in itself generate surplus-value, or even value; it merely realizes profits . . . Merchant wealth is therefore not capital."[46] The common "sense" that Shaftesbury points to—that sensibility that underpins the international balance of power—then, is but a discursive and ideological register of the broader restructuring of social relations favorable for the production of profit. Common sense, in conjunction with market practice, did not produce the kinds of transformation necessary to promote capital accumulation both domestically and abroad. To understand this process in its full historical relevance, I cannot put this more aptly than Teschke does, when he explains that our analysis must not rely solely on the data of changing markets, but must entirely "unpack the *social relations of sovereignty*"[47]

Race and Regulation: Enthusiastic Transport

These social relations can be nowhere more explicitly exposed than in Shaftesbury's own "solution" to the problem of the relativity of common sense. Just after his worrying over the problems of Turkish and French policy, Shaftesbury stages an encounter between an Ethiopian traveler and a crowd of Europeans. He does so, he says, in order to demonstrate the way in which wit's free rein leads to certain knowledge. Sensing his interlocutor's continued disbelief, he delivers the following preamble: "And if you will allow me to carry on their [the friends'] humour, I will venture to make the experiment throughout and try what certain knowledge or assurance of things may be recovered in that very way by which all certainty, you thought, was lost, and an endless skepticism introduced."[48] Wit, for Shaftesbury, can produce "certainty," but there are necessary limits to wit's liberty. To demonstrate this, Shaftesbury engages in a series of speculative anecdotes, the first of which concerns the residents of "Paris or Venice," who meet with an Ethiopian, suddenly arrived on the Continent:

> If a native of Ethiopia were on a *sudden transported* into Europe and placed either at Paris or Venice at a time of Carnival, when the general face of mankind was disguised and almost every creature wore a mask, it is probably he would for some time be at a stand before he discovered the cheat, not imagining that a whole people could be so fantastical as, upon agreement at an appointed time, to transform themselves by a variety of habits and make it a solemn practice to impose on one another by this universal confusion of characters and persons.[49]

In conceiving the encounter, Shaftesbury draws on the rhetorical force of overturning a common critique of enthusiasm: the critique of enthusiastic transport. Here, the Ethiopian's "transport[t]" "on a sudden," recalls the kinds of objections raised to enthusiastic claims about the capacity of visionary bodies to move across space, into the air, and across nations. John Lacy—an English convert to the French Prophets whose work we will discuss at greater length in chapter 4—speaks directly to these objections in a volume framed as a response to the antienthusiast, Reverend Owen of Warrington. In 1715, Owen had written *The Scene of Delusions*, in which he cast a skeptical eye on the Camisard prophesies, specifically the Prophets' claims to enthusiastic transport. In response to Owen, Lacy writes:

> A heavy human Body being lift up and detained in the Air, or carried therein to some Distance, is a Miracle. And touching this, the *Scene of Delusions* tells us, p. 33, the Devil carried many of his Votaries in the Air . . . Conjurors and Witches, and Priests to his Idol Altars; and among the rest, he carried a Man from *Goa* in the *East-Indies* into *Portugal*, in an incredible short time, tho' it be about two thousand Miles . . . And what of this? . . . What if the same occurs to a Man, that taught sound and unreproachable Doctrine only? Why then, this is a miraculous Attestation to him from God. Well; one of the modern Prophets was so lift up and held in the Air, a Yard above Ground, before many Witnesses . . .[50]

If anti-enthusiasts accused enthusiasts of either fabricating such transport or of being guided by the Devil, Lacy claims that such transport is not only possible, but is the confirmation of enthusiastic truth. For Lacy, the miraculousness of lifting a prophet a "Yard" into the air is overlaid with a much farther, faster journey: from Goa to Portugal, a figurative insubordination of the colonial relation. Such a figure is illuminating for us, as it unpacks the temporal and spatial resonances echoing within enthusiasatic tropes. Even enthusiastic experiences that don't appear to "go" anywhere may invoke the geographies and temporalities of transport. For Lacy, this overlay signals the miraculousness of the Prophets' visions.

Extending this reversal in the valuation of enthusiastic transport, Shaftesbury embraces enthusiastic movement and puts it to work, somewhat tautologically, to rehabilitate enthusiasm. Here, the sudden transport of the Ethiopian takes place during Carnival, "when the general face of mankind was disguised, and almost every creature wore a mask." Shaftesbury draws upon the Carnival as a hyperbolic figure for the ridiculousness of cultural custom. The Ethiopian responds with bemusement to the masked city-dwellers, and to the possibility that the authority of custom could generate an event as ludicrous as that of "a whole people . . . [who] at an appointed time . . . transform themselves by a variety of habits, and make it a solemn practice to impose on one another, by this universal confusion of characters and persons."[51] Insofar as the ludic quality of custom is legible even to the untrained eye of a visitor from another country, the Ethiopian figure serves as a figure for the moralist, who regards all culture from a critical distance, and employs raillery as the expression of that critique:

> Though he might at first perhaps have looked on this with a serious eye, it would be hardly possible for him to hold his countenance when he had perceived what was carrying on. The Europeans, on their side, might laugh perhaps at this simplicity. But our Ethiopian would certainly laugh with better reason. It is easy to see which of the two would be ridiculous. For he who laughs and is himself ridiculous bears a double share of ridicule.[52]

Undergirding this evaluation of custom, of course, is Shaftesbury's running critique of common law as inadequate to an international arena of exchange.

The Ethiopian figure, however, is more complex than a simple tropic bolster for Parliamentary sovereignty. Indeed, as we advance through the speculation, we find that the Ethiopian's laughter quickly threatens to undermine his own precarious authority. "[S]hould it so happen," speculates Shaftesbury, "that in the transport of ridicule, our Ethiopian, having his head still running upon masks, and knowing nothing of the fair complexion and common dress of the Europeans, should upon the sight of a natural face and habit, laugh just as heartily as before, would not he in his turn become ridiculous, by carrying the jest too far; when by a silly presumption he took nature for mere art . . .?"[53] In the "transport of ridicule" that initially marked the traveler's incisive eye, this figure is, himself, made ridiculous, and any discriminating faculties that were once attributed to him are disabled. This disabling is in fact, necessary, because Shaftesbury seeks to demonstrate that a limit to "endless skepticism" exists. This limit, it seems, is not cultural difference per se, but skin color—an absolute difference for Shaftesbury, and one that supersedes the cultural distortions of modern society.

As Shaftesbury explains, the Carnival is a figure for the constrainment of character by custom, a social effect that is visible physiognomically:

> ... when men become persecuted ... on every side about their air and feature and were put to their shifts how to adjust and compose their mien, according to the right mode, when a thousand models, a thousand patterns of dress, were current and altered every now and then, upon occasion, according to fashion and the humour of the times. Judge whether men's countenances were not like to grow constrained and the natural visage of mankind, by this habit, distorted, convulsed and rendered hardly knowable.[54]

In this turn on physiognomy, not only individual character, but social force itself is legible in the face. Here the subject becomes a complex cipher for the structure of social relations in general; more than this, the difference of race as skin color begins to function as a hermeneutic that makes legible the constraining nature of social force: "... we must not imagine that all faces are alike besmeared or plastered. All is not focus or mere varnish ... we must remember our Ethiopian and beware, lest by taking plain nature for a vizard, we become more ridiculous than the people whom we ridicule."[55]

Race, Regulation, and Market Freedom

The encounter with the Ethiopian traveler aims to solve ideologically the problem of the endless skepticism that attends both an ethics based in wit and the ideal of the free market. The coding of contact and judgment in terms of skin color constructs a "natural" endpoint to the perils of self-regulating markets and subjects. The traveler laughs (and becomes, himself, ridiculous) when he mistakes the "naturalness" of whiteness for artifice. In doing so, difference as skin color becomes the naturalized limit to the problem of self-regulation, whereas whiteness is itself naturalized to code universal subjectivity. We recall that the figure of the free market had at first qualified the mediation of the enthusiastic subject; this mediation is now supplemented by a logic of racial difference bodied forth in the figure of the Ethiopian traveler. Because the Ethiopian necessarily "carries the jest too far," and proves his own ridiculousness in doing so, Shaftesbury's readers are to rest assured that the critical perspective offered by a cultural outsider does not signal that outsider's ultimate superiority. Rather, the fiction of the Ethiopian's unfamiliarity with white skin color secures the ideological fantasy of a free market—the very "free market" which had become such a disconcerting problem earlier in "Sensus Communis."

In arguing that the Ethiopian figure secures the ideological freedom of the market, I engage in a now longstanding scholarly discussion of the significance of skin color as a marker of racial difference in the early eighteenth century. Although we do not have the space here to review this literature exhaustively, it is worth visiting one of the central junctures of the debate: secularization and skin color. On this topic, Roxann Wheeler has argued that, until 1770, the primary racial distinction in Britain was not skin color but, in fact, categories of "Christian" and "heathen":

> [T]hroughout the eighteenth century, older conceptions of Christianity, civility, and rank were more *explicitly important* to Briton's assessment of themselves and other people than physical attributes such as skin color, shape of the nose, or texture of the hair. Embodied in dress, manners, and language, the concepts of Christianity, civility, and rank were not simply abstract categories of difference; they constituted visible distinctions that are difficult for us to recover today.[56]

Scholars—such as Lynn Festa, Ruth Hill, and G. Gabrielle Starr—have drawn on Wheeler's insights to expand our critical understanding of the multiple articulations of difference within the period.[57] Wheeler's line of reasoning is indeed useful in regarding the expansive signification of difference in the early eighteenth century—particularly her reorientation of scholarship to religious categories of difference, and her demonstration that such religious categories were as vital to the articulation of cultural difference as ideologies of skin color, if not more so.

As Wheeler considers the question of race and emergent commercialism, she finds that skin color becomes unusually significant at a much earlier date than it does otherwise. When "English religious and commercial categories designated the manifold excellence of British civil society," Wheeler argues, "a white and rosy complexion was, on occasion, called on to bolster the picture of British commercial excellence."[58] What, we may ask, is particular to the ideology of commerce that adumbrates the reification of skin color as racial difference—a process Wheeler herself argues did not become dominant in Britain until later in the century? Here, we may offer that, in the transatlantic context, the ideological reinforcement of race as skin color registered the material conditions of capital accumulation—specifically the existence of large, colonial labor forces consisting of indentured and slave labor—quite a bit earlier than in England proper. The labor forces of the colonies, as we argued above, were met with a discursive and legislative racialization as a response to forms of solidarity between workers and to the history of unrest. Even in strictly English texts, it seems, then, that race functioned to signify skin color in a way that anticipated much later calcifications of the concept, insofar as those texts mediated the conjunctures of commerce, geopolitics, and accumulation in particularly acute ways. The importance of the Ethiopian example is not so much that it draws on an abstract ideology of racial or cultural difference, but that it yokes this ideology of race together with social and economic regulation in a manner that can only be described as transatlantic in its conditions of possibility.

In his meditations on Camisard transport, Shaftesbury's figural marriage of race and the market constitutes a nearly exact rendition of the material conditions that produced racial difference as a regulator of the modern social order—a historical constellation that recalls nothing so much as colonial labor conditions. Indeed, Shaftesbury's conceptualization of racial difference as simultaneously the ideological limit to and material precondition for the fantasy of national self-regulation can, in fact, be explained by no other context than the transatlantic one. As I have argued, the ideology, legislation, and historical exclusions of the concept of racial difference operate in very specific ways as the premiere tool of capitalist social control and regulation.[59] We can see a strange but provocative version of this process in Shaftesbury, where, even without an explicit ideology of physiognomic racial characteristics, the conception of difference as skin color functions to promote the self-regulation of the market. The Ethiopian's eventual ridiculousness is, in other words, a demonstration of the viability of market self-regulation, and, although this particular speculative anecdote on the Ethiopian's visit has never before been remarked in the scholarship on Shaftesbury, we must make much of it for this very reason. The analogy of the Ethiopian should finally make clear to us not only how non-self-regulating the "free market" truly is; rather, the potential for accumulation that is the hallmark of the putatively free market is engineered through the deliberate and violent coding of skin color as racial difference, and the legitimation and perpetuation of this coding through the practices of the state. It is *this* material development that most emphatically encodes the shift in social relations and the relations of production that takes place in the colonies. And it is this material development that differentiates the colonial from the British context, while suturing them both in a transatlantic cycle of accumulation that is crucially dependent on the social control of its subjects through their forced racialization in terms of skin color.

The Spatio-Secular-Temporal Fix

Let us put a little more pressure on the transatlantic aspect of this figurative foray by returning to the "suddenness" of the Ethiopian's appearance in Europe. Certainly this suddenness partakes of an aesthetic tradition that performs hypothetical experiments which deliberately and artificially bracket the question of cultural knowledge in order to trace an ontology of beauty. Edmund Burke's example of Cheselden is only the most notorious instance of this tradition:[60]

> Mr Cheselden has given us a very curious story of a boy, who had been born blind, and continued so until he was thirteen or fourteen years old; he was then couched for a cataract, by which operation he received his sight . . . Cheselden tells us, that the first time the boy saw a black object, it gave him great uneasiness; and that sometime after, upon accidentally seeing a negro woman, he was struck with great horror at the sight.[61]

As Srinivas Aravamudan has argued, the Cheselden example functions in Burke to conceal "cultural terror at the sublime's very origin."[62] Much has been written on the Burkean sublime and the racialization of aesthetics. What I want to remark here is that, not only does the Ethiopian figure in Shaftesbury seem a kind of precursor to Burke, but this precursor inverts the relation between observer and observed and, in doing so, demonstrates the degree to which the racial dynamics of aesthetic value are, at their origin, also bound up with the geopolitics of secularization in the early modern period. Indeed, the Shaftesburian scenario invokes the problem with which we began this section: the mediation, in religious discourse, of capitalism's unevenly developing territories and modes of production. Put another way, to the extent that the Ethiopian anecdote attempts to solve the problem of market "freedom," it does so by providing a narrative of spatial movement that is, at the same time, a racialized matrix of regulation. This racial matrix is thus the market's spatialized condition of possibility; to cite David Harvey, this racial matrix is also the "spatio-temporal fix" that is global capitalism's signature.

Let us briefly review Harvey's argument. The spatio-temporal fix is a double-entendre of sorts, signifying both the "fixing" (or addressing) of crises of overproduction by spatial means—relocating production centers to maintain low operating costs, wages, and prices of raw materials—and the "fixing" (or cementing) of fixed capital to certain territories:

> A certain portion of the total capital is literally fixed in and on the land in some physical form for a relatively long period of time (depending on its economic and physical lifetime). Some social expenditures (such as public education or a healthcare system) also become territorialized and rendered geographically immobile through state commitments. The spatio-temporal 'fix', on the other hand, is a metaphor for a particular kind of solution to capitalist crises through temporal deferral and geographical expansion.[63]

The temporal aspect of the spatio-temporal fix refers at first glance to the immediacy and swiftness of the fix as an attempt to counter what Harvey describes as the "chronic" nature of capitalist crisis. The temporal aspect refers as well, however, to the generation of developmental lags or gulfs that are the result of this spatio-temporal fix itself:

> Temporal deferral and geographical expansion "fix" the overaccumulation crises that arise from the chronic tendency of capital to accumulate over and above what can be reinvested profitably in the production and exchange of commodities. As a result of this tendency, surpluses of capital and labor are left unutilized or underutilized. The incorporation of new space into the system of accumulation absorbs these surpluses in two ways. At first, it promotes their utilization in the activities involved in opening up the new space and endowing it with the necessary infrastructure, both physical and social. And then, once the new space has been adequately "produced," the surpluses of labor and capital can be absorbed in the new productive combinations that have been made profitable by the spatial enlargement of the system of accumulation.[64]

Because the spatio-temporal fix is a contradictory construction, the process produces the recurrent crises that it seeks to allay. In particular, the fixing of capital into certain geographical sites creates problems for the mobility of capitalist production and is a drag against which the extraction of global profit strains. Giovanni Arrighi redacts this contradictory logic via Harvey:

> As Harvey notes, this metaphorical meaning of spatial-temporal fix as solution to capitalist crises can and recurrently does enter into contradiction with the material meaning of the expression. For the geographical expansion, reorganization, and reconstruction that absorb surplus capital and labor 'threaten . . . the values already fixed in place (embedded in the land) but not yet realized.' Hence, 'The vast quantities of capital fixed in place act as a drag upon the capacity to realize a spatial fix elsewhere. . . . If capital does move out, then it leaves behind a trail of devastation and devaluation; the deindustrializations experienced in the heartlands of capitalism . . . in the 1970s and 1980s are cases in point. If capital does not or cannot move . . . then overaccumulated capital stands to be devalued directly through the onset of a deflationary recession or depression.[65]

We might see the Ethiopian anecdote, finally, as the invocation of a spatial fix that is simultaneously a racialized logic that pertains in the colonial context. In Shaftesbury, the Ethiopian's arrival in Europe both calls up the fantasy of the immediacy of movement, and the racialized conditions that undergird the extraction of surplus from labor that make the movement of profit possible. This nexus returns us not only to the transatlantic scenario, but also to the question of the Camisards' "sudden" appearance in London, and the figural spectacle of Camisard emigration as a mediation of the spatial collisions that form accumulation's ongoing conditions of possibility. Indeed, insofar as the "suddenness" of the Ethiopian's arrival mirrors the arrival of the Camisards, it trails with it the problem of the increasing—indeed, intensified—proximity of the residual and the emergent that attends the development of eighteenth century capitalism. With due respect to Harvey, we might say that the residual is fact produced by capitalism's spatial fixes, which de-develop and devastate territories, leaving few options for survival other than the selling of one's labor. And, following Raymond Williams—who we will turn to in the next section—we understand the figure of the residual as in dialectical combination with emergent forms.

Might we press all of these connections further, and propose that the trope of enthusiastic transport is made heterotopic in Shaftesbury? Certainly the "transport" of laughter that the Ethiopian figure experiences draws on the heritage of transport in a religious lexicon. However, more than this, insofar as the transporting laughter of the Ethiopian constitutes a kind of self-critique and self-imposed limitation on the freedoms of wit and the market, this laughing transport indexes the transoceanic and international transport of persons, institutions, and capital, the fixes that regulate the production of profit, even as they veer capitalism toward recurrent crises. There is, in fact, a sense in which the latter transport conditions the former and makes it legible. Enthusiastic transport suggests a simultaneously temporal and spatial operation. Spatial because, not only does the subject move, but because the subject's transport suggests the fugitive marks of other movements, such as the historical shifts and alignments particular to the Atlantic in the early eighteenth century. This transport is temporal, not only because it reaches forward oracularly, but also because it reaches back discursively, encoding complex histories of world religions and of statecraft. It is this concatenation of spatial and temporal enthusiasm that we now explore in closing.

Uneven Transport: Enthusiasm and the Political Geographies of Priestcraft

In this chapter's final section, I want to propose that the methodological approach best suited to capture enthusiasm's intricate web of spatiality and temporality is that of uneven development. Uneven development is a simultaneously spatial and temporal theory, a method for political geography and for historical and literary study. At its core, uneven development is the theory of history originally developed by Leon Trotsky to describe capitalism's use of location as a strategy against the organizational power of labor. By producing certain geographical locations as deliberately stagnant nonindustrialized zones, capitalism generates permanent reserves of labor and resources in the periphery—reserves that put pressure on solidarity between laborers, and on the tendency of wages to rise, in the core. Shaftesbury's letters provide a vivid index of this process—one by which the peasantry were removed from a direct relationship to means of production, and the countryside "de-developed" as a precondition for the development of both urban labor in England, and transatlantic settlement in the colonies. As such, the country and city appear to be moving "unevenly" or—as we have marked many times thus far—"forward and backward at the same time." As the city builds its productive capacities, the countryside is ravaged and made unliveable in ways that benefit the concentration of labor reserves in the city. We will discuss this process—particularly as it contributed to urbanization in London, and to the productive force of the English cities, in greater detail in chapter 5—but let us note here the web of institutional transformations that follow from this process of uneven development. As we have just discussed, the vast number of laborers and vagrants in London were met with large-scale transportation to the New World as a means of "venting" England of the incipient threat of collective actions and uprisings. Once in the New World, solidarities between indentured laborers, African slaves, and indigenous Americans again produced forms of pressure from below that were countered in turn by the development of ideologies of racial difference as skin color as a way to drive wedges through labor solidarities.

In his study of historicism in the English Romantic period, James Chandler has elaborated the concept of uneven development in a way that is particularly suggestive for the nexus of forces we have just described. Chandler argues that the concept of uneven development not only returns us to the complex spatio-temporal dynamics of English and Atlantic history, but that it does so in a way that imminently critiques the presumptions of secularization. Chandler argues that "there is another side to the articulation of the historicist code of early nineteenth-century British public culture—not the side of even chronology, the chronology of what might be called 'secularization,' but of uneven development."[66] It will be perhaps surprising to note that, in calling on Trotsky, Chandler demonstrates the degree to which a Marxist account may energize our interrogations of the secularization thesis. Chandler demonstrates that what secularization narratives obscure are the violent practices of uneven development and the tendency for chronologically co-existent but developmentally discontinuous modes of production to work together, if not always in apparent synchronicity, toward the overall accumulation of capital.

The concept of uneven development also serves as a hermeneutical caution about reading Shaftesbury's enthusiasm as, itself, a kind of simple secularization story. That the Camisards are represented, by Shaftesbury, in terms of the perceived "barbarism" of contemporary French inquisitorial law, suggests that their "sudden" and symptomatic arrival signifies more than the secularization of millenarial rapture into either a liberal enthusiasm of self-regulation or, as Irlam would have it, an aesthetics of the sublime. Rather, in aligning the French monarchy with temporally and spatially distant theocratic regimes, "Sensus Communis," in the aegis of a secularizing argument, registers the discontinuous economic and social movements of the system of developing capitalism. It is in this sense that the Camisard debates figure as a cipher for the dynamics of uneven development in this period, and it is in this sense that the problem of religious enthusiasm in early-eighteenth-century England expresses both the historical problem of England's relation to its own revolutionary past, and simultaneously the quite contemporary problem of international relations. In arguing from the example of the Camisards to naturalize the metaphorical fungibility of enthusiasm—from the religious, to the national, economic, and individual—the occasion of Camisard prophesy allows Shaftesbury to reconfigure the question of enthusiastic sovereignty. The result is the affirmation of an exchangeable logic of enthusiasm that underwrites a number of other sovereign powers, such as the power of Parliament to make law, as we saw in chapter 2. And, as the Ethiopian figure has made clear in this chapter, this uncanny fungibility is conditioned on the deepening unevenness and racialization of labor that underscores the spatial logic of early capitalism.

If the figure of the Camisards encodes the uneven dynamics of capital flows in the language of religious passion, it is this concatenation of the theological and the economic that we can uncover using the hermeneutic of uneven development. The time of uneven development does not conform to the presumptions of secularization, that is, to orderly progressions and onward march. Likewise, in the discursive confection of enthusiasm with temporal, spatial, and metaphysical transport, we do not see a competition of residual with emergent forms, but their dialectical combination in the material context of modernity. In this way, the figure of barbaric theocracy in Shaftesbury is not about a simple drag of the residual, nor is it about the transubstantiation of the residual, but rather, and more properly, this residual's intensive mediation of and conditioning by the present. As Raymond Williams has so eloquently demonstrated, the residual is emphatically not the archaic: "The residual, by definition, has been effectively formed in the past, but it is still active in the cultural process, not only and often not at all as an element of the past, but as an effective element of the present."[67] Thus, no matter how arduously *Characteristics* works to present theocracy as an archaic form—albeit haunting, but firmly over—it is ultimately much more invested in the quite contemporary geopolitical and national-historical metonymies that the theocratic residuum generates.

The "currency" of theocracy—if we will accept such a double entendre—is further illuminated as "Sensus Communis" moves from the example of the Ethiopian traveler to more explicit versions of religious historicism of the sort we discussed in chapter 1. In what appears to be a simply proliferative logic, Shaftesbury proposes that we extend wit's mechanism of self-regulation beyond humor to the realm of fear: "Now if a jest or ridicule," he says, "thus strained be capable of leading the judgment so far astray, it is probable that an excess of fear or horror may work the same effect."[68] Although he appears to be applying a straightforward method of multiplying the circumstances of self-regulation to assay its legitimacy in a number of spheres, in meditating on such an "excess of fear or horror" Shaftesbury creates yet another narrative of development that hinges on the figure of religious violence. Via the fantasized history of the Magi, Shaftesbury places readers in a hypothetical ancient Asia and asks them to consider what their relation to Magi priestcraft might have been:

> Had it been your fortune, my friend, to have lived in Asia at the time when the Magi by an egregious imposture got possession of the empire, no doubt you would have had a detestation of the act, and perhaps the very persons of the men might have grown so odious to you that . . . you might have seen them dispatched with as relentless an eye as our later European ancestors saw the destruction of a like politic body of conjurers, the Knights Templars, who were almost become an over-match for the civil sovereign.[69]

The Magi return us to the problem of sovereignty. The Knights Templars stand in for a supranational force that has been crushed by the collaborations of the French monarchy and the Catholic Church. This second speculative anecdote also reorients "Sensus Communis" to the distinction parsed in the "Letter" between the *form* of the letter and the *spirit* of it. As we argued in chapter 2, in many ways the *Characteristics* seeks to eradicate or lessen the qualitative significance of content for morality and to replace the question of belief with a formal relation between subject and the social whole that is legally legible. Such a moral configuration—one encoded in the *legis scriptae*—would require no confession for legal determinations to be made. This process is revived in "Sensus Communis" via the figure of the Knights Templars who, in the eighteenth century, were popularly believed to have been persecuted by Philip IV on suspicion of their infidelity to both church and state, and to have been pressed by the state into making false confessions. The Knights Templars thus serve to demonstrate the unreliability of confession and the impossibility of coordinating speech acts with belief. As with the Ethiopian traveler, the Magi figure a limit case for the self-regulation of sovereignty. More than this, Shaftesbury's hypothetical scenario takes a metadiscursive turn by asking the reader to extend the problem of sovereignty to the question of reading. In this extension, Shaftesbury depicts the Magi as not only religious tyrants, but morally and sexually depraved. Shaftesbury tests the reader, asking if it would be possible to divorce the texts of the Magi from the intentions and behaviors of their authors:

> [I]f it had happened that these magicians in the time of their dominion had made any collection of books or compiled any themselves, in which they had treated of philosophy or morals or any other science or part of learning, would you have carried your resentment so far as to extirpated these also, and condemned every opinion or doctrine they had espoused for no other reason than merely because they had espoused it? Hardly a Scythian, a Tartar or a Goth would act or reason so absurdly. Much less would you, my friend, have carried on this "magophony," or priest-massacre, with such a barbarous zeal. For, in good earnest, to destroy a philosophy in hatred to a man implies as errant a Tartar-notion as to destroy or murder a man in order to plunder him or his wit and get the inheritance of his understanding.[70]

The problem here is one of literalization—the collapse of the content of speech and the spirit with which it is delivered. In an inversion of the critique ordinarily leveled at enthusiasts, Shaftesbury argues that it would be zealous to destroy a philosophy out of a misplaced "hatred" of the culture that produces that philosophy. If it is "zeal" to merge content and spirit in a false immediacy, in the place of such immediacy, Shaftesbury proposes a much more mediated enthusiasm that firms up a distinction between philosophy and philosopher. The attenuations of such an enthusiasm are tested by the extreme circumstance that the philosopher engages in what Shaftesbury represents as the Magi's culture-sanctioned practices of incest: "I must confess that, had all the institutions, statutes and regulations of this ancient hierarchy resembled the fundamental one of the Order itself, they might with a great deal of justice have been suppressed; for one cannot, without some abhorrence, read that law of theirs: *For a Magus must be born of a mother and son*."[71] For Shaftesbury, it is specifically *because* the Magi are imagined to practice incest that their moral law is so exemplary: "But the conjurers (as we will rather suppose), having considered that they ought in their principle to appear as fair as possible to the world, the better to conceal their practice, found it highly for their interest to espouse some excellent moral rules and establish the very best maxims of this kind."[72]

In this example, Shaftesbury stages a scene of reading that "law of theirs." That law, however, is not, in fact, a text of Magi law, but a citation from Catullus. Citing Catullus as the source of Magi law directs us to the already-mediated nature of law in general, and positions in the foreground, the sense in which the law is always for Shaftesbury, a matter of *reading*. In this rather sophisticated exegetical exercise, the "law" that Shaftesbury reads is the absent law, "suppressed" by the Magi, redacted through Catullus. That the law is only available in poetic form affirms Shaftesbury's claim that the Magi law (which Shaftesbury also does not represent to the reader, but rather "supposes") does not correspond with Magi practices. As with common law, legality and morality cannot be derived from custom.

The law of incest that Shaftesbury does read, then, is a historical speculation about the Magi as told through Catullus. In these proliferating mediations, an aesthetics of uneven development subtends the prismatic unfolding of legal discourse. Here, as with the figure of the Ethiopian traveler, speculation thrusts the reader into "sudden" temporal and spatial traverses. The backward temporal movement required to speculate on Magi civil and political society is a kind of historical parfait; the Magi are only presented through the classical context of Catullus. Further, the example of incest itself proves a remarkable trope of uneven development. For Shaftesbury, incest represents the dialectically productive and destabilizing nature of "unnatural" proximities. These proximities do not arrange themselves according to stages but, rather, make "leaps": "*A Magus must be born of a mother and son.*" Such leaps recall the temporal and spatial hurtlings born in the fierce contradictions of global capitalism.[73] The Magi's incestuous leaps represent both the proscribed exterior of culture, as well as the condition of possibility of its quite literal reproduction. In this sense, the Magi allegorize the kind of residual-emergent yokings of the Atlantic circuit that we have been detailing throughout this chapter.

These yokings open another metadiscursive avenue as Shaftesbury utilizes the figure of Magi procreation to introduce the problem of his own inheritance—as a philosopher and citizen-subject—through a narrative transition to the specter of Hobbes. Indeed, for Shaftesbury, Hobbes *is* that subject, so afflicted with horror that it affects his judgment:

> ... an able and witty philosopher of our nation was, we know, of late years so possessed with a horror of this kind [of the philosophy along with the philosophers] that, both with respect to politics and morals, he directly acted in this spirit of massacre. The fright he took upon the sight of the then governing powers [the Commonwealth], who unjustly assumed the authority of the people, gave him such an abhorrence of all popular government and of the very notion of liberty itself that, to extinguish it forever, he recommends the very extinguishing of Letters and exhorts princes not to spare so much as an ancient Roman or Greek historian.[74]

Hobbes's ravenous anti-enthusiasm makes him more of enthusiast than the enthusiasts he so condemns. To read Hobbes in this way is not simply to claim

Shaftesburian enthusiasm and moral philosophy as the successors of Hobbesian political theory. It is, more importantly, to establish a philosophical lineage on the model of the spatio-temporal dynamics of uneven development. Such an interpretation is reinforced as, a bit later on, Shaftesbury conducts a quite masterful reading of Hobbes's notorious diagnosis of the wolfish nature of man:

> What should we say to one of these anti-zealots, [Hobbes and the NeoHobbesians] who, in the zeal of such a cool philosophy, should assure us faithfully that we were the most mistaken men in the world to imagine there was any such thing as natural faith or justice? . . . That there was no such thing in reality as virtue, no principle of order in things above or below, no secret charm or force of nature by which everyone was made to operate willingly or unwillingly towards public good . . . Is not this the very charm itself? Is not the gentleman at this instant under the power of it?' 'Sir!' The philosophy you have condescended to reveal to us is most extraordinary . . . But, pray, whence is this zeal in our behalf? What are we to you? Are you our father? Or, if you were, why this concern for us? Is there then such a thing as natural affection? If not, why all these pains, why all this danger on our account? Why not keep this secret to yourself?[75]

In this symptomatic reading of Hobbes, Shaftesbury points out that if man were naturally wolfish, then Hobbes should, by all rights, keep his knowledge of this nature to himself. Because he has done otherwise, Shaftesbury is inclined to read Hobbes against himself, as inexorably compelled to protect his putative "offspring."

We might be tempted to draw the conclusion now that Shaftesbury establishes a gentle lineage between himself and Hobbes—a Hobbes who has now been recoded as not so wolfish after all. Still, we can't help but reflect on the fact that this lineage is, in fact, backward; it does not extend from father-Hobbes to son-Shaftesbury, but the other way round. In fact, only by reading him symptomatically, does Shaftesbury save Hobbes from the NeoHobbesians and thus rebirth Hobbes for the project of moral philosophy. In doing so, Shaftesbury reverses the direction of chronological progression from son to father. This inversion is much like the Magi's own. The reader cannot help but compare Shaftesbury's invocation of Hobbes, the-father, with the incestuous excision of the father by the Magi son. Reading Hobbes symptomatically allows Shaftesbury to claim he does not "destroy" Hobbesian philosophy, but spawn it anew by reading it against its stated intentions. But this redemptive reading suggests its barely concealed underside of violent supersession. In fact, just such a hermeneutical approach has been held out for us not half a page earlier, when Shaftesbury asks, "would you destroy a philosophy in hatred to a man"?

The significance of this progression—from the national contours of "common sense," to the Ethiopian scene of judgment, the incestuous Magi, and on to the father/son dyad of Hobbes and Shaftesbury—cannot be overstated. It forms the core logic of "Sensus Communis," and indeed reveals the logic of Shaftesbury's work on enthusiasm as a whole. The deep conditioning of philosophical abstraction by the material context of the spatio-temporal fixes and uneven developments of the Atlantic circuit presents itself in the rhetorical movement from the conditions of judgment and trial to the uncannily proximate chronologies of so-called savagery: Ethiopia, ancient Asia, seventeenth-century England. This movement, as Marx would say, "rising from the abstract" (common sense) "to the concrete" (the uneven historical developments conditioning capital accumulation) lies at the heart of Shaftesbury's legitimation of enthusiasm.[76] In raising these particular narrative flourishes to our attention, I hope to have illuminated some of the ways in which geopolitics in general, and the transatlantic context in particular, inform both the dynamics of capital accumulation and the articulation of religious enthusiasm for the project of moral philosophy and the aestheticization of sovereignty.

Chapter 4

A Cry From the Desart

Spatiality and Secularism

"The life of the country and city is moving and present: moving in time . . ."[1]

"*Geography* is here grown into a Supernatural Science, and the Masters of it can tell you to an Inch the Locality of *Heaven* and *Hell*; and some have gone so far in Speculation, as to brag openly, that they have found out the *Latitude* and *Longitude* of both Places."[2]

I open this chapter by way of a perhaps counterintuitive pairing: Raymond Williams's 1973 poetic account of the spatio-temporal integration of early modern urban and rural English life, and John Lacy's critical assessment of modern geography, written in 1712 as part of a longer satirical portrait of natural science, *An Ecclesiastical and Political History of Whig-Land*. This pairing is counterintuitive, first and foremost, because although Lacy, an English convert of the French Prophets, disputes modern geography's approach to mapping Heaven and Hell, he fully embraces the existence of a celestial landscape. Williams's materialist history of the English environment, we are to be sure, would have been hard pressed to accommodate the legitimacy of Heaven and Hell. And yet, the two writers find common cause, across centuries and worldviews, in their critique of empiricist theories of space. In Lacy's work, the inadequacy of modern empiricism is exemplified in geography's reduction of the complex phenomenon of space to calculable units such as "latitude" and "longitude." In the place of statistical units of space, Lacy will offer an intricate historicization of the political landscape of England; this historicization turns on the deployment of enthusiastic rhetoric to critique the language of geography itself. For Williams too, the historicization of country and city life supplies a political account of the landscape that exceeds the possibilities offered by statistical analysis. It is this juncture that I wish to open further in the chapter at hand. In what follows, I will argue that early modern enthusiasm furnished a nonsecular theory of space—one that not only anticipated in crucial ways a materialist critique of empiricist science, but which also provides us now with a register of the ways in which space itself was produced and reconfigured during the early modern period.[3]

This intersection of science and spirituality is well-known to scholars of the period, as Enlightenment religions often synthesized arresting compounds of devotional language and scientific calculation. Newton's belief in the godly mediation of gravity may be the most well known example of such conceptual mosaics. And although Newton's correlation of religious and scientific interests was highly influential in the period—inspiring such theories as John Craig's, in which Newtonian principles were employed to predict the Second Coming in terms of the "velocity of suspicion" of the Gospels[4]—the Camisards, too, fostered a provocative mixture of scientific and reverent thought. The most illustrious example of such mixture is the conversion of Nicolas Fatio, a physicist whose "On the Cause of Gravity" influenced Newton's own theories of gravity and later inspired George Louis-Lesage's better-known *The Newtonian Lucretius*. After his conversion, Fatio became a devotee of the Camisards, and was the only member of the Royal Society ever publicly pilloried for religious enthusiasm.

I mention Fatio by way of the intersection of spatiality and spirituality, and I will address his work in more detail in the closing section of this chapter. In what follows, it will not be my task to unfold a lengthy analysis of science in the early modern period. Such studies have been well and thoroughly performed.[5] What I want to do, rather, is describe the ways in which enthusiastic discourse conceptualized and expressed in unparalleled ways the spatial transformations of the period. To specify what precisely these spatial transformations consisted of, we may begin by turning our attention to the second epigraph at the opening of this chapter, which encapsulates Lacy's deployment of the critical potential of the concept of the supernatural as a charge against empiricist geography: "[g]eography," Lacy observes, "is here grown into a Supernatural Science."

There are a number of ways to interpret the appellation "Supernatural" here, not all of which are necessarily negative: *above nature*, *extraordinary*, and *transcendent* were all significations contemporary to Lacy. But Lacy did not intend the term as a compliment. Indeed, in describing natural science as "Supernatural," Lacy likely drew on the definition of the term most apposite to scientific inquiry: a supernatural phenomenon is one for which a cause can only be attributed to extranatural or divine forces. A supernatural science, then, is a science that has abandoned the question of natural causes and does not seek explanation for its objects of study within the observable facts of the natural world. Certainly as a way of describing empiricist science, the allegation of supernaturalness is damning. Such an allegation attacks the very grounds on which empiricist method authorizes itself through the determination of truth via factual proof.

And yet the inversion by which modern science accrues the devalued connotation of religious fanaticism is nothing particularly unique. It was not at all unusual to refer to Cartesianism or empiricism as enthusiastic methodologies that attempted to circumvent scholasticism and classical humanism in favor of the sorts of experiments and direct assays that appeared as shortcuts to knowledge.[6] What is of particular interest, however, is what happens to the category of space itself in Lacy's indictment. Inches, latitudes, and longitudes, Lacy argues, do not suffice as causal explanations of space. And in their insufficiency, these empiricist designations simultaneously *supernaturalize* the question of cause while *naturalizing* geographic space. In naming as supernatural natural science's empiricist parceling of space into inches, latitidues, and longitudes, then, Lacy introduces the question of cause into the increasingly naturalized concept of geographical space. It is this deployment of enthusiasm to strategically denaturalize space that we wish to focus on in the chapter at hand. More specifically, we zero in on enthusiasm's foregrounding of the conception of *cause* to expose the ways in which natural science, ironically, supernaturalizes space. Here Lacy is found to be in a kind of proleptic solidarity with Williams's own approach, rigorously maintained over an oeuvre of critical material, that space is not an intrinsic, pre-existing terrain on which human history is played out. Rather, this space has been *caused*, produced and shaped through social relationships, the deployment of capital, and the establishment and elaboration of commodity production, exchange, and distribution over land and sea.

The cause of space, of course, is the very historical elision around which Williams asks his readers to wrap their minds. This elision is both exemplified and uncovered by Williams's insistent integration of the dynamic character of urban-rural relations into thinking the constitution of space. Nowhere is the force of this integration more evident than in his claim that these relations constitute a "life" that is "moving," as Williams tells us, "through the history of a family and a people; moving in feeling and ideas, through a network of relationships and decisions."[7] But what does it mean to say that the country and the city, together, constitute a life? The integration and production of the urban-rural network is one that Williams is concerned to denaturalize, to historicize, and to specify as a mutually interpenetrative relationship, one by which the character and productive potential of both city and country were qualitatively reorganized throughout the early modern period:

> The exploitation of man and of nature, which takes place in the country, is realized and concentrated in the city. But also, the profits of other kinds of expoitation—the accumulating wealth of the merchant, the lawyer, the court favourite—come to penetrate the country, as if, but only as if, they were a new social phenomenon.[8]

Although they are frequently defined in contrast to one another, then, the life of the country and the city, together, do not comprise a relationship of contraries. Rather, the country and the city create an intensifying dyad, a relation of "interlocking exploitation."[9] More than this, the life constituted by this "interlocking exploitation" is mediated intellectually in "ideas," affectively as "feelings," socially as "relationships and decisions," and at the sheer level of history itself. Space, as it is defined by Williams in terms of the dialectical interplay of country and city, is thus both produced through the intensification of the effects of each region on the other, and produces the social relationships played out in the country and the city alike.

In regard to this latter claim, I want to anticipate and respond to a possible objection. In his conception of the life of the country and the city, Williams, too, might be said to supernaturalize space; in describing the country and the city as constituting a life, Williams's poetic license attributes to these spaces an uncanny animation—one that links in complex and perhaps contradictory ways with the overarchingly materialist thrust of his study. And yet, far from an antimaterialist mysticism, this life may be more profitably considered as the heritage of the kind of nonsecular spatial thought characterized by Lacy's critical engagement with modern empiricist geography. Indeed, to say that the country and the city together constitute a life, indexes the degree to which this dyad takes on a force and character that exceeds the empirical properties of the country and the city considered singly, or as statistics. This life, then, is a more capacious critical concept than a strict empiricist account of the population, longitudes, or latitudes of either location. As such, the country-city life expresses the ways in which space is both a historical production, and one that shapes and drives the social and material relationships it harbors. Space is at once a product of human history and, itself the "cause" or supplementary force that shapes this history itself.

In this chapter, I take up this intersection of enthusiastic and materialist conceptions of space, and show how early modern debates around enthusiasm came to mediate theories of spatiality and spatial production. In doing so, I pick up the argument of chapter 3, and bring new archival materials to bear on the problem of nonsecular spatiality. In what follows, I delve further into Lacy's enthusiastic theorization of space, and describe the ways in which, for Lacy, enthusiasm dovetails with a nascent materialist critique of empiricist geography. This serious engagement with nonsecular spatial thought intervenes in the widely held assumption that religious discourse, to the extent that it is committed to some conception of celestial space, cannot add a crucial dimension to our histories of early modern spatiality. By way of contrast, I wish to point out the ways in which nonsecular spatial thought, in its very resistance to empiricist methodologies, offers an extensive register of the institutional transformations of the early modern period—developments that were justified and obscured using the very language of empiricist geography that Lacy's work seeks to resist.

This chapter works in tandem with the previous one to produce a larger argument about enthusiasm and spatiality, one that demonstrates the resistance of enthusiastic conceptions of space to the empiricist geography that was deployed to authorize colonial and imperial expansion. These expansions were themselves, as I demonstrated in the previous chapter, encrypted and recoded in enthusiastic rhetoric toward a project of sovereignty and self-management. In this way, the two chapters together ought to show how enthusiasm was utilized to oppositional ends—one more or less a resistance to the ideologies and discourses of developing capitalism, one more or less an apologetics for the same. As early modern space came to be defined by the uneven accumulation and circulation of capital, this process often produced contradictory or uneven connotations of enthusiasm as well.

The London Desert: Camisard Prophets in the City

In 1706, the Camisard Maximilien Misson edited a collection of Camisard prophesies, warnings and reports titled, *Theatre Sacree des Cevennes*, or "Holy Theater of the Cévennes."[10] The volume was first published in French, and in 1707 it was republished in London with a Preface by John Lacy and a new title: *A Cry from the Desart*. The Preface to *A Cry* was the Camisardist text with which most readers would have been familiar and the one to which most readers responded. As the most well-known Camisard text, we must make special mention of the title, which allows us to begin to glimpse the complex spatial dynamics raised by the Camisard presence in London, and to glimpse the ways in which geography and spirituality converged around controversies of religious enthusiasm. For the Camisard refugees in London, the "desert" represents both the arid landscape of the Cévennes. in which they formed as a devout and military unit, as well as the Prophets' spiritual condition, deserted by the monarch, and widely persecuted following the revocation of the Edict of Nantes. In its original, *The Holy Theater of the Cévennes* referred to the theater of guerilla war, as well as to the staging ground of worship that the mountains had become in the peasants' battle with the monarchy. In retitling the collection *A Cry from the Desart*, Lacy both downplayed the militaristic heritage of the Camisards and heightened the significance of Camisard prophesy as a specifically spatial phenomenon. In *A Cry*, the Camisards are discursively framed as always speaking "from" the desert, despite their physical location in London. The "desert" thus signifies the concrete place in which the Prophets cohered as a group, as well as the abstract condition of their spiritual communiqués: a desert, no matter what their physical location. Lacy's title suggests the ways in which geography and spirituality interweave here or perhaps more properly put, the ways in which enthusiasm comes to encode the phenomenon of early modern spatiality itself. Indeed, just as the desert of the Cévennes is posited as somehow always accruing to the Prophets, this same desert describes the Camisard prophesies within British borders. In moving fluidly between its signification as a physical location and a subjective condition, the desert names the interpenetration of subjectivity and space, and perhaps more specifically, the almost counterintuitive possibility that within the rapidly developing urban landscape of London lies a desert, an ancient arid landscape, undeveloped, and holy.

The Camisards' "cry" evinces the complexity of early modern spatial thought in a period of unprecedented movement, and of the unprecedented transformation and differentiation of the built and natural landscapes. More than this, the

Cry returns us to Williams's compression earlier, namely, the "life" of the country and the city. In the Camisards' London, the rural is always within the urban, and the enthusiastic "cry" is an expression of this "interlocking" of one with the other, the conditioning of the rural on the urban, the metropole on the periphery, and vice versa. This spatial palimpsest captures what we described in the previous chapter as the de-development of rural areas as a necessary condition for the productivity of the urban terrain. Let us recall that for David Harvey, the initial processes of primitive accumulation continue into modernity (indeed, for Harvey they continue into the present day). These processes are ongoing, in large part, because capitalism reaches points of crisis wherein the rate of profit begins to drop in relation to pressures from labor for a living wage. In responses to these crises, capitalism intensifies as a spatial phenomenon, ranging around the globe, seeking new sites for profit and predation. As we have argued, often these processes do not only involve building up production centers on previously nonindustrialized land, but also de-developing areas, that is, divorcing the population from its traditional means of reproduction and sustenance, in order to proletarianize the people and drive them into wage labor. Harvey names this process "accumulation by dispossession," and it includes

> The commodification and privatization of land and the foreceful expulsion of peasant populations; the conversion of various forms of property rights (common, collective, state, etc.) into exclusive private property rights; the suppression of rights to the commons; the commodification of labour power . . . colonial, neo-colonial, and imperial processes of appropriation of assets (including natural resources); . . . the slave trade . . . and usury . . .[11]

For Harvey, because capitalist production creates an overaccumulation of goods, and because capitalism also naturally creates masses of organized labor that resist the depredations of the owners of the means of production, profits tend to fall. In order to continue to produce profit, new spaces are dispossessed, made uninhabitable or unsustaining, and traditional social structures made insupportable, as capitalism moves around, within, and between nation-states in an endless movement of de-and re-development. It is in this sense that we may say that, under capitalism, the country interlocks with the city, because it is specifically the dispossession of the countryside that makes urbanization and the generation of an urban labor force possible. Furthermore, it is this interlocking relation that becomes visible under the lens of a nonsecular approach to space—an approach that exceeds the bare, empirical data of statistics in favor of the dynamic interrelationships that, in slipping out of view, condition the visible worlds of urban and rural life.

How is it that the discourse of religious enthusiasm became such a particularly acute register of the politicization of space in the early modern period? Here, we might contextualize the Camisardist "desart" in terms of Henri Lefebrve's immensely clarifying definition of space as a complex metabolic system articulated at a number of often paradoxical or seemingly inconsistent levels at once.

Space, Lefebvre argues, is "indistinguishable from mental space (as defined by the philosophers and mathematicians) on the one hand, and physical space (as defined by practico-sensory activity and the perception of 'nature') on the other."[12] To this set of indistinguishabilities, we might add a religio-political dimension that manifests simultaneously as a mental or spiritual practice and as a sensory one. This is a simultaneity whose alias was, in the early modern period, "enthusiasm." Religious enthusiasm captures the palimpsestic, dynamic relationship between what Lefebvre describes as "mental space" and "physical space," and it does so in large part due to the fluidity, for religious knowledges, between the "mental" and the "practico-sensory." Critics have argued that such fluidity offers us an alternate history of embodiment, one that allows for a more intricate understanding of subjectivity.[13] Building on these observations, we may argue that this fluidity not only revises our histories of embodiment, but, in doing so, encodes the politicization of space as a social phenomenon. The Camisardist "cry" registers precisely the prismatic, politicized spatiality of early modernity. In the Preface, we find the Camisardist Prophet posed, not only as the messenger of millenarial events but also of an unfamiliar landscape and of the strange phenomenon of terrestrial and social overlay: the "seconding" of nature as a social phenomenon.

The Legislated Life of the Country and the City: Lacy and London

A prodigious writer and the lead transcriber and editor of all the Camisard writings, John Lacy was also a trained lawyer, and thus occupied a particularly auspicious position as witness to the Camisard visions. It is perhaps due to this training in the law that, in retitling the volume, Lacy added a lengthy qualifier: *A Cry from the Desert: or testimonials of the miraculous things lately come to pass in the Cévennes, verified upon oath and by other proofs*. The two sides of the title appear unrelated, if not utterly contradictory. The first is a seemingly rapturous, spontaneous expression of divine enthusiasm, the second an ungainly and legalistic substantiation of what ought to need no such prop. The colon holds together the spiritual and legal-scientific accounts of Camisard prophesy in a taut suture. But this is a suture upon which Lacy intends to expand—a contradictory dynamism that he makes fruitful in his writing at large.

In his Preface to *A Cry*, Lacy assures the reader that, although he was not present for all of the prophesies themselves, he is able to verify their legitimacy through the Prophets' narration of these visions:

> The Person who gives this translation of the French, being Present for his own satisfaction, at the times, that the greatest part of the herein contained Certificates, were severally taken. He thinks an obligation to Truth itself . . . to declare, That during his

> Presence, and he believes never else, was there any Indecent Urgencies, or . . . any sort of unjustifiable Practice, used to obtain . . . the Relations herein given; on the contrary . . . every one was desired to say no more than he was able, if legally Required, to affirm upon Oath before Authority.[14]

Here, Lacy deploys the rhetoric of legal oath to undergird his reputation as translator of the prophesies, some of which he has heard only secondhand, some not at all. The law functions to affirm the truth of the prophesies, not because prophesy can be reduced to legal justification, but because the force of the law, the specter of being "legally Required" to swear to the truth of prophesy, has, according to Lacy, served as an incentive for the speakers to delimit their "attestations." Of course, such an assertion could be easily disproved. Even Lacy admits that he can only "believe" that no "Indecent Urgencies" were imposed upon the Prophets. But the invocation of the law does not serve to fortify the claims of the Prophets so much as to ratify the claims of the translator in his ability to bear witness to events that have transpired in the past and over the distance of some miles. In this sense, Lacy redeploys the rhetoric of legal truth as a way of combating not only the potential speciousness of the prophesies, but the simultaneously discursive and geographic problem of translating foreign events to a British public. We would not be mistaken to remind ourselves here of Shaftesbury's own deployment of enthusiasm to shift the grounds of legal truth from an inquisitorial to a statutory basis.

In the Preface to his own *Prophetical Warnings of John Lacy*, Lacy extends his engagement with the tripartite problem of discursivity, legality, and geography. Here, he anticipates and confronts the objection that Camisard prophesy is illegitimate because it doesn't conform to the kind of lengthy, Lockean processes of deduction suitable for empiricist inquiry,

> Having from November last, to the beginning of February following, been present divers times at the Ecstacies of Mr. Marion, Mr. Fage, and Mr. Cavilier, I can say, that their Agitations never did make any Impression upon my Mind or Imagination, such as to promote an Imitation of them, or even an Inclination to it. For the Space of at least eighteen Days before mine came upon me, I had seen none of them; and mine were so entirely different from any of theirs, that it is altogether unlikely that the Force of Imagination (as some without due Consideration have fancied) could produce them.[15]

Rather than narrate the experience of watching the Prophets receive visions, Lacy insists that he did *not* witness these prophesies. This surprising attestation functions, however, as a kind of proof, for it is precisely the lack of empirical evidence that serves, for Lacy, as evidence that the prophesies are true. Against the accusation that enthusiastic prophesy is contagious and causes imitative responses in observers, Lacy draws on the somewhat counterintuitive evidence of things unseen, namely, the geographical and temporal distance between his own prophesies and those of Marion, Fage, and Cavilier which took place at a "Space of at least eighteen Days."

Lacy makes much of temporal and spatial interlacings. Indeed, although the Camisardist visions themselves may appear sudden and therefore specious to outside observers, according to Lacy, the Prophets have been gestating the "organs" of prophesy for months, readying themselves for the transmission of divine knowledge:

> Everyone that is Inspired did undergo a Preparation," Lacy argues, "wherein the Spirit (by Agitations much more frequent in the beginning than afterwards) did form the Organs, ordinarily for one, two, or three Months, before such Person utter'd anything as under Inspiration.[16]

This account of the development of the enthusiastic organs is a direct address to the emphasis on duration called for by Locke in his programme for empiricist knowledge. More than this, Lacy's efforts to articulate a spiritual science of enthusiasm leads him to divulge the complex psychic environment of the Prophets. These inner spaces are represented as evolving proprioceptive topographies that undergird the observable phenomena of the Camisard ecstacies as manifested in the social spaces of the streets and meeting houses. Lacy divulges the mediation of space and subject convoked in the interior terrains of prophetic reception.

Of course, this project of attaching the terrain of the unseen to the phenomena of the visible world is not one that Lacy or, arguably, any Enlightenment thinker would definitively solve. Lacy's allegorization of the problem of spatial knowledge in terms of the physical landscape of enthusiastic interiority, however, is noteworthy. In so doing, Lacy inverts the empiricist account of space. In Lacy, space is not what is visible or quantifiable in inches, centimeters, or miles. Rather, space is a temporally evolving supraempirical phenomenon, one laced inextricably with the "sense" of space, the subjective dimension. This inversion is multiplied by Lacy's service as witness to the prophesies, the "miraculous things" that, as the book details, had taken place in the Cévennes. As London observer, Lacy performs an operation of some rhetorical subtlety in order to serve as witness to prophesies that transpired in the past and over a considerable distance. By testifying to the interior landscape of prophetic organs, Lacy reconfigures and reinstates the terrestrial travels of the Camisards within a theory of enthusiastic spatiality and embodiment. The time lapse, interior geographies of the Camisard bodies operate as a cipher, not only for Godly communication, but for the complex status of national spatial relations, replete with the surprising gulfs and proximities attendant on economic development in early modernity.

What, we might wonder, is the significance of publishing and testifying to prophesies that have in some sense already taken place. Why prophesy the past? As Michael Heyd has pointed out, Camisard prophesy itself provided nothing new at the level of content, and this is a claim that Lacy himself argued: "'This Mission brings no new Doctrine with it.'"[17] In part, the Camisard resistance to issuing new doctrine was an attempt to achieve relevance. If the Camisards' prophesies could be cross-referenced with Scripture, the agreement of Scripture and Camisard prophesy might weigh in favor of Camisard legitimacy. Of course, the problem with repeating accepted prophesy was that the Camisard claims might also appear redundant. This oscillation between redundancy and illegitimacy was one that spun ceaselessly in contemporary debates about the Camisards.[18] For us, the question becomes, not whether the Camisards were legitimate prophets or not, and not even whether the claims of Enlightenment reason could be reconciled with Camisard claims to legitimacy, but rather, what the redundancy of Camisard prophesy itself encoded.

At the most basic level, the prophesies in the Cévennes serve as a record of Camisard oppression, and in this sense *A Cry* serves simply as a historical mark of an otherwise occluded and repressed struggle for self-determination. But what, we need to ask, of the continued relevancy of the prophesies within London some years following the Camisard tenure in the "desart"? Indeed, it is this precise relationship—between the "pastness" of France and the "presentness" of England, or the pastness of the prophesy and the presentness of its publication—that constitutes the significance of the Camisards in London. Camisard enthusiasm serves as a communiqué that performs a double encoding. The dialectically developing relationship of rural and urban spaces is encrypted within a discourse of religious time, of redundant prophesy, and of prophesies of the past. We are reminded here of Lacy's claims regarding the preparation of interior prophetic landscapes and the extent to which, insofar as enthusiastic transport is incubated at length within the enthusiastic subject, this temporal delay reveals all geographies as palimpsestic. Prophesies that are articulated in one "place" evoke the movement of bodies across distances that are simultaneously spans of time. Perhaps more properly put, distances are coded as developmentally "delayed" as the countryside is ritually impoverished under the onward march of urbanization and accumulation by dispossession. The chronological stretch of the interior landscape of enthusiastic prophesy, in other words, encodes and expresses the uneven action of geographical development—the politization of the landscape in new relations of incipient capitalist production. Indeed, if, as we have been arguing, the question of early modern space *is* the question of the newly dynamized relationship between the country and the city (or, the dynamic de-development of the countryside to create the phenomenon of the metropolis), Camisard enthusiasm tropes this new dynamic as a potent overlay of past with present, and of subject with social order. The prophesy of the past, then, functions to communicate some very real political truths about the present, albeit truths that were not available to empirical assay.

Hewing Stones: The City and Value

In 1714, Lacy expanded on linkages he had already made between geographic space and the inward terrain of prophetic knowledge. In the *Ecclesiastical and*

Political History of Whig-Land, a satiric travel narrative published after the Camisard trials, Lacy took an almost Swiftian attitude to the peculiarities of contemporary Whig culture. And this Swiftian tone is no coincidence. Lacy's *Ecclesiastical and Political History* is a woefully overlooked contribution to the somewhat more well-known debate between Swift and Steele over the Hanoverian Succession in 1714—a debate for which Steele was removed from Parliament on charges of sedition for his pamphlet, *The Crisis*, which argued that "pannick" would return to England should the Stuarts return to the throne. Swift, in his turn, satirized Whig propagandizing, and claimed that the Whigs were responsible for generating these "pannicks" themselves. For Lacy, in some contradistinction to both Swift and Steele, the format of writing a satiric "Ecclesiastical History" permitted him to issue a critique of the High Anglican oligarchy from the perspective of an enthusiastic Dissenter.

Lacy's perspective is crucial for our understanding of the political debates of the period. Because eighteenth-century British literary history has been largely cast as a set of struggles between Whig and Tory concerns (such as that between Steele and Swift), our sense of the period has been shaped by an effort to coordinate literary texts with the power plays that unfurled between wealthy interest groups at the level of Parliamentary and Monarchical politics—groups with interests that were not as divergent as some accounts would depict.[19] Indeed, recent histories of the eighteenth century have recognized the limitations of a historical landscape that casts Whig-Tory debates as the polar extremes of progressive and conservative politics. Lacy's perspective adds to our corrective historiographies insofar as it critiques Whig politics by both satirizing and recoding enthusiasm.

In his *Ecclesiastical History*, Lacy describes the inhabitants of "Whig-Land" in all their contradictory and violent aspects. Of particular interest to Lacy's narrator is the origin of the wealth of Whig-Land, and Lacy's text takes an especially salient turn when it describes the foundation of this wealth in the uneven and exploitative relations between country and city within England, and between the English nation and its colonial exploits. Indeed, we might situate the *Ecclesiastical History* within the expanded definition we have already given of narratives of primitive accumulation. Although he was not a political economist, Lacy's description of the intersection of British imperialism with the impoverishment of rural labor in England is uncannily accurate:

> A Remarkable Instance of their [the inhabitants of "WhigLand"] *Charity* towards Foreigners is, that they have taken over a poor depopulated Country, by Thirty thousands as a time, even to the starving of their *own Poor*, whose Mouths were stop'd, instead of Bread, with Arguments to prove, that so many Beggars would enrich their Country. And they are so Charitable, they will receive any, and Naturalize them purely for being the Out-casts and Scorn of other Nations.[20]

In riffing on the Mandevillian claim that a multitude of poor is the surest gauge of national wealth, Lacy reveals the express relationship between English wealth and transatlantic exploit, and between the growth of the English poor and the colonization of the Americas. Here, the expenditure of national resources on colonization projects renders acutely the processes of capital accumulation whereby the reinvestment of profits in production ventures abroad (at the very real cost of the immiseration of national populace, as well as the colonized, enslaved, and indentured persons of the Americas) yields an ever-increasing cycle of revenue that never touches down in the form of food or the satisfaction of material wants. Simply put, as the wealth of the nation increases, so does the impoverishment of the people. Indeed, this impoverishment is critical to the continuation of the cycle, a point that Lacy indicates in referencing the Mandevillian argument that a reserve population of the poor is the surest way to both hold down wages and keep profits high.

On precisely this topic of wages and exploitation, Lacy's *Prophetical Warnings* imagines his speaker supplying what the cycle of accumulation cannot. In fact, the *Warnings* provides one of Lacy's more direct convocations of an insubordinate laboring subject. In the voice of a God who speaks through Lacy, citizens are called on to recognize their exploitation: "Where is the domineering Master of this World, that pays his Servants such wages? Yet they rise, and labour for him. It is a weariness for you, to be but one hour in Prayer with me. Open your Mouths in Prayer, and I will fill them."[21] Anticipating the *Ecclesiastical and Political History*'s concern with the Whig abandonment of the poor, the "Bread" and sustenance that ought to—but do not—fill the mouths of the needy, is instead supplied in the form of an enthusiastic figure of speech. In promising to "fill" the mouth of English subjects, Lacy describes at once a supernatural speech (an enthusiastic vocalization that transpires beyond the will of the subject whose mouth is "filled" with divine communication) and an earthly satisfaction: a full mouth for the laborers who weary themselves in toil for earthly masters.

Much like *A Cry from the Desart*, Lacy's *Ecclesiastical and Political History* posits a speaker who, although technically in the space of "Whigland," is not *of* it. It is almost as if, in his conversion, Lacy too begins to speak "from" the desert—to become alien in his native land. This alienation bespeaks not only Lacy's dissent from Whig establishment and the Parliamentary system of laws to which the Prophets were subjected, but contains an implicit critique of the naturalization of national space. For Lacy, space itself is not a simple empirical quantum of land, but a matrix of political, productive, intellectual, and social relationships. In converting to Camisard Protestantism, Lacy gains a critical distance from Whig policies, and this distance is a trope for a remoteness that is contained within the borders of the nation. In the *Ecclesiastical and Political History*, this remoteness takes the form of a travel narrative conducted by a figure who reveals the mechanisms of imperial exploit. The enthusiastic observer represents his distance from national policy as the span of a metaphorical journey in which he witnesses the nation fanatically populating new colonies while claiming that the interests of the poor coincide with colonial enterprises. This is an illegitimate palimpsest, a false spatial compression, and creates an immediacy to which Lacy's *Ecclesiastical and Political History* hopes to give the lie. One might imagine this immediacy, in which the interests of the poor and of English colonial policy are forced to occupy the same space, as one of the species of false enthusiasm that Lacy seeks to expose.

The ruthless relationship between the wealth of the nation and the poverty of its inhabitants receives a cunning inversion toward the conclusion of Lacy's speaker's trip. In the narrative's only direct address to the historical rise of the Whigs, Lacy satirizes the English Civil Wars and the beheading of Charles I as the founding moment of the contemporary Whig establishment. Via an imagined festival that transpires on every January 30, in commemoration of the day that Charles I was handed to Parliament, a Whiggish "Baccanalia" led by a cadre of high priests sacrifices a calf at "a little Place, to which they gave the Name of a *Prison-House*."[22] In Lacy's narrative, January 30 has become the state's most holy holiday, and a ridiculously solemn occasion on which the Biblical parable of the golden calf is re-enacted to the heights of parody. Here, the living calf is milked to the great ecstasy of the onlookers. The priests, Lacy depicts,

> make upon it a very merry Oath to observe a due Allegiance to the *Calf* as long as he will be able to divert them with those odd Magnificences which they bestow upon him; At last the High Priest makes use of somme Pungent Instrument to make the Calf calcitrate, and then the Company fall into a Passion, and vote him to be carried to their *Banqueting-House*. The Master of the Ceremonies upon his Shoulders brought into the Middle of the Room a Prodigious Log, which they say is Cut off from a Famous Hollow Oak, and upon this they lay down the Calf, and the Chief Preacher of the *Fanaticks* approaches with an Atrocious Butcherly Look; and after staring widely and earnestly with his Eyes to make a sure Aim, and making several Mock Offers with the Ax, He at last with all the Collected Vigour of his Body Hew'd off the Head of the Calf; and at the Stroke Issued forth from his Mouth such a kind of Sound or Groan, as Comes from one that Rives Blocks among us, or beats down the Stones that Pave the Streets, which they account the Hiccoughing of the Spirit, and think it Proceeds from the greatest Ardour of Devotion and from giving an entire Attention of Mind to what they are about.[23]

Lacy's critique harks back to the kind of progressive, communalist objection to Cromwellian rule, an opposition leveled most famously by Winstanley, who noted that the Civil Wars took place under the guise of promised freedoms that never transpired. In truth, they put into place different sorts of oppressions and deployments of power:

> O thou Powers of England, though thou hast promised to make this People a Free People, yet thou hast so handled the matter, through thy self-seeking humour, That thou hast wrapped us up more in bondage, and oppression lies heavier upon us; not only bringing thy fellow Creatures, the Commoners, to a morsel of Bread, but by confounding all sorts of people by thy Government, of doing and undoing.[24]

In his satirical history of the Civil Wars and the institutionalization of the Whig party, Lacy manages to bring together the impoverishment of England, the colonization of the Americas, and the abstraction that was just at this point coming into articulation: the concept of "national wealth." He does so through a lampooning portrait of Cromwellian fanaticism as a program that purports to "true" communication with divinity. This communication, according to Lacy, is nothing more than a "hiccough" that has more in common with the unwilled sounds of urban labor than it does with what Lacy might regard as genuine spiritual knowledge.

The analogizing of fanatical execution to the groans of labor deploys a fantasy about the immediacy of toil and sonic expression in order to disparage the Puritan "fanaticks" as having adopted an unconsidered relationship to their actions. Lacy's analogy is admittedly quite far from an analytically complex or even a sympathetic treatment of the question of early modern labor. Rather, it trades in a number of unproductive stereotypes regarding the split between mental and physical activity. And yet, this analogy situates the problem of enthusiasm in general, and the question of the mediation of divine knowledge in particular, within a quite fascinating interpretive nexus. Here the scene of legal retribution also functions as a negative example of enthusiastic excess. In a fashion that recalls Shaftesbury's recoding of the "Inquisitors," Lacy also locates the expression of false enthusiasm within the theory and practice of the Law. The original beheading has become a state-sanctioned performance that ritually re-enacts the legitimation of what Lacy depicts as a kind of theocratic Whig oligarchy. Although we ordinarily expect this sort of satire about the Puritan Revolution from a conservative and/or Tory perspective, Lacy mounts his critique as an enthusiast and dissenting victim of the retributive justice meted out by the Whig establishment. It is in this sense that Lacy's *Ecclesiastical and Political History* might be said to continue the project from the Preface to *A Cry*, that is, to recode legitimate and false enthusiasms in terms of both a theory of spatiality and a theory of duration. Whereas the enthusiastic body harbors and expresses the long temporalities of divine knowledge, the fanatical one sounds off in a seizure of legislative violence.

Here we are returned to the epigraph with which we began, namely, Lacy's lampooning the claims of geography as a bathetic collision between supernatural entities and the number-crunching empiricism of the new science. And we are reminded, too, of Lefebvre's articulation of the unsatisfactory nature of the endless parceling of space into ever more miniscule sets of empirical data: "There are plenty of reasons for thinking that descriptions and cross-sections of this kind," argues Lefebvre, "though they may well supply *inventories* of what exists in space, or even generate a *discourse* on space, cannot ever give rise to a *knowledge* of space."[25]

The reason why geography cannot seize the expansive significance of space has to do, for Lefebvre, with the political nature of space and the mutual constitution of this political space alongside the discourse of a "science of space," which

> represents the political (in the case of the West, the "neocapitalist") use of knowledge. Remember that "knowledge" under this system is integrated in a more or less

"immediate" way into the forces of production, and in a "mediate" way into the social relations of production.[26]

Translated into our early modern context, we might say that the dangerous "immediacy" is not the enthusiastic communion with divinity, but rather the arrangement of productive forces in accord with the political aims of early capitalism. Certainly Lacy's mediations on intra-national "travel" suggest as much insofar as the speaker's alienation from national space reveals the historical construction of naturalized geographies.

Because the question of true or false enthusiasm raises the rather larger question of the relationship of the utterance to legislative force, the problem of true or false enthusiasm is revealed as political. For what Lacy points out is that the sanction of the law, particularly statute, obviates the need for any duration or reflexivity in an act of government. This act is thus coded as a kind of false enthusiasm. If the French Prophets' interior architectures have, over a length of time, been reconstructed to receive divine communication, the application of legislative force by the Whig establishment requires no such concerted attention or duration. Thus, in Lacy's text there is a complex and contradictory dynamics between the time and space of "genuine" enthusiastic knowledge and the immediacies of legislative fiat that require no reflection and in fact are figured as the empiricist parceling of space delineated by the blocks and stones of the urban landscape. Indeed, we might read the vigorous hewing of the executioner as Lacy's throwing into relief an empiricist concept of not just space itself, but of the construction of the urban terrain more properly. Here, the grotesquerie of the execution is amplified in its contrast with the sheer mundanity of the physical objects. The paratactical compression of blocks and stones with the devout actions of execution produces another bathetic contrast that has the effect of satirizing, not only the execution itself, but, more importantly, the kinds of fanaticism that cannot properly differentiate the value of objects. These sorts of fanaticism are those legitimated by the force of law. Here Charles's head becomes just another block or stone, and the passion that guides the execution swings vertiginously between the "Ardour" of "Devotion" and a "Butcherly" "Beating."

Manufacturing Value: The Body of the Book

For Lacy, Whig-Land's mechanisms of valuation mean that a stone and a head might receive the same treatment. Such vertiginous valuation applies as well to the "chief *Manufactur[e]*" and "*Commodit[y]*" of Whigland—books—and on this topic, Lacy's satiric ire pinpoints the complex weaving together of legislative violence with the worth of literary commodities in a rich parody of state censorship:

There are not more *Corn-Mills* than *Paper-Mills* in this Country. Every body that can Write, Prints his Thoughts; because, let 'em be as bad as they will, they will always meet with proper Readers . . . .And to shew what Encouragement is here given to Letters, in my time of being there, for Copying out an *Act of Parliament*, and adding a Line or two here and there of his own Invention, to stretch the Pamphlet to the size of a *Shilling*, he got by Subscriptions 1500 l, but they wisely inform me, the reason of this was, because 'twas written upon a certain *Crisis*, to raise an *Alarm*, to cause to be set on fire all the Beacons in the Country, to effect an Universal Pannick. All Books are here valuable according to the number and size of the Reports which adorn them; if any Book has one Truth in it, 'tis made a Martyr, and burned to scorch a Fowl, or put into a fiery Furnace under the Pyes by a Pastry Cook, or made Kites of, and thrown down head-long by Children, as from a Pinnacle; some in more solemn manner, if they be all Truth, they will get a Hangman to put in the Flames before their Face. Pillories are there held in great esteem, insomuch that a Man who will skip up upon one voluntarily, and with great flush of Joy, afterwards stiles himself a Martyr for the publick Cause. I have known a Hymn made to it in my time of residing there.[27]

The relationship between legal censure and literary value seems at first to proceed according to a simple arithmetic. The "number and size of Reports" that "adorn" a book—for example, *A Cry from the Desart*, or Steele's *Crisis*, to which Lacy refers earlier—determines the value of a written document. In a manner similar to Shaftesbury's own claims for enthusiasm, Lacy points out that the value of a piece of writing is only inflated by its persecution, and so legal censure inverts its own aims. Just as martyrs are confirmed by the attention they receive in court, so too does a book of "truth" increase in value as it receives the "Hangman"'s attention, putting it "in the flames before their face."

Beyond the Shaftesburian irony that Lacy deploys here, however, this account of literary eminence contains a complex and counterintuitive theory of materiality, one in which, in order to become a "martyr" and thus attain value in Whig-Land, the book undergoes a violent dissolution of its material specificity. This is some departure from the Shaftesburian intervention, for Shaftesbury emphasizes toleration at least in part on the grounds that the punishment of enthusiasts confirms their status as martyrs. Such an argument dovetails in ways that we have detailed with the extension of Parliamentary sovereignty, and as such marks the crucial junction of legal transformation with the birth of aesthetic value. Lacy's analysis, however, exceeds the realm of legal discourse and the application of laws, and ventures into the material substratum of valuation itself in the processes of commodification. For the "number and size of Reports" to add value to a book, the book itself must endure a process by which it is denuded of any supplementary signification and exposed to a variety of literal uses: to "scorch a Fowl," to bake a pie, or to serve as a child's plaything and be flung down from a great height. Here, it is not just that persecution confirms the value of a book. Rather, valuation is founded on the dismantling of the object's material qualities. In this sense, the obscene punishment of books metaphorizes the punishment of the Camisards by the Whig establishment. But more importantly, this punishment dramatizes the counterintuitive processes by which value is invested in material objects under the strange (counter)logic of capitalist accumulation. In being either burned, baked, smashed, or hung, the book's physical body is eroded in the course of its valuation. This sensational process anticipates in important ways Marx's own reflections on the constitution of the value form as a dialectical relation that suppresses the material specificity of the object in order to render it equivalent to a world of other commodities. What is, in fact, a social relation between people is, famously for Marx, thereafter perceived as a relation between things—fetishized commodities that appear to have value (and indeed, a kind of life) in and of themselves. Although this citation is likely familiar, I will reprint it here for the sake of clarity:

> [The] social characters of their [the laborers'] own labours appear to them as social properties pertaining to them by nature, as objective determinations of the products of labour themselves, the equality of human labours as a value-property of the products of labour, the measure of the labour by the socially necessary labour-time as the magnitude of value of the products of labour, and finally the social relations of the producers through their labours appear as a value relation or a social relation of these things, the products of labor.[28]

We do not need to enter into a lengthy discussion of Marx in order to grasp the resonance between his theory and Lacy's parody of literary valuation. In both cases, the object undergoes a kind of dialectical trial by fire by which it is broken down in order to take on a value that thereafter appears to be a natural expression of that object itself. This is to say that the object—in Lacy's case, the book—is attributed a supernatural aura, or worth, through the ritual destruction of its material specificity. Thus the book becomes a "martyr," not just through its juridical persecution, but also through the annihilation of what Lacy describes as its "body." And while we might have imagined a religious enthusiast as the last place to look for such an uncanny adumbration of Marx, it is precisely the religious language of enthusiasm that functions to expose and encode the mechanisms on which the apparently self-evident, self-sustaining forms of market value depend. Such an analogy recalls Derrida's claims—cited in the Introduction—that the abstractions of religious discourse model the abstractions of the commodity form. And so, we might say that all commodities under capitalism are what an enthusiast might regard as martyrs to value. In making a distinction between commodity valuation through the law and what Lacy calls enthusiastic "truth," Lacy reveals the constitution of value through a dual operation of legal censure and the liquefaction of specific characteristics that bequeaths to the object a fetishistic veneer of self-sufficient value. In this sense, the scene of the trial and the martyrdom of the accused—whether that accused be a book or an enthusiast—gives way to reveal the material contradictions of commodification more largely.

In its consideration of manufacture, the *Ecclesiastical and Political History* brings us around to the set of conceptual problems with which we closed chapter 2: the apparent incongruity between ideals of self-management and the extension of Parliamentary law. For Lacy, this incongruity is exposed through the satiric application of enthusiastic "truth" to the institutional interrelationships between the legislative and fiscal arms of Whig-Land. In this sense, enthusiasm's critical leverage lies in its ability to expose the interrelationships between seemingly separate spheres of practice. In doing so, Lacy's work makes a lie of the fantasy of market self-regulation and of liberal ideals of market regulation as well. Enthusiasm, in Lacy's hands, demonstrates the mediated nature of value by articulating the coordination of literary worth with the exercise of legislative power. If for Marx the fetishism of commodities is a way of describing the attribution of a supernatural aura to objects in their constitution as commodities, for Lacy, too, supernatural value is an effect, the processes of which he attempts to trace through the "martyrdom" of the book.

Let us allow the supernaturalization of value to return us to the question with which we began this chapter: that of spatiality and empiricist geography. Although Lacy's work has not been incorporated into traditional historical study of the period, the great virtue of returning his oeuvre to the archive on enthusiasm is that it allows us to link up our study of secularism and space via the problem of value more largely. Indeed, what Lacy demonstrates is the extent to which a nonempiricist approach to travel narrative, far from unscrolling a statistical survey of landscape, uncovers the supra-empirical nature of the space of the nation and its constitution via the uneven relations of manufacture and the dialectical form of value. Indeed if, in Lacy, the debate around enthusiasm reveals the various and often discordant temporal modalities of the national and transnational landscape, enthusiasm exposes the lacunae at the heart of empiricist geography.

Nicolas Fatio and the Ultramundanity of Space

> [M]y Theory proves the Intervention of an Almighty Power governing in the whole Extent of Infinite Space . . .[29]

I want to close this chapter and open the next one by way of another Camisard convert, Nicolas Fatio, who in 1688 announced his theory of gravity before an audience at the Royal Society. Fatio's theory brings together the concerns of this chapter—namely, secularity and the critique of empiricist space—with the concerns of the next, which focuses on the entrenching of spatiality in poetic form. Fatio allows us to bridge these chapters by way of a peek into enthusiastic physics and its application to early aesthetics. Indeed, Fatio's devotional speculative physics not only combats the micronizing techniques of empiricist geography and theories of space, but makes a generic claim: for Fatio, physics was best expressed in poetic form. Closing this chapter with a brief consideration of the connection between enthusiastic spatiality and aesthetics will enable us, in chapter 5, to establish some more general propositions concerning the intersection of poetics, enthusiastic historicism, and the production of the urban spaces that were indispensable to the accumulation of capital.

Nicolas Fatio de Duillier's work with the Royal Society has not received a great quantity of attention from historians, but it certainly garnered significant notice from his peers. Newton himself regarded Fatio as an indispensable theorist, writing in 1692, in a note in his own copy of the *Principia*, that "[t]he unique hypothesis by which gravity can be explained . . . was first devised by the most ingenious geometer Mr. N. Fatio."[30] Ironically, Fatio was indispensable to Newton in part due to his methodological departure from Newton. Where Newton's theory of gravity was predictive—it used the mathematical model of the inverse square law to calculate the gravitational influences of bodies upon one another— Fatio's theory was explanatory; it sought to describe *why* Newton's model would predict gravitational actions accurately. Fatio's theory was the earliest in what is now known as the push theory of gravity. The push theory has recently received renewed attention for its proposition that bodies move toward one another due to a shower of impinging forces.[31] Beyond the latest vetting of the scientific viability of Fatio's thought, however, what interests us is the spiritual component of his theory. Indeed, the push theory was based largely in an enthusiastic speculation about the behavior of "undetectable" particles in the universe, particles that could not be empirically verified. It is this methodology of the supra-empirical that set Fatio apart from natural philosophers, his "willingness," that is, "to propose [theories] . . . based on mathematical principles and calculations, rather than experience or observation."[32]

Although Fatio began his work on gravity before his conversion to Camisard Protestantism, his work continued and deepened alongside his commitment to enthusiastic religion, and it is not contrary, though it may be controversial, to propose that Fatio's conception of divine force is what made possible the highly theoretical and scientifically significant nature of his research. The most striking illustration of this may, in fact, be a generic one: Fatio chose to communicate his theory of gravity, not in scientific prose, but rather in the form of a poem. In 1731, Fatio explained his stylistic decision thusly:

> It was natural that such a treatise be written in Prose, and not in Verse. But partly because I knew the Academy was not altogether in good earnest . . . and partly because my Theory proves the Intervention of an Almighty Power governing in the whole Extent of Infinite Space, I did write it in the Form of a Poem.[33]

Fatio's belief in divine determination is not at issue here. Neither are the internal debates of the Royal Society, or Fatio's suspicion that his work would not be taken seriously. What is of interest, however, is Fatio's assertion that divine determination both allows him to speculate on the massive "Extent of Infinite Space," and necessitates the formal capture of these speculations in a poem. He writes in the form of a poem, that is, because the expansive, supra-empirical quality of his object—gravity—finds its syncopation in the supra-empirical deixes of poetry itself. Indeed, by Fatio's account, it is enthusiastic belief that allows him to synthesize the endlessly unfurling details gathered by empirical assay—what he terms the "singular and otherwise unaccountable effects" (155) available to observation—into a universal theory of gravitational force that finds its aesthetic equivalent in poetic form.

Let us briefly review Fatio's theory of gravity. Fatio proposed that gravity was the effect of innumerable, unseen particles (termed "ultramundane," or beyond human observation) raining constantly upon bodies and driving them together. This theory reconciled a Cartesian mechanistic view of space as composed of bodies with Newton's dynamic theory of "action at a distance." Was it enthusiasm that served as the inspiration for Fatio's complex scientific analysis? Georges LeSage certainly thought so. Upon buying the scientist's papers from Fatio's last landlord in London, LeSage discovered Fatio's poem regarding gravity and wrote an accompanying introduction, explaining what distinguished Fatio's theory from those of the empiricist astronomers, who have

> [n]o clear view of this chaos [the universe] (of which the first glance is, I admit, frightful) . . . [They] have not known how to disentangle it and subject it to their calculations . . . [They have] lacked sufficient love of truth or courage of their convictions . . . [T]hey have failed to become impressed with the strength and fecundity of this beautiful system so distinctly as to lead them, in their enthusiasm, to sacrifice to it their other views and projects.[34]

In LeSage's view, it is Fatio's enthusiasm that conditions his pathbreaking claims. And this is because enthusiasm allows Fatio not only to devote himself to divine and scientific truths, but to believe that these truths are woven together in a larger "beautiful system." Indeed, it is enthusiasm that, according to LeSage, makes sense of an otherwise tangled heap of information.

Let us put a little more pressure on LeSage's formulation. What did it mean to say that enthusiasm "disentangle[s]" the "frightful" sight of the universe? Or that it permits Fatio a "clear view" of "chaos"? Based on LeSage's redactions of Fatio, we may offer two linked hypotheses. First, it is enthusiasm that allows Fatio to systematize the complex, contradictory phenomena of the universe, to propose their causes, and to produce "calculations" based on data otherwise illegible. Enthusiasm here is less a matter of apprehending singular items of scientific (or divine) data, and rather more the ability to speculate upon the co-ordinating relations that are themselves not apprehensible as such. Our second hypothesis has to do with LeSage's sense that the empiricist philosophers have been unable or unwilling to "sacrifice" to the "beauty" of the universe "their other views and projects." In this, LeSage draws on the language of religious passion to name the "sacrifice" of individual data necessary to the attainment of scientific truth. By an enthusiastic comprehension of the overarchingly systematic nature of the universe (its inexorable "strength") Fatio is sufficiently "impressed" and able to grasp what the empiricists cannot.

Might enthusiasm offer a unique perspective into the formation of poetic form? In addressing this question, we will leave our consideration of poetry's specific qualities for the next chapter, and mark instead Fatio's own attestations regarding gravity, a topic that recurrently turns to the "beauty" of physical principles. In first encountering Newton, for example, it is the beauty of Newtonian systematicity that most impresses Fatio. In 1687 he writes, of Newton's *Philosophiæ Naturalis Principia Mathematica*,

> Il traitte en general de la Mechanique des Cieux; de la maniere dont les mouvemens circulaire qui se font dans un milieu liquide se communiquent à tout le milieu; de la pasanteur et d'une force qu'il suppose dans toutes le planetes pour s'attirer les unes les autres . . . Ce traitté que j'ay veu en partie est assurement tres beu, et rempli d'un grand nombre de belles propositions.[35]

What do we make of this scientifico-poetic sense of beauty? Let us situate it in terms of Fatio's conception of space as "ultramundane." Unlike Descartes, Fatio did not hold that space and substance were equivalent. Fatio's way of illustrating this nonidentity was to argue that an object (his example is gold) might contain "a trillion times more void than substance." To argue that no identity obtains between substance and space is to strike at the root of empiricist theories of geography, population, and statistics. Such a radical nonequivalence between space and substance in turn entails a theorization of causality that exceeds the visible and the quantifiable fields and edges into the realm of universalizing speculation. Here, enthusiasm is not only a "mania," as Clement Hawes describes it, or a style, as Shaun Irlam proposes, but a systematization of universal order more largely—a systematization of the "communication" of movements "in all the medium." This is a communication that both Fatio and LeSage describe as "beautiful." Fatio's exulting in this beauty has significance, I would argue, for the history of aesthetics. Because for Fatio, enthusiasm is not only a systematizing method of thought; it is also the capacity to render that system in aesthetic form. In this sense, poetic form becomes not simply an addition to the theory of gravity, but that theory's formal incarnation.

We might now offer that Fatio's enthusiasm offers an uncanny adumbration of a Kantian enthusiastic worldview, or systematizing method of thought. Jameson clarifies this connection: in "[w]hat Kant characterizes as 'enthusiasm', the intensity of affect signals the transformation of empirical experiences into transcendental ones . . . the looming sense of the proximity of totalities beyond the immediate particulars."[36] This conception of enthusiasm as a comprehensive worldview ought to remind us of Shaftesbury. Indeed, in redacting Fatio on this point, LeSage extends a Shaftesburian thread that names the ability to exultantly glimpse the interconnectedness of phenomena beyond the empirically verifiable. For Fatio, the ability to conceive the universe as a whole that is made up of more than visible, verifiable empirical data requires the accompaniment of an ultramundane theory of space.

If what we mean by enthusiasm is, in part, the perception of the systemic nature of space and of the social world, then not only does an enthusiastic poetics give aesthetic form to spatiality, such a poetics gestures toward the politicization of that space, encoding in intricate ways the historical and spatial dimensions of capital accumulation. It is this encoding that concerns us as we move into chapter 5. If the final chapter brings together the concern of the four that precede it—enthusiasm, historicism, secularization, accumulation, spatiality, and the law—it will do so specifically as a matter of the aestheticization of all these concerns in poetic form.

Chapter 5

Poetic Enthusiasm

The City, the Country, and Extended Accumulation

> What emerges from the ruins of universal History is a "rhythmology" of capital, a conceptualization of crises, and a historicity in which politics "attains primacy over history."[1]

What did an enthusiastic poetics look like in the early eighteenth century? At first glance, this is hardly the thorniest question that we have asked thus far. After all, poetry and religious sentiment have long shared a number of defining qualities, perhaps most recognizably the allure of transcendent passion and the promise of surmounting the constraints of the physical world. From the Renaissance to the Romantics, poetic history boasts a roster of official enthusiasts that would not surprise any serious student of literature. Indeed, the lineage that spans John Donne, George Herbert, Christopher Smart, and Percy Shelley, traces a purported secularization by which the rapturous address to God sheds its otherworldly addressee to become a rapturous apostrophe to sublime nature, and devotional poetic tongues evolve into dizzying fidelities to beauty.

Poetry has long appeared to be the repository of religious feeling in a rapidly secularizing world. But if this is a secularization—and at this point in our analysis I trust we have cast that category well in doubt—then it is one that seems to leave a blooming poetic passion as its trace. Such a literary history converges with a critique of secularization by installing the vestiges of religion within poetry itself. In the place of a secularization narrative about the sweeping of magic from the world, the humanities have installed a melancholic correction: religion is not gone; it is remembered in aesthetic form. But in replacing divine with poetic passion, do such literary histories counter a secularization thesis or continue one? In what follows, I want to offer that, in the poetic whiff of godliness, we detect one of the latent presumptions of both secularization and its critique: that the passion for God must go *somewhere*; that it must land somewhere even if its referent is increasingly cast in doubt. And so this lost or receding referent is said to dwell not simply in the flowering of modern aesthetics, but more precisely within poetry's exquisite address.

The presumption that the surplus energies of social life range continually in search of an object upon which to alight ought to be questioned in itself. Such an economy of passion partakes of a fungible logic that replaces one ardor with another, a substitution characteristic of capitalist modernity. In questioning this deputizing of poetry as the storehouse of religion, we ask: How is it that the unfolding of poetic passion has come to seem the trace of religion, the grotto within which faith and feeling have taken refuge? How is it, in other words, that poetic passion and the extraempirical deixes of poetry have come to appear to substitute for the extraempirical deixes of spiritual passion?

In asking such a question, I mean to point to the fact that the transubstantiation of religious passion has become, to some extent, the presumed content and telos of literary history that questions the validity of the secularization thesis.[2] Such an approach arranges itself around the (quite correct) position that religious passion was not simply wiped from the world. The elaboration of this position, however, tends to posit that while religious passion was not obliterated, it came to rest within a particular literary medium, and that medium is poetry. This presumption, I would like to insist, is common to both secularization and its critique, and because it is common to both, it is in need of further historicization.

One of the best considerations of enthusiasm's poetic sedimentation is Shaun Irlam's *Elations*, and we can take his argument as exemplary of the recent shift in literary studies toward a complex account of secularization. Irlam advances the claim that enthusiasm represents one mode of a dialectical tension informing epic poetry of the mid to late eighteenth century. In an outstanding reading, Irlam argues that Thomson's *The Seasons* is composed of a dual and contradictory conception of the imagination—one a "mimetic and seconding imaging agency," and the other "a more daemonic conception of the imagination as an autonomous, originating agency."[3] The former mode, asserts Irlam, "derives from a secular, empirico-descriptive, and scientific ethos," whereas the latter "partakes of an archaic, theological *mythos* of the poet—of the kind repeated in discussions of religious and poetic enthusiasm."[4] For Irlam, these two urges are reconciled in Thomson's "rational enthusiasm," or the transformation of the "daemonic urges" into a hermeneutical-interpretive urge that, in regarding and composing the super-phenomenal aspects of the earthly world, produces a "divinized"[5] imagination. In fine deconstructive fashion, Irlam concludes that the inevitable failures of such an imagination inscribe the contours of the modern subject: a "rational" enthusiast composed equally of a theological and an empirico-scientific comportment continually, but productively, at odds.

We may appreciate Irlam's mastery of poetic form while taking a step back from his historicization of aesthetic sensibility as the renovation of religious sentiment. Our concern is more metahistorical. How, we wish to know, is it that such a renovation came to stand in for the movement of history itself? I will take the liberty to suggest now, in advance of a chapter that shall seek to demonstrate precisely this argument, that those literary approaches that seek to find in the rapturous unleashing of poetic passion a sophistication of religious sentiment into a poetic sensibility that gilds the objects of the earthly world, while they deliver a complex and indispensable analysis of poetic sensibility, simultaneously ensnare poetry as an alibi of secularization itself. Poetry, that is to say, serves as the worldly otherworldly object for a passion that has been betrayed by the mundanization of modernity. In this regard at least, the secularization thesis and its extant literary critique share a conception of history as an economy of emotion.

If we seek to challenge both the historicization of modernity by the movement of its passionate gestalts, as well as the joint custody of this passion by secularization and its current critique, perhaps we are best off approaching the problem from the standpoint of the poetic form that had the most attenuated relation to passion of its period. Indeed, if poetry is presumed to be the hideaway of religious feeling, this has left Augustan poetics in a peculiar position. At the very moment that it seems enthusiasm began to inflect poetic passion, we are told that Augustan poetry repelled religious fervor, sealing itself off from enthusiasm's infectious zeal with an impenetrable sheen of formal rigor and an antipathy for the perceived populism of enthusiastic excitement. In the chapter at hand, I propose to unsettle this literary-historical presumption, and—via a close, contextualizing reading of Jonathan Swift's notorious sewer poem, "A Description of a City Shower"—to reunite our now considerably expanded understanding of the discourse of enthusiasm with the formal concerns of Augustan poetics. In doing so, I do not mean to speculate on whether Swift himself would have seen the "City Shower" poem as anything like an enthusiastic expression. Rather, I mean to consider the implications of enthusiasm as a theory of form. To argue thusly is to attempt a relationship to the secularization thesis that departs from the extant critiques and, rather than tracing the career of enthusiastic passion, analyzes the formal capture in poetry of those material contexts that, as we have shown, defined enthusiasm in the period of our concern.

We have demonstrated at some length that enthusiasm was a meeting point in which the major institutional transformations of the early modern period were given discursive form. As we have already shown in our work on Shaftesbury and the Camisard debates, enthusiasm experienced a shift in the early eighteenth century wherein it began to center less on belief and rather more on self-regulation as the defining property of systems—specifically the systems of discourse, trade, and the law. We maintained, furthermore, that these systems were anything but self-regulating; rather they functioned as a network of institutions calibrated, at least in part, through the agency of the state. As the discourse of enthusiasm began to weave together the urge toward universal knowledge with the specific institutional developments that conditioned that knowledge, the immediacies of enthusiastic passion dialectically encoded early modern social and economic transformation. If enthusiasm is best described as a systematizing mode of thought, a way of gesturing toward the relationships between the defining institutional transformations of the early modern period, then to trace the absorption of enthusiastic rhetoric in poetry will not be an enterprise that takes place at the level of content. Rather, in turning our attention from moral philosophy and political theory to Augustan poetics, we begin to explore the aesthetic crystallization of what we may call *the enthusiastic nexus*: the concatenation of economic, legal, and spatial transformation with the shifting status of religious ideology.

In the chapter at hand, I propose that Swift's notorious refusal to idealize geographical space—a refusal exemplified in the "City Shower"—produces what we might see as an enthusiastic spatialization: a composition of the spatial complexities of capital accumulation into poetic arrangements. This, indeed, may be what Daniel Bensaid has suggested by a "rhythmology of capital." To execute this reading, I will rely heavily on our already-established sense of enthusiasm as a mediatory discourse that encrypts the contradictions and linkages between the different registers of social and economic development in the early eighteenth century. What I will add to this extant argument is a proposal about how aesthetic mediation engages enthusiastic discourse specifically. In this effort, I approach the "City Shower" via another poem, the 1727 "Stella's Birthday." I do so because "Stella's Birthday" offers a metameditation on both the limits and the prismatic unfurling of poetic mediation. Reading the "City Shower" through the lens of "Stella's Birthday" dynamizes both poems, and ultimately allows me to contend that Swift, perhaps the eighteenth-century's most notorious poetic anti-enthusiast, executes a remarkable adaptation of the logic of enthusiasm to poetic structure. He does so, not as a matter of content, but through the exemplary constellations of enthusiastic form.

Swiftian Enthusiasm

To raise the problem of Swiftian enthusiasm is to engage a long-standing debate within Swift scholarship, a debate unresolved to this day. If the Dean loved the apparati of order, poetic as well as religious, he also reveled in the threat of its undoing, and these vexed dyads of the Swiftian oeuvre are no secret.[6] Indeed, Swift's final position on any number of his obsessions has been long deemed irretrievable from his texts' expert dodges and feints. Swift's work on excrement, social value, and the body, for example, remain in an eternal oscillation, and the Anglican author whose depictions of debauchery famously form an argument for virtue's "permanence"—as Ronald Paulson puts it—over the fallible nature of the body, is the same Swift who obsessively returns to the nooks and crannies of degenerate flesh with a seemingly unstoppable fascination.[7] On the topic of enthusiasm, this oscillation becomes vertiginous, as Swift appears to tilt ceaselessly from condemnation to abandoned enjoyment. It is Swift, after all, who chides readers on the signature troubles of enthusiastic excess, all the while describing in ornate detail the enchanting temptations of inspired thought and belief. Indeed, if zealous Grub Street hacks and fanatical quixotes receive a rigorous drubbing from the Dean, it is still Swift himself who bares with an unconcealed glee the dirty laundry of London, and it is still Swift who lingers on the base pleasures of the body and the enticements of ecstatic forms of knowledge.

Despite a broadly Hobbesian anti-enthusiasm, then, the lure of pandemonium is strong for Swift. Perhaps so strong that its valence in his oeuvre is to this day unresolved. In virtually all the criticism, enthusiasm and excess are regarded as agents of a compelling but ultimately destructive mania that is only partially reined in by an ethical faculty, expressed, particularly for the poetry, in the regulatory strictures of Augustan form.[8] For quite some time, critics have sought to reconcile Swift the sermonizer—the reverend Swift who made sure never to utter the name of God in one single sermon, never to imply a direct relation or the felt experience of spirit—with Swift the loving expert of the flesh, of excrement, and of the chaos of enthusiastic comportment. About this fundamental ambivalence, at least, the critics have long been in agreement.

In what follows, I will propose a somewhat different thesis regarding Swiftian enthusiasm, one that has specifically to do with the figure of waste, and one that will allow us to accept his seeming ambivalence around dangerous ecstasies (spiritual as well as erotic) as part of a much larger question. This much larger question has to do with the conjuncture we have been tracing all along: that between accumulation and enthusiasm. Regarding this conjuncture, I will show that Swift's singular attentiveness to waste marks an enthusiastic politico-poetics of space. In this effort, I follow Carole Fabricant and Warren Montag who have each shown that the figure of waste threads through Swift's landscapes such that it marks not only the specificity of both London and Edinburgh as twinned cities in a colonial dyad, but the politicization of space in general. Indeed, for Swift, aesthetic form becomes a prism within which the singularly sour waft of political geography is refracted. As Warren Montag has argued, reading and the politics of space are inextricably interlaced for Swift, as exemplified in *A Tale of a Tub*:

> Even this species of critic seemingly set up as a prescription for the activity proper to the critic, must in the course of reading exercise "The caution of a man that walks through Edinburgh streets in a morning who is indeed as careful as he can to watch diligently and spy out the filth in his way; not that he is curious to observe the colour and complexion of the ordure, or take its dimensions, much less to be paddling in, or tasting it; but only with a design to come out as cleanly as he may."[9]

Swift's reader/observer marks the urban geography by its filth. He does so, however, not in order to calculate, count, or describe the filth in itself. Indeed, this filth-scrutinization is not a project for an empiricist approach. Rather, the observer "watches diligently" "with a design to come out . . . cleanly." This distinction between an eye for design and one for detail has been perhaps most strongly articulated by Adorno, for whom no object can be explained by or reduced to its classification: "The name of dialectic says no more, to begin with, than that objects do not go into concepts without leaving a remainder, that they come to contradict the traditional norm of adequacy."[10] Though not himself an Adornian, Swift does reject the classificatory mode, or what Adorno called the "identity thinking" that, as Simon Jarvis lucidly explains, "seeks to know its object by the sum total of correct classifications of it."[11] In the place of classificatory thought, Swift sketches out the objects (here, filth) of the urban landscape via a "design" that is at once integrated into the object and on which the object depends for its identity. In this sense, filth is key to a process of analytical abstraction or systematization. The path of filth, that is, is crucial to conceiving not only the contours of the whole, but also the way *out of* what might otherwise seem an entrapping and endless catalogue of specifics: "colour," "complexion," "dimensions," taste.

Let us then provisionally think of waste in Swift as bearing some relation to systematizing thought. This is to propose that we provisionally think of waste as bearing some relation to the connection of objects and observing subjects, a relation only comprehensible, according to Swift, from the abstracting perspective of the "design." Such an approach to the question of waste allows us to bracket, for the time being, that age-old debate on the finer points of Swift's satiric methodology, and on whether Swift's voluminous satires of enthusiasm ultimately partake of enthusiastic excesses.[12] Montag can continue to assist us in such a bracketing via his analysis of the "Proposal." This text, argues Montag, "like *A Tale*, exhibits a singular fascination with the corporeality of language, its physical properties. But the corporeality of language is not the same as its materiality. The former is rather a sign of the latter, a way of conceptualizing the inconceivable or of figuring the unimaginable and the unthinkable."[13] The unimaginable encoded within the gleeful corporeality of Swift's language is, I want to argue, the politicization of space and its integral relation to the unfolding of historical transformation. This process is unimaginable because every visible change to the built or natural landscape entails a simultaneous erasure and concealment of the institutional and social relations upon which such physical transformation depends. Such relations, nonetheless, are the material context figured by what Montag describes as linguistic "corporeality." In this light, and in the context of England's colonial relationship with Ireland, such corporeality is, in Montag's lexicon, "the sign of," the dialectical combination of visible infrastructural development with the rendering invisible of the architectures of oppression.

Carole Fabricant has restored the political import of these architectures to us by arguing that the built environments of Dublin and London are never offered up by Swift without a proximate corrective, that is, the physical rearrangement of the countryside. In *A Tale of a Tub*, for example, Swift delivers barren Irish fields that signify not simply the inescapable catastrophe of the conversion of arable land to pasturage, but also the somewhat less visible stripping and blighting of Irish land by the English military encampments paid for by Irish taxes: "Mean while, the neighbouring Fields trampled and beaten down, become barren and dry, affording no Sustenance but Clouds of Dust."[14] Fabricant shows that the rendering invisible of the English military occupation of Ireland—with its myriad vampiric dimensions ranging from the unleashing of sheer force upon the Irish population, to the financial draining of Irish taxpayers—is mediated in the "corporeality" of Swift's language. But it is not mediated as a direct representational relation. Rather, the enthusiastic nexus is encoded in the architectures of Swift's poetry itself. How, then, did the discursive history of enthusiasm guide the ways that Swiftian form came to encode history and historical change?

Mediation and Accumulation

> What is peculiar to the early modern period is neither an apprehension of the problem of mediation nor a confidence of its solution, but an unprecedented intensification of both.[15]

For Swift, the history that informs his poetics is one that is bound up with England's jurisdictional relationship to Ireland and with Irish resistance to English commercial and colonial enterprises. This resting of English nation building and financial expansion on the Irish colonial project was not always a relationship that was immediately legible. Indeed if, as John Brewer has argued, the "founding of the Bank of England in 1694, its circulation of paper currency, and its management of a national debt by which a permanent standing army could be financed had made Britain the first modern 'fiscal-military state,'"[16] this consolidation of commerce and politics could be hard to discern and articulate. As Sean Moore has pointed out, Swift—in part because of his vantage point as Anglo-Irish—has a unique perspective on this otherwise occulted national entanglement. Swift, argues Moore, "was among the first to articulate how currency and credit . . . fueled this imperial war machine."[17] As an Irishman continually traveling between London and Dublin, Swift was privy to a critical perspective on the fortification of the English state through colonial plunder and profiteering. Carole Fabricant has exhaustively detailed the ways in which Swift's "general critique of capitalism and its adverse effects upon the British landscape increasingly gave way to a more specific (as well as more impassioned) exposure of the ills inflicted on the Irish soil by England's colonialist policies"[18] As we will see, not only did Swift's writing register this imbrication, it also registered the legislative transformations that sustained the development of financial expansion, accumulation, and the political sovereignty of the nation.

These are not new claims. Swift has long been regarded as a vociferous critic of early capitalist consumer culture, and of the complicity of the Whig oligarchy with the enhancement of trade over traditional, land-based wealth in property.[19] I hope to complicate or broaden some of these claims by contextualizing the visible field of consumerism within a larger matrix of capital accumulation. I do so by returning the discussion of Swift and capitalism to the problem of mediation, or the problem of how the historical and economic changes against which

Swift railed found their way into the form of his poetry. I want to suggest that the transformation and development of these institutional systems is registered in Swift's poetic form as the problem of mediation itself and of the capacity of language to capture the specificity of historical phenomena.

As Michael McKeon has argued, in the later seventeenth century, spiritual truth became bound up with concepts of historicity through the structure of mediation: "the emergence of the claim to historicity as a formal feature at once vital and problematic to the mediation of spiritual truth."[20] For Swift, it is through space, in general, and *landscape*, in particular, that such historicity is mediated: "for Swift, the geographic and architectural aspects of his environment were invariably linked to prevailing social and economic conditions . . . It was an inescapably and pervasively *political* landscape that regularly caught Swift's eye."[21] Mediation, however, is a uniquely complex concept in Swift's oeuvre. Notoriously obsessed with the question of the social whole and of order, divine or worldly, Swift was also committed to the impossibility of direct knowledge of this whole. In this sense, Swift's Anglican conservatism underwrites a legacy, not just of ambivalent materiality, but of a concerted attitude toward the thorny problem of the understanding of these directly unknowable truths. Although proto-realist work, such as Defoe's, may have articulated one very explicit approach to the problem of mediation in which "[d]octrines of literary realism, which rise from the ruins of the claim to historicity, reformulate the problem of mediation for a world in which spirituality has ceased to represent another realm to which human materiality has only difficult and gratuitous access, and has become instead the capacity of human creativity itself,"[22] for Swift the question of mediation was compounded by an Anglican antagonism to "naïve empiricist or enthusiastic beliefs in the possibility of an immediate access to truth."[23] This resistance to immediate knowledge meant that, for Swift, the problem of mediation was an extremely live one that found expression in the intricacies of poetic form. Indeed, as McKeon argues, the uncertainty of the direct translatability of political meaning, "provides Swift and his contemporaries with a crucial focus for investigating the problem of mediation."[24] In other words, Swift's convictions about religious enthusiasm were channeled into poetic architectures that constantly tested the limits and possibilities of the mediation of meaning.

If McKeon's work has gone quite far in establishing mediation as the defining feature of Swift's oeuvre, I want to build on these claims to consider the degree to which the historical conjuncture named by capital accumulation converges with, not only the highly-wrought Anglican conception of mediation, but also with the specific obfuscations monumentalized in the landscape of urban development. The inexorable vanishings that accompany and undergird the establishment of the institutional apparati of capitalism find their discursive complement in the Anglican attenuations of mediation and their architectural complement in the assemblages of the early modern city. Accordingly, in what is to come, I read "A Description of a City Shower" in terms of the contradictions sewn into the fabric of urban development, colonial nationalism, and the legislation of capital accumulation. Toward this goal, I begin, in somewhat perverse manner, by leading the reader through an exploration of Swiftian mediation via a poem that focuses, not on the urban landscape, but rather on the landscape of human relations. That poem is Swift's "Stella's Birthday," and it provides an exemplary introduction to Swiftian mediation in general.

Poetic Mediation

We might say that the broadest conception of any poetic project necessarily entails the question of mediation as it is commonly understood: the transcription of an ungraspable or unimaginable object, context, or concept into the specificity of aesthetic form. But mediation, as we have marked, is a much more complex matter than this. We will take our most thorough account of Swift's approach to the problem of the legibility of social order in our analysis of the Shower poem, shortly. But the problem itself is perhaps more immediately visible in Swift's 1727 "Stella's Birthday," and it behooves us to acquaint ourselves with the question of poetic mediation and the problem of history, articulated in "Stella's Birthday" in terms of the history of the individual, here first.

In many ways, the Birthday poem is a bare meditation on the problem of mediation. After all, the poem's driving aim is to grasp after its receding referent (Stella) while she grows ill and prepares for death on the occasion of what would be her final birthday. "Stella's Birthday" appears to begin with an assertion about the predominance of spirit over matter in the face of the loss of the loved object:

> This day/whate'er the Fates decree,/Shall still be kept with joy by me:/This day then let us not be told,/That you sick, and I grown old;/Nor think on our approaching ills,/ And talk of spectacles and pills./To-morrow will be time enough/To hear such mortifying stuff./Yet, since from reason may be brought/A better and more pleasing thought,/Which can, in spite of all decays,/Support a few remaining days;/From not the gravest of divines/Accept for once some serious lines./Although we now can form no more/Long schemes of life, as heretofore;/Yet you, while time is running fast,/Can look with joy on what is past.[25]

However much Swift seems to be privileging the dominance of spirit, the poem's immediate foregrounding of the physical clutter of "spectacles and pills" leaves essentially ambiguous the ultimate hierarchy of spirit over matter. We would expect precisely this from the Anglican skeptic who brings from "reason" a more "pleasing thought" that itself appears to go against all reason in its supersession of the seemingly insuperable fact of "all decays." But perhaps this is the signature quality of Anglican reason that ultimately aims toward acceptance rather than understanding.

Indeed, in place of immediate understanding, an ethical happiness is proposed to compensate for the miseries of illness and death, replacing the anticipated demise of the subject with the comforts of a long narrative arc, a discursive life that extends past the living. More than this, the problem of aesthetic mediation merges here with the question of futurity and historicity; the speaker acknowledges that neither he nor Stella can "form" "Long/schemes of life, as heretofore." The use of "scheme" here suggests the "rhyme scheme," which is to say the form itself of the poem, which mirrors the prospects of its referent, to whom length and futural speculation are foreclosed. The rhyming couplet—certainly not a "long scheme"—is here, according to the speaker, that form most apposite to a life quickly coming to a close. But ironically, the couplet also appears to be the form best suited to historicity. If Stella no longer can form "long schemes," she is exhorted to "look with joy on what is past." The rhyming couplet incarnates the history of a life when that life no longer can be projected into the future in "long scheme," but must rather "run fast" down the page.

As Stella (and the poem "Stella") spiral toward a close, the speaker implores her to achieve the correct comportment toward her past expenditures and the effects that those expenditures will manifest in the future:

> Your skillful hand employ'd to save/Despairing wretches from the grave . . . Must these [good deeds] like empty shadows pass/Or forms reflected from a glass?/Or mere chimaeras in the mind/That fly, and leave no marks behind?

Here, the poem does not simply encode the question of mediation in this reaching toward Stella. It thematizes this motion itself, in asking Stella (and the reader) to consider the translation of a life into its linguistic avatar: "Say, Stella, feel you no content," the speaker asks just a few lines further, in one of the poem's signature exhortations, "Reflecting on a life well spent?"[26]

The preceding lines have long held a vaunted place in Swift's considerable corpus of inquiry into the relation of spirit and matter, soul and body. A particularly agonized and personal account of this dyad, posed to the ageing and considerably ill Stella, Swift's query unleashes one of neoclassical poetry's more moralizing instances of the rhetorical question. Surely this is a feat of some magnitude for a tradition that obsesses on the refinements of virtue, and has offered us such famous reflections as Pope's dedication to his patron, no less than Queen Anne's Secretary of War: "Granville commands; your aid O Muses bring!/What Muse for Granville can refuse to sing?"[27] But even Pope's straightforward acknowledgment of the presence of force at the heart of the rhetorical question is outdone by Swift's inquiry, which articulates one of the signature demands of modernity: namely, the demand that social convention correlate with a "correct" individual feeling. For moderns, it is not enough to behave correctly; one must feel correctly, too. It is not enough to brave the event of one's impending death; one must feel the satisfaction of having lived a rapidly closing life well. More than this, although we may not have expected Swift's anxious set of claims urging Stella to "feel" herself to partake of the Shaftesburian tradition of enthusiastic ethics, in the proprioceptive hailings of "Say, Stella, feel you," Swift recalls the enthusiastic component of moral self-regulation, which takes the subject's sensation of self as the basis of her calibration with the world at large. Indeed, Swift's command to Stella recalls a Shaftesburian virtue grounded in self-relation; to this, Swift adds a canny poetic comment on the apparatus of enthusiasm in the form of a double entendre that highlights the typically feminine mediation of this "self"-feeling: the overheard "cunt" of "content" is doubly accented by the demands of octosyllabic tetramater, which comes down hard on the "ent," leaving the whispered "cunt" echoing in the background.

In instructing Stella to feel herself on the brink of death, Swift points at still another signification of "content," which waits palimpsested behind the first. Indeed, the insistence on Stella feeling her "content" leads us to the poem's more specific injunction: the "cunt" of "content" reminds us of the matter—the CONtent—toward which the proprioceptive self reaches in a series of ultimately unsatisfying sutures. In invoking the "cunt"-ented relation of the self to itself, the poem drives toward its more general set of concerns. That set of concerns that circles around the problem of mediation: not just the encoding in poetic form of an always-receding referent, but also the dialectical relation between form and content—visibility and invisibility—upon which the poem's signification rests.

The poem highlights the question of aesthetic form by producing proliferating levels of signification through clever but simple shifts of stress. Even at the outset, to achieve the basic conversational rhythms that "Say, Stella" demands, we instinctively inject metrical interruptions into the poem's octosyllabic format, introducing pauses just after "Stella" and just after "you." The lines' tonal patterns refract prismatically, and feminine caesuras reveal themselves sprinkled in the forward drive of the tetrameter. In thus playing with the overheard implications within the tonally sanctioned one, Swift readies the reader for the "CONtent" behind "conTENT." Readies the reader, that is, for the fractal significations made possible by poetic form.

Accordingly, the significance of "Say, Stella, feel you" does not inhere in the lines themselves, does not attach itself to content per se, but rather to a form that becomes especially striking when we stray from it. This second meaning thus draws out the essentially elegiac keen at the heart of the poem, which dreams of meaning's perfect conduction while wrestling with the interposing mediations of poetic form itself: "SAY, StellA, feel YOU no CONtent/REflecTING on . . ." It is not without a certain amount of deliberate, melancholic irony that, despite his own interdictions on enthusiastic immediacy, Swift's poem longs for a direct conduit from sound to soul, from the word "Stella" to the person Stella, with no content "reflecting" between the two.

If only Swift could "Say" Stella and "feel" her, indeed. This wish drinks deeply of the eighteenth-century fantasy of the feminine as a perfect, reflection-less transmission of meaning. As a sort of commentary on the complexities of this fantasy, "Stella's Birthday" plays on the traditional religious signification of enthusiasm—the "dialectical immanence of the spirit within the letter which in Protestant thought applies also to the world at large."[28] In good Anglican fashion, the poem recognizes the impossibility of this immanence: the "content reflecting" between reader and referent registers the estrangements of social life, with its interposing, incomplete identifications and mirroring beguilements, and simultaneously transcribes the historical conditions of this estrangement into an aesthetic arrangement.

The real historical Stella, the dying one, who lies beyond the reach of the poem, thus poignantly occasions Swift's larger reflection on the function of poetic form. The poem reaches toward Stella, insisting that she will be attainable after her death because she will be translated into an iterable "mark," secured for history and etched in language. The form of "Stella's Birthday," the poem insinuates, is, thus, not something as simple as matter itself—that which could be "reflected from a glass"—but rather constitutes the very nonreflective stuff, that real transubstantiation of what was always beyond the tangible touch of the poem itself: the real Stella, formally encrypted into "Stella's Birthday." These alchemical powers of formal relation return us to the Shaftesburian conception of enthusiasm, that felt relation to a social whole, which is, itself, unpicturable and untouchable. If, for Shaftesbury, this social whole is transcoded in the calibrations of subjective feeling, for Swift, this relation to a larger outside unscrolls in the contingencies of language and in the arrangement of discursive meaning. More than this, it is the combination of Swift's Anglican and baroque understanding of the relation between content and context, with his consciousness of the political geographies of English-Irish relations, which organizes this transcoding. Together, these dual commitments result in a mournful circling around the problem of mediation that is, at the same time, a spectacular formal rendering of the poetic problematics of historicity, as we shall see in the next section.

Short-Scheme Historicity, or Urban Mean Time

Let us now attempt to accelerate our understanding of temporality in "Stella's Birthday" to establish a number of speculative links between poetic form and the specific historical context that Swift knew so well: that of early capitalist development. There has been much work done on the coeval development of historicity and the novel form. Here, McKeon's work is only one in a long tradition linking the rise of realism to the rise of historicist consciousness. And there has been, as well, a significant body of work exploring historicity and the epic poem as well. Laura Brown's reading of Pope's "Windsor Forest" is exemplary here, though we might also include Suvir Kaul's reading of James Thomson's "Rule, Brittania!" as representative of this recent push to establish poetry as the premier register of social and cultural change in the eighteenth century. What "Stella's Birthday" adds to these conversations is a connection between historicism and the rhyming couplet that produces a structure we might call short-scheme historicity. Riffing on Swift's own bracketing of the "long schemes" in "Stella's Birthday," we might say that what the rhyming couplet manages to do in its pithy pairings and striking, rhythmic jolts, is to produce, not only a counterintuitive historicism within the poem, but, more specifically, a staggered-motion historicism that recalls the temporo-spatial compressions and gulfs characteristic of early capitalist development. As we detailed at some length in the previous two chapters, the compressions and adjacencies of city life were accompanied by the widening gulf between urban and rural production processes. And yet, even as the country and the city—and the center of empire and the metropole—differentiated into increasingly distinct spheres, they were yoked together into one, internally contradictory and yet superproductive zone of profit. This is a spatial process with a temporal mediation. Those rural and peripheral spheres come to represent a kind of past-in-the-present, a "backwardness" that is based in the development and utilization of space. Such a spatio-temporal plait recalls Lacy's work, in which, as we saw, this process of urbanization is dialectically upended; as the "desert" comes to occupy the city, the logic of the urban inner core is exposed as necessarily dependent on the de-development and making barren of the countryside. Swift, too, was well aware of the perverse and cruel suturing of urbanization to rural degradation.

We will explore these themes in greater detail shortly. For now, let us consider that it is this temporo-spatial logic that is given affective form in "Stella's Birthday." Indeed, when the speaker asks, "Does not the body thrive and grow/ By food of twenty years ago?"[29] does Swift not yoke together both the long-scheme fortifications that seem to stitch together a life sustained by actions taken in the past—actions that themselves become memories of oneself at different temporal junctures—with the productive disjunctures generated between rural production, which appears to produce food "twenty years ago," and an urban consumption that takes place in what seems to be an ever-present "now"? Such a phenomenon, indeed, represents what we might call "urban mean time," that is, the calibration of contemporaneity to urban sites that always appear to exist in a "present" to which rural landscapes must catch up across the developmental gulfs of capitalism. These gulfs exist in the present, but consign urban and rural topographies to timescales that are distinct, and yet entirely interdependent in being so. In the temporal concussion detonated when the "food of twenty years ago" meets the technologies of consumption in the now, the poem convokes, not the linear time of bourgeois history, but the redemptive and inscrutable logic of Anglican mediation, which encrypts in poetic form the staggering superpositions of an uneven development that destroys in order to create, and dispossesses to enshrine and protect private possession. These superpositions are mirrored in the temporal wheeling and spinning of the individual life—Stella's—that is being not only anticipatorily mourned and consecrated, but increasingly abstracted and attenuated in the process. Here, it is the rhyming couplet freed from the expectations of long-scheme historicity—the novel form, for example, which stitches together a life's progress across time and space in a variety of logical ways—that encodes the palimpsestic lurches that comprise the early modern landscape.

In the gulfs generated and intensified by Swift's pairings of matter and spirit, historical context begins to peek through. If this claim feels unmoored, let us avail ourselves of a brief return to the extant debates around Swiftian enthusiasm. The *Tale of a Tub* will be apposite for us here, as debate has long ranged around whether Swift's satire of Protestant enthusiasm itself partakes of an enthusiastic— or, as Clement Hawes argues "manic"—style. The question here has to do with whether Swift is purely satirizing enthusiasts or whether his own writing becomes, in the process, enamored with enthusiastic rhetoric and style, so much so that it imitates it or takes on its essential properties. If the former—that is, if Swift is "simply" satirizing enthusiasm—then, the argument runs, Swift sides with "spirit" over the vulgarity of enthusiasm as represented by a kind of corporeal or bodily excess (indeed this is a conflation Swift delights in and repeats often). If the latter—that is, if Swift's satire partakes of the pleasures of enthusiastic materiality—then, the argument goes, Swift has found himself so drawn to this materiality that his work cannot be disentangled from this driving obsession. This debate, as is well known, has spun ceaselessly for some time.

Montag, however, moves us considerably forward in this debate, not by landing on one side or the other, but by demonstrating that the opposition constructed between enthusiastic and anti-enthusiastic style is something of a false one. Indeed, for Montag,

> *A Tale* . . . does not simply reduce the world to matter and matter to excrement. While it is true that the work constructs a materiality (conceived negatively as the absence of spirit) to which it reacts with horror and disgust, this construction in no way entails a reduction of the complexity of the world and the plurality of its forms and modes. Instead, *A Tale* initiates a rethinking of this complexity without reference to the opposition of matter and spirit.[30]

Without a simple opposition between matter and spirit, Swift's satire of enthusiasm is reopened to a different set of framing questions, and a different set of hermeneutical and literary-historical possibilities. Let us begin with the proposition that Swift's poetry manages to inscribe the material complexities of early modern development into the intricacies of poetic language and form. In a great many ways, this claim is not unique. As Fredric Bogel has demonstrated, satiric forms have long been understood to be historically deictic. Indeed, Bogel argues, via Edward Rosenheim, that "the assertion that satire is 'an attack upon discernable, historically authentic particulars,' could be understood as a description not of satire's relation to historical reality, but as a claim that is an important convention of satire itself: the implicit assumption that there exists a historical world, 'out there,' elements of which are both solidly specifiable and distinct from the order of discourse in which they are specified."[31] For Bogel, the search for these historical particulars is split from the rather more deconstructive project to examine the deictic mechanisms themselves: "To look automatically for the particulars attacked, however, is somewhat like searching for the real god invoked by an epic poet instead of investigating the nature and significance of the invocation."[32] The distinction Bogel draws, however, is not necessary. Our reading of Swift will show that the historical particulars are mediated by the "invocation" embedded within the formal structures of the poem itself.

Perhaps the long-standing debate over Swift's relationship to the immediacies of enthusiasm can be clarified by a dialectical approach. To readers of Swift, it has appeared that his Anglican commitment to the attenuations of divine meaning is at odds with his attraction to the immediacies of enthusiastic, excerememental materiality. However, as we have shown, Swift's meditations on immediacy do not favor either attenuation or attraction so much as they encode a theory of historicity within the poem's formal structure. Such an encoding is not to dodge the problem of mediation, but rather to refer it to its appropriate signification. Let us allow Adorno's redaction of Hegel to illuminate our approach to this problem.

For Adorno, Hegel intervenes into the fantasy of enthusiastic immediacy by insisting that all immediacies are mediated. The "principle of Experience," argues Hegel, "carries with it the unspeakably important condition that, in order to accept and believe any fact . . . we must find the fact united and combined with the certainty of our own selves."[33] Our belief in immediate knowledge of divinity—or of any object—is, insists Hegel, always already mediated since we ourselves intercede onto some fantastically transparent grasping of the object. As Adorno points out, however, Hegel does not simply dispense with the fantasy of immediacy. Rather, this fantasy is integral to the processes of mediation itself: "One can no more speak of mediation without something immediate than, conversely, one can find something immediate that is not mediated . . . [I]n Hegel . . . the two moments . . . produce and reproduce one another reciprocally."[34] The urge toward immediacy, insists Adorno, is integral to mediation and cannot be disposed of. Dialectical thinking does not seek to outdo this immediacy, then, but is the demonstration of the insufficiency of immediacy, and the laying out of the historical conditions and conjunctures that give rise to such fantasies.

As Jarvis points out, Adorno's illustrative example for the "identity-thinking" undergirding the fantasy of immediacy, is commodity exchange. In the exchange of commodities, items are reckoned as identical to one another through the reduction of all qualitative differences to quantums of labor-power: "In the exchange of commodities Adorno finds the epitome of an identificatory judgment. That which is not merely quantitatively unequal but qualitatively incommensurable is misidentified as though it were equal and commensurable."[35] It would be revisionist to insist that the solution to this violent commensuration is to halt exchanges altogether. Adorno's approach, rather, is to demonstrate the ways in which the moment of equivalence—or identification—always falls short and, in doing so, offers us an avenue for understanding the specific social relations upon which the valuation of the commodity is based.

If enthusiasm represents a theory of mediation, we are coming to see that this is not only because enthusiasm names the relation between things, but more specifically, that it encodes the relation internal to the concept itself, that is, the constitutive contradiction at the heart of both the subject and the object. It is in this sense that we can say that mediation—the aching suture that predicates the subject as the subject *of* specific material relations—and the fizzy immediacies connoted by enthusiasm, together describe, as Jameson has put it, the "dialectical nature of the encounter with History."[36] What this dialectical relationship between mediation and immediacy means for "Stella's Birthday" is that historical context is not immediately legible but is rather mediated—or encrypted—within the immediacies longed for by the poem.[37]

In the section that follows, I want to expand on some of the analyses we've drawn from "Stella's Birthday," specifically my proposition that the rhyming couplet, in Swift, becomes a deixis of historicity in general and of the uneven action of capitalist development in particular. This relationship will become much clearer in the generic innovation in "City Shower," namely, the urban georgic.

An Urban Georgic

As an instance of conservative ideology, the "City Shower" poem has been taken as exemplary of the critique of monied interest, commercial dominance, and the moral decay of city life. It attacks the ephemeral values and surface enchantments that the longing for subjective "content" in "Stella's Birthday" is also designed to counteract. Accordingly, perhaps, the "City Shower," too, partakes of a byzantine relation to its ungraspable referent—although this referent is nothing so personal as Stella herself. In the case of the "City Shower," the referent is the historical context of London, specifically, and urban development, in general.

The London of the late seventeenth through the early eighteenth centuries is the period of immediate reference for Swift, and indeed it was a period that saw immense infrastructural development, capital accumulation, and legal transformations. In 1710 Swift traveled to London as an ambassador for the Church of Ireland in order to lobby for the right of First Fruits, which would remit government taxes for the church of Ireland. His voyage to London was of legislative urgency, and one that staked its claim on the privileges and power of the Church, as well as on the Irish claim to self-determination and self-regulation. Swift traveled as an emissary, vested with translating into legal language Anglican prerogatives and doctrine. We might risk saying, then, that he traveled under the mantle of mediation, charged with the task of encoding Church ideology into legal, Parliamentary language.

Swift's daily life was filled with constant sense of the vastness of the political, ecclesiastical, and social worlds of London and of Dublin. The work of negotiating these worlds was but one piece of a larger effort to manage the effects of what Catherine Roncaglia has called the dual pillars of that "gigantic experiment in primitive accumulation": the massive confiscation of land from Irish Catholics in the seventeenth century in conjunction with the ideology that secured the legality of this proprietorship: "religious conformity in the form of the penal laws and test acts designed to prevent Catholic or Dissenter land ownership, service in government or education, and the practice of religion."[38] It was these two engines that, as Sean Moore has argued, "brought about the surplus value necessary to raise the third pillar: finance capitalism by the state itself in the form of the debt of the nation."[39] As Moore and Roncaglia make clear, the visible world of finance is but the tip of a much larger project in primitive accumulation. This project is in many ways all but invisible, but Swift's specific perspective—not only as transnational traveler, but as a poet with an eye to the "design" of the city—places him in a unique position vis-à-vis the ordinarily occulted social relations that undergird the "pillar" of finance. The "City Shower" is, in many ways, a kind of mournful walk through these landscapes of primitive accumulation. As the speaker traverses the passages of the city, the depredation upon which urban development depends—both the colonial deployment of primitive accumulation within Ireland and the rural primitive accumulation within England—shadows his perambulations. Put in the language of "Stella's Birthday," we might say that the "content" of these depredations are not "reflected" in the poem; at the level of the form of the poem, however, the etchings of these geopolitical relationships become clearer.

The "City Shower," in its basic movement, tracks the effects of a storm on London's inhabitants and on its famously foul open sewer system. This focus on the elements made the "City Shower" recognizable in its time as mock georgic in the style of Virgil. Like the Georgic, which observes the weather, the abundance of agriculture, and the daily specifics of rural life, Swift's mock georgic tracks the weather, the abundance of London's animal, vegetal and proto-industrial waste, and the specifics of city life. For these reasons, the "City Shower" has been received as a generically difficult innovation: an urban georgic. At its root, the real punchline of the Shower is the poem's form itself; the umbrella joke (so to speak), the one that enables all the satires that unfold within the City Shower, is that of the transposition of rural rituals to an urban setting.

From the first two lines, Swift's poem recalls Virgil's: "Careful observers may foretell the hour/(By sure prognosticks) when to dread a shower." As Laura Brown has shown, "In the seventeenth century ... 'sewer' was also spelled 'sure' and 'shewer.'"[40] Where the Virgillian Georgic prognosticates in order to coordinate the harvest schedule with the rains, then the urban georgic prognosticates in order to sound an alarm about the impending tidal wave of waste that will course through London when the rains cause the open sewers to overfill, and feces, debris, dead animals, and loose property will be borne along by the waters. This is the joke at its most basic level. But where most critics understand this formal transposition as Swift's way of highlighting the equalizing proximities and moral vertigo of the city, few have yet discussed at length the ways in which, in herding the rural genre into London's thoroughfares, Swift does not simply satirize city life, but issues a sweeping, formal contextualization of the poem's own historical conditions of possibility.

To recognize that this is the case, we have simply to consider the signature quality that makes a georgic a georgic, and distinguished Virgil's Georgics in particular: unlike the pastoral's emphasis on rural leisure, the Georgic focuses on rural labor. In situating the city content within a rural form, Swift thus references the modus of early British capitalism: the geographic "renovation" of country and the city, the transformation of rural labor into urban poor. Capitalism harvests this fruit, precisely. Dispossessing the laborers of the land through the historical event of enclosure, capital develops and de-develops different geographies in accordance with the demands of production. The resultant wave of metropolitan immigration constitutes a permanent reserve of labor in the core. These historical events, in conjunction with the development of legislation prohibiting "combination"—or early forms of unionization—kept the wages of the eighteenth-century workforce extremely low through the constant threat of the substitution and replacement of laborers. It is in this sense that the urban georgic is, at least in part, what Carole Fabricant has termed an "anti-pastoral," or "an extended poetic and epistolary statement that Eden no longer exists in contemporary topography; it can be characterized only by images of an emphatically post-lapsarian garden."[41] For Fabricant, this antipastoral tendency is the formal incarnation of Swift's anticapitalist critique:

> Swift's anti- and mock-pastoral depictions also constitute an important aspect of his continuing, as well as developing, political and social commentary on contemporary society. His mock-pastoral verses are offered as one of the very few types of expression appropriate for an age witnessing the systematic debasement of the land. On the broadest level, the one especially evident in his writings before 1715, they form part of Swift's devastating critique of capitalism . . .[42]

Fabricant argues that Swift's oeuvre builds from the poetic representation of an antagonism between country and city to a more nuanced conception of their dialectical imbrication. Her argument traces a movement by which, at first, the country is seen to have been decimated at the hands of the stockjobbers and the speculators of the city. Fabricant turns to Swift's *The Run Upon the Bankers* as an example: "'The bold Encroachers on the Deep,/Gain by Degrees huge Tracts of Land,/'Til Neptune with a Gen'ral Sweep/Turns all again to barren Strand.'"[43] We see this same sort of critique again, in *The Bubble*, "Thus the deluded Bankrupt raves,/Puts all upon a desp'rate Bett,/Then plunges in the Southern Waves,/ Dipt over head and Ears—in Debt."[44]

Much as these works construct a binary tension between country and city, as Fabricant shows, this antagonism does not hold. Indeed, for Swift, both country and city are ravaged by the effects of capitalist development, even as this "development" produces the architectures, social spaces, and productive potentials of the urban landscape: "But the contrast Swift drew here between a landed gentry and a class of urban capitalists. . . . gradually gave way to his far more significant and original insight that, in the final analysis, the traditional distinction between country and city no longer applied."[45] For Fabricant, we might say that Swift's work registers the Buffonian "second nature" we discussed in chapter 3. "It may well be," Fabricant argues, "that originally (as Cowper put it) 'God made the country and man made the town,' but Swift's writings continually underscore the fact that, in eighteenth-century England and Ireland, the country along with the town was being created (or, to be more precise, uncreated and recreated) by man . . . ."[46] Swift's commitment to the antipastoral drives his landscapes toward the dystopic. As Swift is quite aware, neither the country nor the city flourishes under incipient capitalism:

> The *Grazier's* Employment is to feed great Flocks of *Sheep*, or *Black Cattle*, or both . . . And, the Good of it is, that the more *Sheep* we have, the fewer human Creatures are left to wear the *Wool* or eat the *Flesh* . . . The other Part of the *Grazier's* Business is, what we call *Black-Cattle*; producing *Hides, Tallow*, and *Beef* for Exportation . . . However, to bestow the whole Kingdom on *Beef* and *Mutton*, and thereby drive out half the People who should eat their Share . . . is a most peculiar and distinguished Piece of publick Oeconomy; of which I have no Comprehension.[47]

Swift's recognition of the dialectical syncopation of urban and rural sites of production suggests that Fabricant's "anti-pastoral" might be expanded to signify the specifically predatory movement of capitalism as it accumulates architectures, commodities, and productivity at the one end, and, as Marx noted so aptly, depredation, "misery, and the torment of labour" at the other.[48] These poles are not simply divided between country and city, but rather vein through both landscapes. Indeed, the geographies of domination that severed rural laborers from the land made possible a reserve pool of labor for urban production—that pool of persons, to which I referred earlier, who served as a constant reminder to workers that, simply put, if they would not work for minimal wages, someone else would. In this way, early capitalism was able to manage the threat of combination on the part of labor while keeping wages low and profits high. This, precisely, is one key means by which early English capitalism was able to reap the benefits of the dialectical imbrication of rural and urban geographies. And it is this historical concatenation—of legislation, geographical contortion, proto-industrial production—that the "City Shower" transcodes into a problem of form.

The Non Finito/The Legislated Against

Critics have not infrequently claimed that the "City Shower" presents a "slice of life" portrait of the gritty dailyness of the city. But it does much more than this. In demonstrating that urban rituals depend on the harvesting of waged labor from the countryside, the urban georgic registers the historical context for the production of the new urban habitus. It does so because it reveals, at the level of form, the material basis for the eighteenth century phenomenon of "city life" itself.

Here let us be more specific. British geographies could not have developed in the way that they did without legislation designed to support and extend the events of enclosure and urbanization. Swift's poem makes this historical fact legible by articulating its "sure prognosticks" within in a legal lexicon. Consider, "Returning home at night you find the sink/Strike your offended sense with double stink." Until now, these have never been controversial lines. Whereas in the Virgillian Georgic, the prognostics come in the form of natural oracles—the winds rise, the seas close in, the leaves whisper, the mountains whistle—in the Swiftian georgic, the "sure"/sewer prognostic comes in the bathetic form of pungent waste. And yet, there is more to say than simply to note the clever mimicry of Virgil's prognostics. To begin, there are few couplets in this poem that make such explicit use of the *non-finito* as these lines do, and it is here that we begin to see the poem's canny conjuring of its historical context through a series of artful pauses and lapses.

The non-finito was a popular classical and eighteenth-century sculpting technique by which the artwork is left deliberately unfinished. Art historians have long argued that the non-finito increases the pleasure of the viewer who is recruited by the work to imaginatively finish it himself.[49] The non-finito informed visual artworks from Donatello to Michelangelo, and was enormously popular throughout the Renaissance.[50] But the non-finito had a discursive life as well, and one that extended past the early seventeenth century. As Aulay Macaulay reminds us, Virgil made great use of the non-finito to extend the scope of his poetic reference. Virgil's first pastoral, Macaulay argues, "concludes with a thought, which raises in the mind a grasp of the finest images in nature."[51]

Eric Rothstein has thoughtfully detailed the significance of the Virgilian non-finito in eighteenth century poetry, arguing specifically of neoclassical verse that it demonstrates a "tendency ... to extend the phenomenology of the non finito ... to works that are formally completed."[52] By tracing the aesthetic heritage of the non-finito, Rothstein shows that seemingly tight neoclassical couplets swell in signification under the influence of the non-finito. In citing Macaulay on Virgil, Rothstein also traces the specific lineage on which Swift bases the "City Shower." Indeed, in the "City Shower," we find a poem that is Virgilian not only in its themes, but also in its pointing to an "outside" that is formally evoked through explicitly unfinished referents—an outside that far exceeds the poem's explicit content.

When we take the non-finito out of the exclusive realm of the visual arts and consider its place in the literary arts, the non-finito not only asks to be completed but broadens the question of "completion" by expanding the imaginative work to the problem of the mediation of historical context. Consider the particulars of Swift's non-finito; "Returning home at night you find the sink/Strike your offended sense with double stink" (ll 5–6).[53] Line 5 could be read hermetically: "Returning home at night you find the sink," which in its initial read likely signifies cesspool or sewer, and so reads, *Returning home at night, you find the sewer*. But this line becomes unfinished after we read the following line, and realize that the "sink" in "Returning home at night you find the sink," does not conclude the action, but is only the initial mise en scene, recaptured in the next line by "strike." Indeed, the actor of line 5 shifts once line 6 has been read, as the movement sink/strike retroactively changes the meaning of the prior line. Where line five had previously laid its emphasis on the addressee finding the sink, we now find the central actor is the sink itself which strikes the reader/stroller with such force that it rolls the poem temporally backward.

"Strike" performs a subsitution of agency: the "sink" for "you," and in doing so, it enlists the reader in a necessarily recursive structure: the meaning of the poem is only achieved by revisiting and altering claims that have already been made. The play of the non-finito here recalls the kind of supraempirical, "ultramundane" historicity of enthusiasm we saw in Fatio. More specifically, the enthusiastic action of poetic recursiveness—or de-development—reflects the uneven action of early capitalism, which gluts the city with unemployed labor by upending traditional modes of production and ravaging extant forms of rural subsistence. The "double stink" of the sewer is this double strike of capital, which plunders the countryside of its laborers while developing the industrial-wage bondage of the city and the pool (or "sink") of reserve labor at the same time. Indeed, in substituting "the sink" for "you," the poem suggests a baleful collectivization: In this city, we then find the "sink"—the cesspool, the sewer—but also, importantly, as the OED confirms, the "scum or dregs of a place or set of persons." Here in London—itself another "sink" (the OED again has a sink as the "place where things get lost")—we find ourselves "struck" by the sink, the smell of which forces an imaginative reconstruction, a recognition that the poem itself, this tight neoclassical coupleting, contains cunningly deliberate non-finitos, which point deicdically toward what lays, disappeared, or "sunken," within.

If the non-finito, in its expansive capacities, is a kind of poetic enthusiasm, this enthusiasm suggests a larger whole generated through the sensorious impact of a signifying absence. Here Swift's conjuring of signifying absences within and between the lines recalls Kames's notorious "ideal presence," that mimetic action by which absences are invested with a potent significatory force. Indeed, in reading the "City Shower," the reader feels herself to be experiencing what Kames describes as a "non reflective waking dream" in which, as Blackmore expanded, "'a true and bright Idea' stamp[s] an impression on words so strongly 'that the absent Object'" seems to be somehow "present."[54] For Swift, the absent object comes to mediate the spatio-temporal contexts of Swift's London—a logic legible in the temporal injunctions of lines 5 and 6, which impel a retrospective movement that organizes this absence as a historical relation, never ontologically present but always determinant. This force of history is mediated in that most formal framework of the poem—itself a "double stink"—that necessarily loops backward/rurally in order to describe the sensory event of city life.

The Sewer and Paving Act and Those Struck from the Historical Record

It will be serve us well now to review the etymological meanings of *strike* as well, which exceed *blow*. The traditional meaning of *blow* is important here because certainly the blow or strike of line 6 accomplishes the formal directive of mimesis. However, *strike* also hearkens back to the tradition of the georgic and what would have been, within the early eighteenth century, a still-contemporary resonance: a bundle of flax or hemp; a measure or denomination of dry measure. By *strike*, we are thus returned to the scene of rural labor, but only to be reminded of the now inextricable relation of this rural labor to the "offended." Those "offenders," indeed, are those erstwhile rural laborers whose subsistence has been deemed criminal because it relies on forms of now-illegal appropriation. A prime example of such forms of appropriation, as we will shortly see, was sewer gleaning. In this way, the sink most certainly does strike the sense with a "double stink"—a double meaning most impressively foul. For the double meaning of the strike connotes not just the mimetic-sensory blow of poetic form, not just the long lost simple measurements of grain, but finally the specifically juridical meaning of strike in the early eighteenth century, which was that of the torture of prisoners. If we investigate the legal history of sanitation law, we can see most clearly this double stink in action.

In 1670, Parliament passed the "Sewer and Paving Act," which, at first glance, appears to have had the function of legislating improvements to the open sewer system after the Great Fire of London. When we read the 1670 Act closely, however, we find that it does not describe many improvements on the sewers at all, but rather outlines in exhaustive detail the legal boundaries of sewer maintainance and upkeep:

> [T]he said Maior Aldermen and Commonalty in Common Councell assembled shall from time to time authorize and appoint under their Common Seale or the more part of them, Which said persons soe authorized and appointed or any seaven or more of them together with the said Surveyours or some or one of them within his or their Precincts repectively shall at their Meeting have power and authority to order and direct the makeing of any new Vaults Draines and Sewers, or to cutt into any Draine or Sewer already made, and for the altering enlargeing amending cleansing and scowring of any old Vaults, Sinks or Common Sewers. For the better effecting whereof it shall and may be lawfull to and for the said persons soe authorized and appointed as aforesaid or any seaven or more of them [at theire said Meeting] to impose any reasonable Taxe upon all Houses in the said Citty and Liberties thereof in proportion to the benefit they shall receive thereby, for and toward the new makeing, cutting, altering enlargeing [amending] cleanseing and scowring all and singular the said Vaults Draines Sewers Pavements and Pitching aforesaid.[55]

What the Act did, in the main, was to appoint a body of persons to attend to sewer improvement and upkeep. Such work was, in fact, quite necessary after the Great Fire, when Christopher Wren famously set about widening the lower end of the Fleet River in an attempt to create an open canal system and commercial area. However, Wren's plan did not alleviate the problem of the Fleet's choked upper reaches, and it certainly did nothing to improve the disease-ridden quality of the open sewer system. Indeed, the task of "sewer improvement" did not appear to have much at all to do with rebuilding the infrastructure.

The Act states further, that

> ... the partyes therein offending contrary to this present Act shall and may be proceeded against, and thereof convicted by Indictment at the next Sessions of the Peace to be held for the said Citty and Libertyes. Thereof, according to his or their severall Offences, unlesse they shall submitt to the Judgement and Censure of the persons soe to be authorized and appointed as aforesaid or any seaven or more of them, and shall satisfye and pay such mulct or penalty as by them shall be sett and imposed for such Offence into the Chamber of the City of London, to be imployed for and toward the Workes in this Act mentioned. Any Law, Statute, Usage or Custome to the contrary notwithstanding.[56]

The Act, then, did not improve much on the sewers; indeed, it is a commonplace of sewer historians that London sewers did not advance technologically until the mid-nineteenth century crisis of the "Great Stink." In light of this technological stagnation I wish to advance the proposition that one of the perhaps surprising aims of the Act had little to do with sewer engineering. Rather, what the Act articulated into statute were the precise persons who could and could not make incursions on the open channels of waste that ran through the city. In legalizing and centralizing the civic office of city sanitation, in other words, the Act described as illegal any incursions onto the sewers by any persons not employed to tend to them. Why this latter should need to be legislated is something of a question. After all, the poor had been gleaning from the sewers for some time, and this economy of scavenging suited city sanitation fairly well, since the sewers were notoriously overflowing with carcasses, rotten vegetables, casks of ale, and any number of other things.[57] In this way, the poor would have functioned as unpaid sanitation workers. It was they who ran the risks of proximity to the diseased matter floating by, they who often alleviated the clogged, narrow channels of waste and debris, and they who lived off their paltry and fetid booty.

Why, then, would the city wish to pay people to do what was already being done? Why not continue to sacrifice the urban poor to address the myriad problems in civic design? The answer to this question becomes clearer when we turn our attention to the Appendix to the 1671 Act. The Appendix, whose subtitle spirals ominously to its specific referent—Act of Common Council for Paving and Cleansing, and Preventing Nuisances in the Streets of London—details exactly who cannot be in the streets at particular times:

> And farther, that from henceforth no beggars or vagrants, tankard bearers, porters, or other persons whatsoever, bearing any kind of burthens on their heads, backs, or arms, horses, or any kind of cattle, shall be permitted at anytime of the day, from six of the clock in the morning until nine of the clock at night, to go or pass, or be led upon the said flat pavements in any street between the houses and the posts adjoining to the said flat pavements, except only for going into the said houses directly cross the said pavements, under the penalty of five shillings for every horse, or other kind of cattle whatsoever, and three shillings and four pence for every tankard-bearer, porter, and other person carrying burthen as aforesaid, for every offence, and the said

beggars and vagrants to be punished according to the laws already in force: and that all constables within this city and liberties thereof, and other officers, employed or to be employed by the said commissioners, or any seven or more of them (who shall have power, and are hereby authorized and directed to employ such persons accordingly) and all marshals and their men, and warders, are to take special care to prevent the said offences, and to apprehend all such offenders. And, in case the said marshals or their men, or warders, shall be negligent in doing their duty herein, it shall be lawful for the lord mayor for the time being, and his successors, upon due proof of such neglect, to move such marshals and their men, and other inferior warders, and others to put in their places.[58]

As English legal historiographers have shown, the bulk of English statute law in the late seventeenth and early eighteenth centuries was devoted to criminalizing customary forms of appropriation and subsistence. It was at this time, in fact, that the legal status of gleaning was transformed into the punishable crimes of embezzlement and pilfering. In *The London Hanged*, Peter Linebaugh details the Acts that applied to customary appropriation in the workplace: the waste products of production that traditionally had been the unspoken spoils of the laborer, were now addressed by, for example, The Bugging, Clicking, Watch-Scraping, and Cabbage Acts, which applied to pelts, leather, metals, and linens, respectively. The waste products of production were now to be the property of the owner of the means of production, and his to throw away. Why would waste be legislated in this manner? Wouldn't it be more efficient to allow the citizenry to dispose of, recycle, re-function this waste? Quite simply put, however, to the extent that laborers were prohibited from subsisting on these customary forms of waste, the need to sell one's labor time was intensified.

But what of the unemployed pool, or sink, of labor who subsist on the waste of the waste? Although Linebaugh's study applies to gleaning at the workplace, we can see that this tidal wave of eighteenth-century legislation was intimately related to the fate of such wastes as carrion, the dregs of ale production, and household scraps. Set adrift on the open channels of the Fleet, such waste, too, was prohibited to the vagabond. When read with the Appendix, we realize that the Sewer Acts perform what Robin Blackburn has termed "extended accumulation," or what David Harvey might call "accumulation by dispossession." After having expropriated the land in the countryside, the state addresses those persons now "freed" to vagrancy in the urban core. And dispossesses them again. This dispossession serves a double purpose. It legally estranges the urban poor from the customary forms of appropriation on which they had subsisted, thus "freeing" them/forcing them into wage labor. And it creates the occasion for expenditures of capital on urban development; such expenditures return an investment, but do not, themselves, necessarily improve the living conditions of the people. As David Harvey explains,

> The eighteenth century in Britain was characterized . . . by a capital surplus much of which went into the built environment because it had nowhere else to go. Investment

in the built environment took place primarily for financial rather than use-value reasons—investors were looking for a steady and secure rate of return on their capital. Investment in property . . . in turnpikes, canals, and rents . . . as well as in state obligations were about the only options available to rentiers.[59]

In light of Harvey's analysis, we can regard the development of the sewer system after the Great Fire in direct relation to those demands of capitalization that produce forms of infrastructure development that do not serve the needs of the people, but rather that of capital.[60] This is one way of understanding why the "improvements" on the sewer system after the Great Fire were not improvements at all, and why despite the available technology for covered sewers, it was not until the nineteenth century that such improvements were instituted. The goal of improving on the sewers in the late seventeenth and early eighteenth centuries was not the welfare of the people, finally, but rather the creation of opportunities for capital investment and return, and the continued dispossession of the urban poor of any means of subsistence except the selling of their labor. We will return to the relation of infrastructure development and accumulation later in the chapter. For now, however, we must return to the "City Shower"'s representation of the effects of such expenditures on the London economy.

The Commodity's Stink

With our piece of sewer legislation in mind, we recall the "double stink" of the shower, the dual strike of capital that severs the peasantry from their traditional work "striking" bundles, and criminalizes/strikes at their subsistence on the waste products of the city. This geographical double stink carries over to lines 7 and 8, where it is submitted to the abstractions of calculation, presumably the calculations of a new bourgeois who is advised, "If you be wise, then go not far to dine,/You spend in coach-hire more than save in wine."

It would have been impossible to read the advisement, "If you be wise" without reflecting on Swift's satiric replacement of rural work with urban consumption: The georgic is typically conceived as a poem of advice to the laborer. Here, rather than being advised on how to produce, the "you" is advised on how to consume. As such, the "double stink" of the stricken laborer carries over, permeating this exchange as well; here, the London consumer, the nameless "You" who is advised by the speaker, shimmers into view over the absent presence of rural labor, a substitution that calls up the double nature of the commodity form itself, which stinks of doubleness, and duplicity, as well.[61] As we know from Marx, the commodity is double, and this dual, dialectical character inheres in the value form itself: "As use-values, commodities differ above all in quality, while as exchange values they can only differ in quantity, and therefore do not contain an atom of use-value."[62] Moishe Postone explains that this double character of the commodity form is rooted in the double character of labor: "concrete, useful labor, which produces use values, and abstract human labor, which constitutes value."[63] Because it is rooted in the double character of labor, sameness and difference are dialectically concatenated in the commodity, which "does not contain two different sorts of labor; the *same* labor, however, is determined as different and as opposed to itself, depending on whether it is related to the *use-value* of the commodity as its product, or to the *commodity-value* as its mere objectified expression."[64]

In comparing "coach-hire" to "wine," Swift presents us with two notorious luxuries, which is to say that they each appear incontrovertibly unique and valuable in and of themselves. The exchange is thus grounded in the pairing of two commodities that exhale a strong waft of singularity: service work and an imported indulgence. The wine, of course, was produced by the French peasantry, and traded through a class of French merchants that created miniature guild-style monopolies. It was consumed almost exclusively, in England, by the ruling classes. Indeed, wine production represented a long-term resistance on the part of the *ancien regime* to the encroachments of industrialization and the flattening equivalences of mass-production. Wine was, however, ripe for the picking for early merchant capital, which traded specifically on wine's culture of connoisseurship and patina of "local flavor." Thus, what the wine trade lost in productivity, it gained in appeal to consumers who longed to taste the specificity of each bottle.[65] However, wine prices were notoriously unstable and "personal"; that is, they appeared to reflect the negotiations of the merchants. Indeed, the price of wine was, itself, something of a fetish, because it appeared to register any number of contingencies—such as whether or not British, German, or French barrels were used to store and sell the wine, or if British traders had managed to strike a deal with French vintners before the French monarchy could intervene.

So, too, did coach hire appear to be an individually negotiated value. For those new bourgeois who did not keep a coach on a regular basis, coach hire represented a seemingly personal transaction, because it involved an apparently direct negotiation between two parties. Here in the "City Shower," the coach hire and the wine confront each other as directly exchangeable goods, an interaction predicated on the division of labor, the mediation of money, and the magical disappearance of labor. The poem reiterates this disappearance formally, as the London consumer occupies the position of the Georgic laborer who receives advice from the poet about how to conduct his work.

Both the early modern wine trade and the service industry wore their individuality loudly and proudly. But both were structured, like all commodities, according to the general demands of the price system. In the encounter of coach hire and wine, we have two distinctly different goods being exchanged. Both carry their patina of specific value strongly on their backs. But in choosing these commodities in particular, and in pitting one against the other on the heels of the double stink, Swift's poem drives toward the inescapable conclusion that all commodities under capitalism, even the most seemingly different, exist within the grips of the double character of the commodity form, which not only permits but encourages the equivalence of qualitatively different goods. Indeed, these commodities are so different qualitatively, they might as well be Marx's famous coat and linen, whose difference grounds the event of exchange: "Coats cannot be exchanged for coats, one use-value cannot be exchanged for another of the same kind . . . Only the products of mutually independent acts of labour, performed in isolation, can confront each other as commodities."[66] Simply put, the social division of labor makes commodity exchange necessary, because the laborer can no longer provide for himself the necessities of his own subsistence. Here, too, the coach hire and wine appear precisely to confront each other directly, but this seemingly direct confrontation is only the form of appearance of the social division of labor upon which commodity production and exchange depends.

The exchange value of qualitatively different goods is not reckoned in terms of use, but in terms of the money form, which is invoked in Swift by its glaring absence: "You'll spend more in coach-hire than save in wine." The seemingly direct exchange of "hire" for "wine" is an elision that is made more poignant by the slant rhyme, which sonorously evokes the fleetingly qualitative difference that is being always suppressed by the demands of equivalence. The poem suggests, against the melancholic echo of difference, that the addressee is already making impossible calculations, and has already made equivalent the coach hire and the wine. In doing so, the poem recalls the invisible yet potent reach of the commodity form, which subsists on yet another violent abstraction, that of labor itself. The laborer-addressee of the Georgic has become, bathetically, the urban would-be connoisseur, with his impossibly small calculations and fantasies of direct, personal exchanges.[67]

In as much as the coach hire and wine appear to confront each other head-on, then, the "City Shower" rains down the mystifications of the commodity form itself, whose magic is made possible by a system of production that keeps laborers radically separated from each other. Insofar as commodities are "products of the labour of private individuals who work independently of each other . . . producers do not come into social contact until they exchange the products of their labour, [and so] the specific social characteristics of their private labours appear only within this exchange."[68] Finally, famously, this mystification is naturalized such that, "the mysterious character of the commodity-form consists therefore simply in the fact that the commodity reflects the social characteristics of men's own labour as objective characteristics of the products of labour themselves, as the socio-natural properties of these things."[69]

The "strike," that erstwhile rural measure of value, has now fully met the exigencies of the commodity form, which measures qualitatively different goods, such as imported wines and service rendered, according to a much different formula.[70] Even the service economy, with its appearance of being able to be directly negotiated by individual persons, is subjected to the law of value and the abstractions of the commodity form. And of the wine industry—which at this point continued to represent the fantasy of direct negotiation on a world-historical scale—even this pastoral legend succumbs here to the predations of the commodity form, which equalizes everything in its path.

Accumulation by Dispossession: "Mean while the South rising with dabbled wings . . ."

Swift's critique of capitalist consumer culture can be said to take two predominant forms at once: the poetic efflorescence of chaotic equivalences and exchanges, as we saw earlier, and the "scatologization" of circulation, as we will see later. In eighteenth-century England, the conception of the economic system as a circulatory system had entered public consciousness with the publication of William Harvey's *On the Circulation of the Heart and the Blood in Animals* (1628). And, as is well known, Swift has seized on this bodily metaphorics to great, grotesque effect in "Cassinus and Peter." So, too, in the "Shower," the exchanges of coach hire and wine are troped as a toxic, inabsorbable excess regurgitated by the body. In this way, the poem reflects the threat, inherent in the circulation of equivalent commodities, of overproduction and of the social order's inability to consume the masses of produced goods. Lines 33 and 34 register the effects of overproduction in their iconic turn to the weather: "Mean while the South rising with dabbled wings,/A sable cloud a-thwart the welkin flings,/That swilled more liquor than it could contain,/And like a drunkard gives it up again." The South, of course, is the South Wind, and can be understood here as a reference to the rise of colonial production. As such, it represents the relation of British to colonial manufactures as a crisis of overproduction: the British market is glutted, unable to consume further. As David Harvey explains, overaccumulation is the signal condition of the capitalist mode of production, and "can within a given territorial system mean a condition of surpluses of labor (rising unemployment) and surpluses of capital (registered as a glut of commodities on the market that cannot be disposed of without a loss, as idle productive capacity, and/or as surpluses of money capital lacking outlets for productive and profitable investment)."[71] The regurgitated glut is Swift's troping the increasing financialization of the British economy.

That British manufactures had been stagnating in the face of colonial production is clear. Part of this had to do with the tie-up of English resources in managing Ireland, rather than investing in the colonies. Clearer still is England's increasing transformation into a nation of consumers.[72] Swift was well aware of the threat of overaccumulation—his opinion of the South Sea Bubble was well-known. In the "City Shower," too, we see the South's "rising" as a sign of the crises of production that accompanied and undergirded developing capitalism. The scene of regurgitation—the cloud that "swilled more liquor than it could contain,/And like a drunkard gives it up again" (ll 15–16)—further marries the rich hermeneutics of location with the centrality of the problem of consumption. This narration of vomit, which has been to this point largely overlooked, must be considered in terms of the geopolitical resonances of overconsumption in this period. The "South rising" recalls the rise of colonial production (we might even be so pedantic to read this production as that of rum, particularly in the context of the ensuing drunken regurgitation), and imagines that colonial context returned to the metropole in the inescapably threatening figure of "rising." Swift's figure of the "South rising" thus invokes a double resonance: at once calling up colonial revolutions and rebellion, and at the same time generating a scatological but accurate sketch of the capital relations between metropole and colonies. If the shower is the drunkard who "gives it up again," the sewer is that channel that receives the waste products of capital accumulation. Let us recall Harvey's argument that the eighteenth century British economy was "characterized by a capital surplus much of which went into the built environment because it had nowhere else to go." And recall, too, that the specific legislation for sewer "improvements," mainly centered on moving the sewers from the sides to the center of the streets, and not on substantive, quality-of-life changes. The sewers were, in this way, a receptacle for capital waste as much as for debris proper. Such "useless" investment is the hallmark of a fully glutted home economy, a drunkard economy that immediately "gives up" again what it has absorbed in the form of labor and investment in fixed capital.

As we argued in chapter 4, for Harvey, the concept of "accumulation by dispossession" is an extension of Marx's original concept of primitive accumulation, and it is the key to understanding how capitalism manages to reproduce itself as a system despite recurrent crises of overproduction and overaccumulation: "such crises are registered as surpluses of capital and of labor power side by side without there apparently being any means to bring them profitably together to accomplish socially useful tasks. If system-wide devaluations (and even destruction) of capital and of labor power are not to follow, then ways must be found to absorb these surpluses. Geographical expansion and spatial reorganization provide one such option."[73] In the early eighteenth century, sewer and criminal legislation met in the concept of accumulation by dispossession, and ensured that the urban poor were dispossessed of even their ability to subsist through customary appropriations of waste products. Statute laws were developed to criminalize sewer gleaning, and if transportation presented itself as the solution to "venting" this vagrant population to labor to the colonies, "the South rising" suggests the circuit of labor and capital accumulation in which England finds itself inextricably bound. The products of this cycle—in the form of unrest and overaccumulation—are returned back to the metropole, where they are regurgitated in the form of more infrastructure production, a dumping of capital waste that facilitates the expansion of bureaucracy and legislation far more than sanitation or the well-being of the urban residents. The urban poor, unable to subsist on the common waste products of urban capitalism, are forced to sell their labor, or "give it up again," to the sewer project, an instrumentalization of the capital waste of this particular economic circuit. Lines 13–16 finally demonstrate this complex transatlantic movement of capital investment and production, and the dispossession and criminalization on which this depends. We will return to the subject of criminal law later on. In order to do so, however, we must follow the movement of the poem into the particulars of domestic labor.

Brisk Exchange: The Poetics of Labor

Along with its connotations of southern-hemispheric production, lines 13–16 ready the reader for a poetic exposition of the imbrication of transatlantic with domestic production. The multiple significations of "south wind" chiasmatically carry the weight of this discursive task. The "South Rising" heralds not one, but two areas of uprising: the West Indies and South London.[74] Here, the "sable cloud" of southern-hemispheric uprising is yoked together with protoproletarian English uprisings in one solidaristic "fling." Such a reading of the "South Rising" is, I believe, warranted by the South Wind's neoclassical significance as a Virgilian augur of war. Swift elaborates further on this bellicose reference beginning in line 17, where the rising South wind wakes a vengeful female actor—"Brisk Susan"—who is in the midst of completing some household labor. Here, Susan's self-reproduction (whipping linen from a rope) sprinkles dirty water violently upon the poet. But this scene of labor instantly multiplies, and Susan herself becomes immediately, eerily substitutable for "some careless quean," who, in "whirl[ing] on her mop," also drenches the peripatetic narrator. The two female figures labor at distinct tasks, but their interchangeability is, to borrow the language of Swift's description, queasily "brisk." As the equivalences wrought upon the laborer herself mirror those demanded of the commodity, the poet becomes a receptacle for the violent exfoliations involved in the reproduction of labor power. The fragmentation of the waste product of labor itself is screened as a bathetic interplay of incalculably small bodily excrescences (dust) with the impersonal and relentless rain. As this battle is made up of particulate matter, it represents an incalculable exchange: "Twas doubtful which was rain and which was dust." The battle is generally read as simply another satirical flourish on the mock epic, yet the particulars of the particulate matter here are important. The combatants are indistinguishable from/exchangeable for each other, and yet the struggle is "unequal," signaling an exchange that recalls the commodity form's double character, its simultaneous equivalence and inequality.

Ultimately, the detritus of this laborer bonds together with the celestial event of the rain, and, together, they "invade" the poet's coat. The coat is utterly singular—"Sole coat"—and the poet makes much of its ruination. In doing so, the formerly illegible combination of dust and rain become suddenly available to a properly chronological account: "dust cemented by the rain/erects the nap, and leaves a cloudy stain." After the indistinguishable whirl of dust and rain, the sky is seemingly dragged down to earth, and the "sable cloud" of the opening of the stanza is imprinted, with the help of the "dust," onto the poet's clothing. Just what is this "cloudy stain"? The singularity of the coat—its extremely personal and qualitative nature—becomes the screen against which the dust/rain coagulate is comprehensible, making available to the reader a distinction that was previously illegible. At first glance, it appears that the intensely personal nature of the coat causes each character of the battle to also become personal and distinct. So "personal" is this transformation, in fact, that the exchange takes on sexual characteristics, "[e]rect[ing] the nap" and leaving "a cloudy stain."

These lines are memorable for the gender inversion that this female laborers' sprinklings effect, forcing an erection of the poet's inanimate "body," and causing it to stain itself. We might note as well the emasculation of the poet figure in precisely these lines, as his coat is made to stand up on its own and ejaculate. But let us not stop here. For we can press this analysis further if we consider it in the context of the exchanges that have marked the poem from its outset. In fact, we cannot fail to note the resonance of this passage with Marx's magnificent description of the quantitative reckoning of two qualitatively different goods:

> Hence, in the value-relation, in which the coat is the equivalent of the linen, the form of the coat counts as the form of value. The value of the commodity linen is therefore expressed by the physical body of the commodity coat, the value of one by the use-value of the other. As a use-value, the linen is something palpably different from the coat; as a value, it is identical with the coat, and therefore looks like the coat. Thus the linen acquires a value-form different from its natural form. Its existence as value is manifested in its equality with the coat, just as the sheeplike nature of the Christian is shown in his resemblance to the Lamb of God.[75]

In the "City Shower," too, the bodily nature of the coat reveals the dialectical nature of its "singularity," which is, in fact, not singular at all, but radically substitutable in the field of exchange. The embodiment of the coat reveals the casting of this "singularity" in the fires of a labor that is itself highly abstracted and subject to substitution. Indeed, the final two lines of stanza three are dense with significance, as the labor sprinklings raise the coat and, in a quite typical performance of the commodity as fetish, cause it to ludically imitate the movements of a physical body. This scenario, in which the output of labor—the "sprinklings"—animate the coat, iterates the movement of value itself, which, as Marx argues, "is constituted only by the socially necessary expenditure of direct human labor time."[76] As labor is occluded into the exchange process, the "sable cloud" imprints on the coat, reminding the reader of the imbrication of this transatlantic matrix with domestic production—and reminding us, as well, of the wellsprings of resistance birthed by such occlusions. Inasmuch as the coat's embodiment is a reflection of this expenditure of labor time, the fetish of physical embodiment is only the outermost layer of a relation of value, in which the parties are at once "unequal" and indistinguishable from one another.

180   SPACE

"Now" Time: The Commodity-Form

The "Now" of the next stanza alerts the reader that we are firmly within the field of onward chronologies, as mirrored in the relentless rain, the massing of the water in "contiguous drops," and the sharp turn to "shops": "To shops in crowds the daggled females fly,/Pretend to cheapen goods, but nothing buy."[77] Of some interest here is the "pretend" bargaining in which the women engage. At once a simple parody of female consumption, this performance also reflects growing fears about the falling rate of profit and the incessant reduction of any commodity's value under developing capitalism. The female consumer's bargaining is the ostensible cause of the falling rate of profit, and yet the pretense of bargaining is itself a performance in the service of shelter. The contradictions of capital come to the fore in this spectacle of female consumption without any actual exchange. This abstract detailing of acts of exchange, which blazes on, even as the actual exchange is subtracted from the performance, is Swift's conservative parody of commercial value. The mass of female bargainers ape acts of exchange while revealing that the value of commodities is radically severed from the materiality of the commodity itself. Indeed, even the bargainers themselves take second seat to the act, as "daggled females" are forced to the back of the line by the enjambed actor, "To shops in crowds."

Critics have interpreted these lines as a more or less basic satire of the city's ridiculous inflations of value. Although such inflations are symptomatic of the development of London as a consumer society, Swift's satire exceeds a simple contrast of ancient virtue with modern depravity. Indeed, the anxious relation of the city dwellers to the oncoming shower might be said to reflect the anxiety at the heart of capitalist production, that is, the anxiety of overaccumulation and the devaluation of the currency and commodities on which this production depends. As we will see, the poem concludes with just such a threat, unfurled as the tumbled massing of these accumulated goods.

Accumulation and Poetic Form

We close our reading of this poem by following Swift's commodity-logic to its end, where it returns to the scene of the law and of the regulation of property. In bringing together the commodity form with the question of legislative transformation, Swift touches on one of the central convergences of the early eighteenth century: the deepening associations between the rise of statute and the rise of the commodity. As Peter Linebaugh explains:

> In the middle ages what had been legally important was not the monetary value of the property stolen, but the fact that theft indicated a violation of the feudal bonds. Theft was a betrayal of the hierarchical personal relationship in a society where everyone was kept in his or her place, but there was a place for everyone. By the

1690's, in contrast, the personal relationship was concealed in and through the commodity-form. Relationships that were formerly personal, such as those of lord and vassal, or master and apprentice were converted into exchange relationships. These developments in the law of larceny may be understood, therefore, as allowing human sacrifice to the fetishism of commodities. In legally defined circumstances private property became so significant that its violation broke the most important taboo of capitalist society and required the sacrifice of life.[78]

The eighteenth century witnessed a huge increase in the number of crimes that became occasions for capital punishment. Theft was one of them. This coeval development of an increase in capital punishment and the criminalization of waste gleaning is reflected in the litanies and geographies of the final lines of the poem, because the route described here is precisely the route taken by prisoners from Newgate prison to their execution. We know this much from Brendan O'Hehir's 1960 exposition of the Shower, in which he refutes Williams's canonical reading of the final lines as representing "The garbage and offal from the sheep and cattle pens, then standing to the west of West Smithfield, washing down to meet the overflow from the neighborhood of St. Sepulchre's . . ."[79] By some contrast, O'Hehir insists that the significance of this route is that it is the route to execution, "precisely the route of Swift's torrent: from St. Sepulchre's down Snow Hill to its junction with Cock Lane and Cow Lane—the site of Holborn conduit . . . and thence to Holborn bridge."[80]

Why not both readings? In fact, the "City Shower" gives poetic form to precisely this convergence: the simultaneous efflorescence of the waste products of capital accumulation and the rise of statute in the criminalization of customary forms of subsistence. In returning to O'Hehir, we can reconnect the sewer with the history of imprisonment and capital punishment that the poem aesthetically reformulates. The significance of Swift's sewer is that it reveals the imbrication of new legislation around commodities, with the production and regulation of waste. If the category of waste itself was a concept produced by capitalism, what was waste for one was most certainly not waste for another. Linebaugh expands,

> For the mass of the people . . . dirt was very much a part of their lives. For many working class people, wastes were essential. Nightsoil men and dung farmers earned their livings recycling London's animal and human wastes by removing them to Pimlico and Victoria to replenish the vegetable garden and orchard soils. The mudlarks derived their livings from coal wastes. Recall the case of Boroughs: what was waste to Deponthien was life to Boroughs. As one author has written, "Nature admits no waste. Nothing is left over; everything is joined in the spiral of life."[81]

As customary appropriation was increasingly criminalized, waste became an industry: "The criminalisation of custom on the land was accompanied by a redefinition of crime in the workplace, as the new capitalism sought to end the feudal tradition of artisans' and others' rights to a proportion of their labour."[82]

Such a perspective on waste allows us to engage another canonical reading of the final line of Swift's poem, which offers twelve syllables to the rest of the poem's ten: "Sweepings from butcher's stalls, dung, guts, and blood/Drowned puppies, stinking sprats, all drenched in mud,/Dead cats and turnips-tops come tumbling down the flood."[83] For centuries, critics have regarded these last lines as a poetic retort to Dryden who was fond of the alexandrine, perhaps to a fault. In stuffing his last line with trash—it is said—Swift makes a comment on Pope's form, and points out that anything at all can occupy an alexandrine. A puppy, a cat, or a turnip will do. Beyond this squabble with Pope, however, O'Hehir's analysis brings to the fore the degree to which Swift's breaking the laws of verse is mirrored by a catalogue of other law-breakings and law breakers that occupy the final lines of the poem. If the intensification of capital punishment throughout the century functions as the legislative handmaiden to securing private property and capital investment, this intensification also goes hand in hand with the criminalization of forms of customary appropriation such as waste gleaning. This concatenation encapsulates the institutional transformations we have been charting all along—transformations rather famously described by Marx as the "Bloody Legislation Against the Expropriated":

> The proletariat created by the breaking-up of the bands of feudal retainers and by the forcible expropriation of the people from the soil, this free and rightless proletariat could not possibly be absorbed by the nascent manufactures as fast as it was thrown upon the world. On the other hand, these men, suddenly dragged from their accustomed mode of life, could not immediately adapt themselves to the discipline of their new condition. They were turned in massive quantities into beggars, robbers and vagabonds, partly from inclination, in most cases under the force of circumstances.[84]

Swift's poem delivers the bloodiness of these convergences to us in the sedimentations of its form. Consider that the accumulation at the end sounds uncannily like that list of things legally prohibited from the sewers:

> That no man shall cast or lay in the streets, lanes, or common passages, or channels within this city or liberties, any dogs, cats, inwards of beasts, cleaves of beasts feet, bones, horns, dregs or dross of ale or beer, or any noisome thing, upon pain of ten shillings for every offence.[85]

Here, we are reminded of the prohibited and the proscribed—the criminal and the vagabond—at the heart of capital accumulation. In the end, the sewer poem traces a ghost topography of the condemned, as objects themselves seem to tell their own story, appearing animate in the face of the dead humanity that either walks this same course to their death, or has been forbidden to walk it, and from thence to glean subsistence.

The Dry Transatlantic

In this analysis of the closing lines of the "City Shower," I follow recent work in Critical Geography that has added much to our extant historical research into the fields of consumption and of production. The birth of consumer culture has been, moreover, well charted by historians and literary critics such as John Brewer, Adela Pinch, and Colin Nicholson. Indeed, the cross-fertilization of history and literary analysis is much showcased in work on the history of consumption, the marketplace, and of early modern trade. Work on the literary mediations of eighteenth-century production, however, has been somewhat thinner. In turning to Swift—who has been typically analyzed as a critic concerned most of all with consumption and its ills—I seek to show the ways in which his poetry registers the changing worlds of eighteenth-century production, particularly the advent of capital accumulation.

Recently, the "City Shower" has become a touchstone for transatlantic study. This disciplinary embrace of the poem is, in large part, due to the poem' central figure of water. Laura Brown and Joseph Roach exemplify a tendency to guide Swift studies in a westerly direction: Brown has introduced the idea that Swift's poem represents what she calls the "fable of oceans and floods," that is, a pervasive eighteenth-century trope of fluidity that registers the expansion of transatlantic trade routes and the growth of the British empire overseas. Brown argues that the sewer represents the imbrications of urban development with the transoceanic commodities and slave trades. It is on the basis of the historically relevant etymology that Brown connects the "City Shower" with the transatlanticization of British commerce more largely. In a chapter titled "Fables of Oceans and Floods," the sewer poem figures prominently alongside other clearly transatlantic odes, such as Pope's "Windsor Forest" and Thomson's "Seasons.": "Images of fluidity—rivers, waterways, and seas—carry a distinctive charge in the poetry of this period. This is a trope with a broad and rich cultural significance extending from the fable of the sewer ... to another corollary, contemporary fable: the fable of torrents and oceans, a collective story of imperial expansion."[86] Brown's reading is a critical departure from the traditional work on Swift, because it connects transatlantic studies' interest in figures of water to the contradictions of domestic development. By linking the filthy particulars of the urban infrastructure to the world of transatlantic commerce and empire, Brown moves us closer to a transatlantic studies that is not simply additive in nature but rather transformative in scope, and one that must yoke, no matter how difficult it is to do so, the dialectical development of the nation-state (including all of its apparati of force and expropriation) with the international development of British commerce.

We might follow Brown's lead in regarding Swift's sewer as a critical contribution to a compendium of transatlantic literature: certainly a less sublime body of water but inevitably a rich, historically specific one. Yet if recent work in trans- and circumatlantic studies tracks the proliferating tropes of water through eighteenth-century literature, no one has yet asked what these seemingly ever-present figures of water might in fact occlude. Indeed, my chapter has followed Brown's important work but argues that, if Swift's Shower represents a kind of dirty, urban transatlantic sluice, recent work in empire and Atlantic studies requires a redoubled account of the interior of the nation-state to keep step with our ever-growing bodies of work on border crossings and Atlantic transitions.

Along these lines, the Shower's bringing together the antinomies of commodity production and the commodity form with the violent and cruel legislation of territorial depredations upon which national sovereignty depends, produces what we might think of as a kind of Anglican enthusiasm. Or, at least, it generates an Anglican answer to the problem of enthusiasm. This answer takes the form of a materialist mediation of the spatio-temporal secular fixes of capitalism and the allegorization of these fixes in the "short-scheme" historicity of the rhyming couplet. Such couplets repeatedly unleash formal contradictions and conceptual ruts against the expectation of linear equivalence and complementarity. And they permit, too, the kinds of compressions, lags, and surprising contiguities that return the poem, formally speaking, to the landscape of early capitalism in non-finitos that intercede starkly onto our expectations of tight coupling, historical progress, and tidy rhymes.

The material mediations of Swift's London offer a rich poetic history of urban development and production, one that, in many ways, answers David Harvey's call for a many-layered history of urbanization: "Whatever else it may entail, the urban process implies the creation of a material physical infrastructure for production, circulation, exchange, and consumption. The first point of contact, then, is to consider the manner in which this built environment is produced and the way it serves as a resource system—a complex of use-values—for the production of value and surplus value."[87] Just so, we see that Swift's sewer allegorizes, in the fetid water, the processes of accumulation and the history of urban development that feed and sustain the commercial veins of the city.

In the tumbling trash of the final alexandrine, we cannot fail to recognize the return of the threat of the sable cloud—the "rising" of the South: the "torrent," the "force," the "huge confluent" all remind us of the latent power of the oppressed who shoulder the burdens of capital development. The final, notorious alexandrine brings this point home, and the "pile" of the dead that Swift curates here is the inexorable horizon of history. Indeed, the route of the sewer-water allegorizes not only an expansive, oceanic England, but also the land route of the condemned within the borders of the nation. In this sense, it is the combination of the transoceanic with the land route ghosted by the sewer, that evokes, most dialectically, the historical forces of capital accumulation.For it is this combination that records for history, in the steps of the prisoner, the conjuncture traced throughout this book: the fetid concatenation of infrastructure, the transformation of the relations of production, and that "bloody legislation" of which we have already said so much.

NOTES

Introduction

1. Clement Hawes, *Mania and Literary Style: The Rhetoric of Enthusiasm from the Ranters to Christopher Smart* (Cambridge: Cambridge University Press, 1996); Shaun Irlam, *Elations: the Poetics of Enthusiasm in Eighteenth-Century Britain* (Stanford: Stanford University Press, 1999); Jon Mee, *Romanticism, Enthusiasm, and Regulation: Poetics and the Policing of Culture in the Romantic Period* (New York: Oxford University Press, 2003).

2. Talal Asad, *Genealogies of Religion: Discipline and Reasons of Power in Christianity and Islam* (Baltimore: Johns Hopkins University Press, 1993), and *Formations of the Secular: Christianity, Islam, Modernity* (Palo Alto: Stanford University Press, 2003); Tomoko Masuzawa, *The Invention of World Religions: Or, How European Universalism was Preserved in the Language of Pluralism* (Chicago: University of Chicago Press, 2005); Russell T. McCutcheon, *Manufacturing Religion: The Discourse on Sui Generis Religion and the Politics of Nostalgia* (New York: Oxford University Press, 1997), Gauri Visvanathan, *Outside the Fold: Conversion, Modernity, and Belief* (Princeton: Princeton University Press, 1998).

3. Alberto Toscano, "Beyond Abstraction: Marx and the Critique of the Critique of Religion," *Historical Materialism* 18, no. 1 (May 2010), 21. I share Toscano's concern to develop a dialectical approach to the philosophical and political uses to which the idea of religious passion has been conscripted, and I share as well Toscano's orientation to Marx's work on religion in general an d the spectralization of life under capitalism more specifically. Toscano's superb literary and historical critique of fanaticism extends the observations of "Beyond Abstraction" to a number of historical situations, beginning with the German Peasants' War. See, Alberto Toscano, *Fanaticism: On the Uses of an Idea* (London: Verso, 2010).

4. Marx, "Theses on Feuerbach" in Karl Marx and Friedrich Engels *The German Ideology* (New York: Prometheus, 1998), 570, cited in Toscano, 8.

5. I take the phrasing, "critique of the critique of religion" from Toscano, "Beyond Abstraction," 6.

6. Karl Marx, *Capital: A Critique of Political Economy, Volume 1,* trans. Ben Fowkes (New York: Penguin, 1992), 186.

7. Karl Marx, "Theses on Feuerbach," *The Marx-Engels Reader*, ed. Robert Tucker (New York: Norton, 1978), 144. Toscano's citation of Marx's "Leading Article" supports a similar claim: "It is the greatest irreligiousness, the wantonness of worldly reason, to separate the general spirit of religion from the positive religion; this separation of religion from its dogmas and institutions is equal to asserting that the universal spirit of right must reign in the state irrespective of the definite laws and the positive institutions of right." Karl Marx, "Leading Article in No. 179 of the *Kolnische Zeitung*," in *Karl Marx and Friedrich Engels on Religion* (Mineola: Dove Publications, 2008; Moscow: the Foreign Languages Publishing House, 1957), 33–36.

8. See José Casanova, *Public Religions in the Modern World* (Chicago: University of Chicago Press, 1994).

9. Ann Pellegrini and Janet Jakobsen identify this fantasy of secularism precisely. They argue that the hallmark of secular ideology is its self-conception as a uniquely impartial—and necessarily nontotalizing—form of knowledge. From the standpoint of liberal secularism, "[o]nly a secular view of religion as an object of knowledge can provide the external perspective that reveals any religious claim—despite its own assertion of universalism—to be particular." "World Secularisms at the Millennium," *Social Text* 18, 3 (Fall 2000): 9.

10. Asad, *Formations of the Secular*; Dipesh Chakrabarty, *Provincializing Europe: Postcolonial Thought and Historical Difference* (Princeton: Princeton University Press, 2000); Simon During, *Modern Enchantments: The Cultural Power of Secular Magic* (Cambridge: Harvard University Press, 2004); Jonathan I. Israel, *Radical Enlightenment: Philosophy and the Making of Modernity, 1650–1750* (Oxford: Oxford University Press, 2002); Charles Taylor, *A Secular Age* (Cambridge: Belknap Press, 2007), Viswanathan, *Outside the Fold*.

11. The most comprehensive account of this history is to be found in Michael Heyd, *'Be Sober and Reasonable': The Critique of Enthusiasm in the Seventeenth and Eighteenth Centuries* (New York: Brill, 1995). Locke's famous critique of enthusiasts is found in *An Essay Concerning Human Understanding*, which I will discuss at greater length in chapter 1.

12. J.G.A. Pocock, "Edmund Burke and the Redefinition of Enthusiasm: The Context of the Counter-Revolution," in *The Transformation of Political Culture 1789–1848*, eds. Francois Fuet and Mona Ozoof, vol. 3, *The French Revolution and the Creation of Modern Political Culture*, ed. Keith Michael Baker (Oxford: Pergamon Press, 1989), 25.

13. Irlam, *Elations*, 6.

14. William Wordsworth, "Tintern Abbey," in *William Wordsworth: the Major Works*, ed. Stephen Gill (New York: Oxford University Press, 2008), ll. 93–102.

15. See Mee, *Romanticism, Enthusiasm, and Regulation*. We are not in a position here to arbitrate on these seemingly opposing senses of enthusiasm in the nineteenth century, one in need of regulation, and the other an auspicious early model of the modern, self-reflexive subject. Though I will posit that it may well have been the case that enthusiasm enjoyed a simultaneity of contradictory significations in this period. On this topic, see also Hawes, *Mania and Literary Style*.

16. Markman Ellis, *The Politics of Sensibility: Race, Commerce, and Gender in the Sentimental Novel* (Cambridge: Cambridge University Press, 1996); Julie Ellison, *Cato's Tears and the Making of Anglo-American Emotion* (Chicago: University of Chicago Press, 1999); Lynn Festa, *Sentimental Figures of Empire in Eighteenth-Century Britain and France* (Baltimore: Johns Hopkins University Press, 2006); Ann Jessie Van Sant, *Eighteenth-Century Sensibility and the Novel: The Senses in Social Context* (Cambridge: Cambridge University Press, 1993).

17. Although I do not have the space here to review the literature on "alternative modernities," it should be clear that my account of enthusiasm is indebted to recent work in

alternative modernities that has revived the study of secularization. At the same time, I seek to avoid the micronizing tendencies of some work within this tradition. Although I build on the excellent research and analytic strategies that have been developed to address the still-dominant force of religion in the contemporary world, I depart from alternative modernities studies at the point that it replaces an encompassing analysis of capitalist development with a number of proliferating but incommensurable "social worlds." For more on alternative modernities, see Arif Dirlik, *Postmodernity's Histories* (London: Rowman and Littlefield, 2000), and Dipesh Chakrabarty, *Provincializing Europe*. For an alternate perspective on alternate modernities, see Fredric Jameson, *A Singular Modernity: Essays on the Ontology of the Present* (London: Verso, 2002).

18. This claim may be seen to sit in some relation to Charles Taylor's dissatisfaction with what he calls "subtraction stories," or those accounts that regard secularization as the result of a withdrawal of religious belief from public life. My book departs from Taylor in two main regards, both methodological. The first is that although Taylor's philosophical project tracks the refiguring of "belief" in what he understands to be the "immanent frame" of a modern world in which religious transcendence is one option among many, my own project operates its critique at a literary-critical level, and thus understands belief largely in terms of its discursive articulations. The second departure has to do with the dialectical nature of my project. Where Taylor regards secularism as having been generated, at least in part, out of a shift in religious practices and "social imaginaries," I detail a materialist account of secular ideology rooted in the advent of new economic formations. On extensions of and departures from Taylor's argument, see also Michael Warner, Jonathan VanAntwerpen, and Craig Calhoun, eds. *Varieties of Secularism in a Secular Age* (Cambridge: Harvard University Press, 2010).

19. See, for example: Walter D Mignolo, "The Enduring Enchantment: (Or the Epistemic Privilege of Modernity and Where to Go from Here)," *South Atlantic Quartlery* 101, 4 (October 2002); During, *Modern Enchantments*; Colin Jager, *The Book of God: Secularization and Design in the Romantic Era* (Philadelphia: University of Pennsylvania Press, 2007); Joshua Landy and Michael Saler, eds., *The Re-Enchantment of the World: Secular Magic in a Rational Age* (Palo Alto: Stanford University Press, 2009); Mark A. Schneider, *Culture and Enchantment* (Chicago: Chicago University Press, 1993); Michael Taussig, *The Magic of the State* (New York: Routledge, 1997).

20. Chakrabarty, *Provincializing Europe*, 89.

21. On moral philosophy as the concatenation of a range of discourses that we now consider as separate, see John Guillory's field-defining account in *Cultural Capital: The Problem of Literary Canon Formation* (Chicago: University of Chicago Press, 1993).

22. Ann Taves, *Fits, Trances, & Visions: Experiencing Religion and Explaining Experience from Wesley to James* (Princeton: Princeton University Press, 1999); Leigh Eric Schmidt, *Hearing Things: Religion, Illusion, and the American Enlightenment* (Cambridge: Harvard University Press, 2000).

23. Ian Baucom, *Specters of the Atlantic: Finance Capital, Slavery, and the Philosophy of History* (Durham: Duke University Press, 2005), 25. The bibliography on capital accumulation principally includes Samir Amin, *Accumulation on a World Scale: A Critique of the Theory of Underdevelopment*, trans. Brian Pearce (New York: Monthly Review Press, 1974); Giovanni Arrighi, *The Long Twentieth Century: Money, Power, and the Origins of Our Times* (London: Verso, 2010); and David Harvey, *Spaces of Global Capitalism: Towards a Theory of Uneven Geographical Development* (London: Verso, 2006).

24. John Keay, *The Honourable Company: A History of the English East India Company* (New York: Harper Collins, 1993); J.H. Elliott, *Empires of the Atlantic World: Britain and Spain in America, 1492–1830* (New Haven: Yale University Press, 2006).

25. Marx, *Capital: Volume 1*, 709.

26. Arrighi, *The Long Twentieth Century*, 81.

27. Baucom expands, "Serving to link one place to another and so to define the operative territories of capital, the geographies of circulation that supersede and interrupt the borders of the nation-state, these spaces-of-flows thus belong less to the particular cities and states that they link or to the individual places in which they happen to have come to rest than to the expensive territories of circulation that they govern. They exist by serving the needs of sovereign polities but exist to serve the sovereign principles of exchange they embody, the financial flows they regulate, the capital imperative which they incarnate and whose chief purpose is the conversion of endless variety into a single, general equivalent: money," Baucom, *Specters of the Atlantic*, 36.

28. John Brewer, *The Sinews of Power: War, Money and the English State, 1688–1783* (Cambridge: Harvard University Press, 1990).

29. Robin Blackburn, *The Making of New World Slavery: From the Baroque to the Modern, 1492–1800* (London: Verso, 1998), 513. Blackburn argues against an orthodox Marxist tradition—particularly that represented by the work of Robert Brenner—that an expanded version of primitive accumulation that includes an account of the plantation system is necessary to our understanding of the origins and development of capitalism, and is warranted by Marx's own analysis.

30. Blackburn, *The Making of New World Slavery*, 374–375.

31. Saree Makdisi, *Romantic Imperialism: Universal Empire and the Culture of Modernity* (Cambridge: Cambridge University Press, 1998); Peter Linebaugh and Marcus Rediker, *The Many-Headed Hydra: Sailors, Slaves, Commoners, and the Hidden History of the Revolutionary Atlantic* (Boston: Beacon Press, 2001).

32. Marx, *Capital, Volume I*, 735.

33. Fredric Jameson, *The Political Unconscious: Narrative as a Socially Symbolic Act* (Ithaca: Cornell University Press), 127.

34. Baucom, *Specters*, 20.

35. When, in *Gravity's Rainbow*, Seaman Bodine—the prototypical "chemical enthusiast"—sings "The Doper's Dream," he treats us to a near-perfect précis on this sense of enthusiastic pleasure: "Last night I dreamed I was plugged right in/To a bubblin' hookah so high,/When all of a sudden some Arab jinni/Jump up just a-winkin his eye./'I'm here to obey all your wishes,' he told me./As for words I was trying to grope./'Good buddy,' I cried, 'you could surely oblige me/By turnin' me on to some *dope!*'" The enthusiastic dream is that of unmediated communion: with the genie (who "suddenly" appears), with the drug, with the hookah (to which the Doper is "plugged right in"). The Doper's loss for words amplifies the communion, as the mediations of language are erased in the intimacies of dope and in the Orientalist fantasy of luxurious embodiment. These sensory immediacies dilate in the ocular consumption of a radiant landscape of pills and hash, spied while flying through the air: the trees were "a-bloomin' with pink 'n' purple pills," and the "Romilar River flowed by/To the magic mushrooms as wild as a rainbow." The conclusion of the Dream completes the enthusiastic cycle, with the Doper having been duped by the "jinni," who turns out to be a "narco man," who busts, then imprisons the Doper. Like all enthusiasms, the enthusiasm for drugs is represented as the inspiration for actions that may run counter to other goals and needs: "And I wonder," the Doper laments in closing, "will I ever go free?" Thomas Pynchon, *Gravity's Rainbow* (New York: Penguin Classics, 1995), 369.

36. Colin Jager, "Is Critique Secular? Thoughts on Enchantment and Reflexivity," Published by the Doreen B. Townsend Center for the Humanities, University of California, Berkeley. *townsendcenter.berkeley.edu/pubs/Jager.pdf*.

37. Ibid.

38. By this distance barometer between religious affiliation and state sanction, in the United States, The Branch Davidians, Heaven's Gate, and the People's Temple have been

almost routinely classified as "enthusiastic"; Mormons, Roman Catholics, and Eastern Orthodox Christians less so, and, finally, denominations with still-tighter ties to governmental support, such as the Presbyterian Church, The Evangelical Lutheran Church in America, and United Church of Christ, less frequently still. On the Peoples Temple and enthusiasm, see David Chidester, *Salvation and Suicide: An Interpretation of Jim Jones, the Peoples Temple, and Jonestown* (Bloomington: Indiana University Press, 2003). On Heaven's Gate and enthusiasm, see Brenda E. Brasher, "The Civic Challenge of Virtual Eschatology: Heaven's Gate and Millenial Fever in Cyberspace," in *Religion and Social Policy*, ed. Paula D. Nesbitt (Lanham, MD: Alta Mira Press, 2001). The description of the Branch Davidians as enthusiastic was routinely articulated in the press coverage of the siege of Waco. See, for example, "Editorial," *The Progressive*, June 1, 1993. On the Branch Davidians and enthusiasm, see also Eugene V. Gallagher, *The New Religious Movements Experience in America* (Westport: Greenwood Press, 2004).

39. Slavoj Zizek, *In Defense of Lost Causes* (London: Verso, 2008), 52. Jean-Francois Lyotard's recently translated *Enthusiasm* also takes up the Kantian conception of enthusiasm as a sublime sentiment spurred by spontaneous or incalculable political acts or transitions. See Jean-Francois Lyotard, *Enthusiasm: The Kantian Critique of History*, trans. Georges Van Den Abbeele (Palo Alto: Stanford University Press, 2009).

40. Alain Badiou, *Ethics: An Essay on the Understanding of Evil*, trans. Peter Hallward (London: Verso, 2001), x.

41. Ibid., 2.

42. G.W.F. Hegel, *The Phenomenology of Spirit*, trans. A.V. Miller (New York: Oxford University Press, 1979), 23.

43. Ian Balfour describes this nexus precisely when he redefines "prophesy" in the Weberian tradition: "One could go further than Weber and specify that the decisive factor in the prophet's relation to the divine word is its immediacy," Ian Balfour, *The Rhetoric of Romantic Prophesy* (Palo Alto: Stanford University Press, 2002), 4.

44. Marx, *Capital, Volume I*, 125.

45. Ibid., 128.

46. Ibid., 165.

47. Ibid., 128.

48. David Harvey, *A Companion to Marx's Capital* (London: Verso, 2010), 17.

49. Marx, *Capital, Volume I*, 163.

50. Jacques Derrida, *Specters of Marx, the State of the Debt, the Work of Mourning, and the New International*, trans. Peggy Kamuf (London: Routledge, 1994), 165–166, cited in Toscano, "Beyond Abstraction," 15.

51. Toscano, "Beyond Abstraction," 25.

52. Raymond Williams, *Marxism and Literature* (New York: Oxford University Press, 1978), 244.

53. Mary Poovey, *A History of the Modern Fact*: Problems of Knowledge in the Sciences of Wealth and Society (Chicago: University of Chicago Press, 1998).

54. See Laura Brown, *Fables of Modernity: Literature and Culture in the English Eighteenth Century* (Ithaca: Cornell University Press, 2001).

Chapter 1

1. See Ann Pellegrini and Janet Jakobsen, "World Secularisms at the Millennium," *Social Text* 18. 3 (Fall 2000).

2. J.G.A. Pocock's massive *Barbarism and Religion* charts at great length the role of religious discourse in crafting modern consciousness in Edward Gibbon, and in the work of Gibbon's contemporaries, Smith, Ferguson, Robertson, and Hume. J.G.A. Pocock,

Barbarism and Religion, 4 vols. (Cambridge: Cambridge University Press, 2005). See also J.I.A. Champion, *The Pillars of Priestcraft Shaken: The Church of England and its Enemies, 1660–1730* (Cambridge: Cambridge University Press, 1992); Clement Hawes, *Mania and Literary Style: The Rhetoric of Enthusiasm from the Ranters to Christopher Smart* (Cambridge: Cambridge University Press, 1996); Shaun Irlam, *Elations: the Poetics of Enthusiasm in Eighteenth-Century Britain* (Stanford: Stanford University Press, 1999); Jon Mee, *Romanticism, Enthusiasm, and Regulation: Poetics and the Policing of Culture in the Romantic Period* (New York: Oxford University Press, 2003). Isabel Rivers, *Reason, Grace and Sentiment: A Study of the Language of Religion and Ethics in England, 1660–1780*, 2 vols. (Cambridge: Cambridge University Press, 2005); David Sorkin, *The Religious Enlightenment: Protestants, Jews and Catholics from London to Vienna* (Princeton: Princeton University Press, 2008).

3. Such, Marx argues, were "just so many . . . methods of primitive accumulation. They conquered the field for capitalistic agriculture, incorporated the soil into capital, and created for the urban industries the necessary supplies of free and rightless proletarians," Karl Marx, *Capital: A Critique of Political Economy, Volume 1*, trans. Ben Fowkes (New York: Penguin, 1992), 895.

4. Max Weber, *The Protestant Ethic and the Spirit of Capitalism*, trans. Talcott Parsons (New York: Routledge, 2001), 119.

5. Ibid., 18.

6. See, for example, Christopher Hill, *The World Turned Upside Down: Radical Ideas During the English Revolution* (London: Penguin, 1984). Or, from a different angle: Keith Thomas, *Religion and the Decline of Magic: Studies in Popular Beliefs in Sixteenth and Seventeenth Century England* (New York: Oxford University Press, 1997); Hans Blumenberg, *The Legitimacy of the Modern Age*, trans. Robert M. Wallace (Boston: MIT Press, 1983).

7. A particularly instructive instance of the debate around enthusiasm is Hobbes's engagement with Boyle over the production of knowledge. Both parties accused the other of grounding a concept of social order in an enthusiastic theory of substance and knowledge. On this critical debate, see Steve Shapin and Simon Schaffer, *Leviathan and the Air-Pump: Hobbes, Boyle, and the Experimental Life* (Princeton: Princeton University Press, 1985).

8. Mandeville's claims about the passion of consumption are so well known that they do not bear repeating here. However, his appreciation for the efficiency of the division of labor is worth another look, and I will do so in chapter 2.

9. John Locke, *An Essay Concerning Human Understanding* (New York: Oxford, 1975), 699.

10. Ibid., 43.

11. Hegel, *The Phenomenology of Spirit*, trans. A.V. Miller (New York: Oxford University Press, 1979), 16.

12. Ibid., 25.

13. Locke, *Essay*, 151.

14. It seems Tristram has anticipated this claim: ". . . did you ever read such a book as Locke's *Essay upon the Human Understanding?* . . . I will tell you in three words what the book is. – It is a history-book, Sir . . . of what passes in a man's own mind," Laurence Sterne, *Tristram Shandy*, ed. Howard Anderson (New York: Norton, 1960), p. 61.

15. Michael McKeon, *The Origins of the English Novel, 1600–1740* (Baltimore: Johns Hopkins University Press, 1987), 40.

16. Ibid.

17. J.G.A. Pocock, *Barbarism and Religion, Vol 2, Narratives of Civil Government* (Cambridge: Cambridge University Press, 2001), 225.

18. Ibid., 227.

19. David Hume, *The History of England: From the Invasion of Julius Caesar to the Revolution in 1688* (Chicago: University of Chicago Press, 1975), 145–46.

20. Francis Hutchinson, *A Short View of the Pretended Spirit of Prophesy* (London, 1708), 39; Quoted in Michael Heyd, *'Be Sober and Reasonable': The Critique of Enthusiasm in the Seventeenth and Eighteenth Centuries* (New York: Brill, 1995), 170.

21. Heyd, *'Be Sober,'* 170.

22. Ibid., 211.

23. As Jonathan Israel notes, historians have "frequently emphasized the importance in European cultural and intellectual history of the exodus of Huguenot *erudits*," and "their forming a European diaspora in exile with its intellectual and publishing headquarters in the Netherlands." Israel, *Radical Enlightenment* and *Enlightenment Contested: Philosophy, Modernity, and the Emancipation of Man, 1670–1752* (New York: Oxford, 2009), 575.

24. Hillel Schwartz, *The French Prophets: The History of a Millenarian Group in Eighteenth-Century England* (Berkeley: University of California Press, 1980).

25. Narcissus Luttrell, *A Brief Historical Relation of State of Affairs from September 1678 to April 1714,* vol 6, (Oxford: Oxford University Press, 1865), p. 188. I thank David Alvarez for assistance with this citation.

26. Samuel Parker, *Censora Temporum: The Good or Ill Tendencies of Books, Sermons, Pamphlets, etc., Impartially consider'd, in a Dialogue Between Eubulus and Sophronius* (London: Printed for H. Clements, for the Month of August 1708); Edward Fowler, *Reflections upon a Letter Concerning Enthusiasm, to my Lord *****. In Another Letter to a Lord.* (London: Printed for H. Clements, 1709); Mary Astell, *Bartlemy Fair, Or An Enquiry After Wit: in which Due Respect is had to a Letter Concerning Enthusiasm, to my Lord ***** (London: Printed for R.W. Wilkin, 1709).

27. Anthony Ashley Cooper, Third Earl of Shaftesbury, *Characteristics of Men, Manners, Opinions, Times*, ed. Lawrence E. Klein (Cambridge: Cambridge University Press, 1999), 15. All references to Shaftesbury will be drawn from this volume unless indicated otherwise.

28. Shaftesbury, "Letter," *Characteristics,* 20. For more on the usage of John 4:1—"test the spirits to see whether they are from God"—by a range of authors, from John Tillotson to Calvin, see Heyd, *'Be Sober and Reasonable',* 176–185.

29. Shaftesbury, *Characteristics,* 22.

30. Ibid., 9.

31. In this, Shaftesburian enthusiasm participates in what Jon Mee, following Foucault, has described as the modern development of regulatory norms. Rather than regard enthusiasm as the increasingly abjected object of a secularizing society, Mee proposes that enthusiasm grounds an ever-more relevant set of discursive regulatory norms—norms by which aesthetics and politics tested their own limits. Mee argues that enthusiasm forms the basis for modern, "secular" self-management. The seeds of this regulatory discourse, I offer, were first sown by Shaftesbury. See Jon Mee, *Romanticism, Enthusiasm, and Regulation: Poetics and the Policing of Culture in the Romantic Period* (New York: Oxford University Press, 2003).

32. See John Guillory's field-defining account of moral philosophy in *Cultural Capital: The Problem of Literary Canon Formation* (Chicago: University of Chicago Press, 1993). For Guillory, moral philosophy "gestates" the two discourses of political economy and aesthetics: moral philosophy is their prehistoric shell, and the range of concepts that it considers within its ken seems impossible to us now because moral philosophy presumed to discuss economic matters—which forever after would be the province of political economy—in aesthetic terms.

33. Champion, *The Pillars of Priesthood Shaken,* 23–24.

34. Shaftesbury, "Letter," *Characteristics,* 27–28.

35. John Guillory, *Cultural Capital,* 305.

36. J.B. Schneewind, *The Invention of Autonomy: A History of Modern Moral Philosophy* (Cambridge: Cambridge University Press, 1998), 305. For Schneewind, the order that is revealed is ultimately that of the classical republic. In this sense, Schneewind, like Pocock, traces a Harringtonian model in Shaftesbury's Whigghism. This is in some contrast to theorists like Poovey, Guillory, and Caygill who understand Shaftesbury's theory of social order in terms of early attempts to envision and legitimate the modern liberal state.

37. Shaftesbury, "The Moralists," *Characteristics*, 274-275.

38. Ibid., 277.

39. Poovey *History of the Modern Fact*, 178.

40. Mary Poovey, *A History of the Modern Fact*, (Chicago: University of Chicago Press, 1998), 178.

41. For Fredric Jameson, a "cognitive map" enables "a situational representation on the part of the individual subject to that vaster and properly unrepresentable totality which is the ensemble of society's structures as a whole." Jameson, *Postmodernism, or the Cultural Logic of Late Capitalism* (Durham: Duke University Press, 1992), 51. Literary historians such as Guillory and Poovey argue that cognitive mapping was central to the experience of eighteenth-century subjectivity, and focus on the ways in which the newly capitalist world system was cognitively indigestible. This claim has been elaborated by Jonathan Kramnick, and it has been developed extensively by Terry Eagleton. See Jonathan Kramnick, *Making the English Canon: Print Capitalism and the Cultural Past, 1700–1770* (Cambridge: Cambridge University Press, 1999) and Terry Eagleton, *The Ideology of the Aesthetic* (New York: Wiley, 1991).

42. Suvir Kaul, *Poems of Nation, Anthems of Empire: English Verse in the Long Eighteenth Century* (Charlottesville: University of Press of Virginia, 2000). See especially Kaul's extension of James Chandler's argument about historicism to the early eighteenth century "historical poem" (p. 276).

43. Benedict Anderson, *Imagined Communities: Reflections on the Origin and Spread of Nationalism,* rev. ed. (London: Verso, 2006);

44. Ian Balfour, *The Rhetoric of Romantic Prophesy* (Palo Alto: Stanford University Press, 2002); Dipesh Chakrabarty, *Provincializing Europe: Postcolonial Thought and Historical Difference* (Princeton: Princeton University Press, 2000); James Chandler, *England in 1819: The Politics of Literary Culture and the Case of Romantic Historicism* (Chicago: University of Chicago Press, 1998); Pocock, *Barbarism and Religion*. Pocock points out that, later in the century, Hume would take up enthusiasm again as a way of organizing the transitions of history. See also, Clifford Siskin, *The Historicity of Romantic Discourse* (New York: Oxford University Press, 1999). Hobbes' crucial early work, for example, *A True Ecclesiastical History from the Time of Moses to the Time of Martin Luther*, marries historical inquiry with biblical tradition. More than this, the foundational nature of religion to theorizing civic order is also to be found in the oft-neglected second half of the *Leviathan,* which contains a strenuous argument against the inflated power of the clergy, and a lauding of the theological liberties of the Interregnum. On this topic, see Champion's discussion of Hobbes in *Pillars of Priestcraft*.

45. John Locke, *The Reasonableness of Christianity* (London, 1696), 111.

46. On the emergence of the "fact," see Poovey, *History of the Modern Fact*.

47. Francis Fullwood, *A Parallel: Wherein it Appears that the Socinian Agrees with the Papist* (London, 1673), Quoted in Champion, 112.

48. Anon., *Discovery of 29 Sects here in London* (London, 1641). The text lists, as well, Seekers, Familiasts, Adamites and Anti-Scriptarians. As David Cressy argues, "sectarianism represented the antinomian nightmare of an ecclesiastical polity slipping into chaos," David Cressy, *England on Edge: Crisis and Revolution* (Oxford: Oxford University Press, 2006), 227.

49. Nabil I. Matar, *Islam in Britain, 1558–1685* (Cambridge: Cambridge University Press, 1998), 48.

50. Linda Colley, *Captives: Britain, Empire, and the World, 1600–1850* (New York: Anchor Press, 2004); Barbara Fuchs, *Mimesis and Empire: The New World, Islam, and European Identities* (Cambridge: Cambridge University Press, 2004); Nabil I. Matar, *Turks, Moors, and Englishmen in the Age of Discovery* (New York: Columbia University Press, 2000); Daniel Vitkus, *Piracy, Slavery, and Redemption: Barbary Captivity Narratives from Early Modern England* (New York: Columbia University Press, 2001).

51. See, esp., Matar's readings of Charles Blount and George Sandys in *Islam in Britain*.

52. Perhaps the most well known satire of the discursive portability of Islamic enthusiasm is Jonathan Swift's *Discourse on the Mechanical Operation of the Spirit*, about which much has been said.

53. Henry Stubbe, *An Account of the Rise and Progress of Mahometanism, with the Life of Mahomet: And a Vindication of Him and His Religion from the Calumnies of Christians*, ed. Hafiz Mahmud Khan Shairani (London: The Islamic Society, 1911), 81.

54. John Harrison and Peter Laslett, *The Library of John Locke* (Oxford: Oxford University Press, 1971).

55. Stubbe, *An Account*, 105.

56. Ibid., 1.

57. See Israel, *Radical Enlightenment* and *Enlightenment Contested: Philosophy, Modernity, and the Emancipation of Man, 1670–1752* (New York: Oxford, 2009), and Margaret Jacob, *The Radical Enlightenment: Pantheists, Freemasons and Republicans* (Boston: Allen and Unwin, 1981).

58. This allegory became particularly strained around the concept of commerce and its typological congealment in the figure of the Jews—a topic to which I will devote much more commentary in the second half of what follows.

59. Ian Baucom, *Specters of the Atlantic: Finance Capital, Slavery, and the Philosophy of History* (Durham: Duke University Press, 2005), 150.

60. Giovanni Arrighi, *The Long Twentieth Century: Money, Power, and the Origins of our Times* (London: Verso, 1994), 6.

61. Ibid., 79.

62. See J. G. A. Pocock, *Virtue, Commerce, and History: Essays on Political Thought and History, Chiefly in the Eighteenth Century* (Cambridge: Cambridge University Press, 1985).

63. See Adam Sutcliffe, *Judaism and Enlightenment* (Cambridge: Cambridge University Press, 2005), 68–73 for a fuller account of the variety of Deist accounts of Egyptian and Hebrew history.

64. Sutcliffe links Toland's Spinozist deprivileging of the Jewish past—made possible "by providing a purely secular, historicist reading of the Old Testament"—with his seemingly contradictory interest in James Harrington. Toland published an edition of Harrington's works, "including such intensely Hebraic texts as *The Art of Lawgiving*." Ibid., 199.

65. Shaftesbury, "Letter," *Characteristics*, 16.

66. Ibid., 15.

67. Ibid., 28.

68. Ibid., 360. For much more on priestcraft and the history of religious discourses within the seventeenth and eighteenth centuries, see Rivers, *Reason, Grace and Sentiment: A Study of the Language of Religion and Ethics in England, 1660–1780*, vol. 2, *Shaftesbury to Hume* (Cambridge: Cambridge University Press, 2005).

69. Sutcliffe, *Judaism and Enlightenment*, 200.

70. John Toland, *Letters to Serena* (New York: Garland Publishing, 1976), 174.

71. Joel Reed, introduction to *The Agreement of the Customs of the East-Indians With Those of the Jews*, by John Toland (New York: AMS Press, 1999), ix.

72. Shaftesbury, "Miscellany II," *Characteristics,* 360.

73. Sutcliffe, *Judaism and Enlightenment*, 154.

74. Ibid., 205.

75. Shaftesbury, "Miscellany II," *Characteristics,* 44–45.

76. This argument is made at length in the Introduction to *Provinicalizing Europe*.

77. Robin Blackburn, *The Making of New World Slavery: From the Baroque to the Modern, 1492–1800* (London: Verso, 1998), 513.

78. Fredric Jameson, *The Political Unconscious: Narrative as a Socially Symbolic Act* (Ithaca: Cornell University Press, 1982), 28.

79. Karl Marx, introduction to the *Contribution to the Critique of Hegel's Philosophy of Right*, in *The Marx-Engels Reader,* ed. Robert C. Tucker, (New York: Norton, 1978), 18.

80. Under feudalism, wealth is produced through the extraction of *surplus* product; under the wage-labor system of capitalism, surplus value is extracted by paying laborers a wage that is not equivalent to the value of the product that they produce. See David Harvey, "Production and Consumption, Demand and Supply and the Realization of Surplus Value" in *The Limits to Capital* (New York: Verso, 1999).

81. Karl Marx, *Capital: Volume 1*, trans. Ben Fowkes (New York: Penguin, 1992), 874-875.

82. Adam Smith, *An Inquiry into the Nature and Causes of the Wealth of Nations* (London: Penguin, 1979), 437.

83. Karl Marx, *Grundrisse: Foundations of Political Economy*, trans. Martin Nicolaus (New York: Random House, 1973), 45.

Chapter 2

1. Anon., "Satyr on the French Prophets," 1707.

2. Karl Marx, *Capital: A Critique of Political Economy, Volume 1,* trans. Ben Fowkes (New York: Penguin, 1992), 742.

3. Narcissus Luttrell, *A Brief Historical Relation of State of Affairs from September 1678 to April 1714* vol 6, (Oxford: Oxford University Press, 1865), p. 188.

4. See Derek Hirst, *The Representative of the People?* (Cambridge: Cambridge University Press, 1975), 175–194. The language of the Act makes clear that it is designed to abort unauthorized mass gatherings of whatever sort: "An act against tumults and disorders, upon pretense of preparing or presenting public petitions or other addresses to his majesty or the parliament . . . Be it enacted . . . that no person or persons whatsoever shall from and after the first of August, 1661, solicit, labour, or procure the getting of hands or other consent of any persons above the number of twenty or more to any petition, complaint, remonstrance, declaration, or other addresses to the king, or both or either houses of parliament . . ." Charles II, *Statutes of the Realm.*, V., st. 1, c.5, 308:13.

5. Elie Marion, *Prophetical Warnings of Elias Marion, heretofore one of the commanders of the Protestants, that had taken arms in the Cévennes* (London, 1707), 189.

6. See Georgia Cosmos, *Huguenot Prophesy and Clandestine Worship in the Eighteenth Century: The Sacred Theatre of the Cévennes* (London: Ashgate, 2005).

7. The tight connections between the French Protestants in London and the Philadelphians, for example, evince this shift. See Paula McDowell, "Enlightenment Enthusiasms and the Spectacular Failure of the Philadelphian Society," *Eighteenth-Century Studies* 35, 4 (Summer 2002): 515–533.

8. John Lacy, *A Relation of the Dealings of God to his Unworthy Servant, John Lacy* (London: 1708).

9. See Catherine Randall, *From a Far Country: Camisards and Huguenots in the Atlantic World* (Athens: University of Georgia Press, 2009), and Ann Taves, *Fits, Trances, & Visions: Experiencing Religion and Explaining Experience from Wesley to James* (Princeton: Princeton University Press, 1999). Also Clarke Garrett, *Spirit Possession and Popular Religion from the Camisards to the Shakers* (Oxford: Oxford University Press, 1999).

10. Lacy, *A Relation.*

11. David Lemmings, ed., *The British and Their Laws in the Eighteenth Century* (Rochester: Boydell Press, 2005), 8–9.

12. Christopher Hill, *The Century of Revolution, 1603–1714* (New York: Routledge, 1980), 265.

13. David Lieberman, *The Province of Legislation Determined: Legal Theory in Eighteenth-Century Britain* (Cambridge: Cambridge University Press, 2002), 26–27.

14. Matthew Bacon, *Abridgement of Law and Equity* 3rd Edition. (1768), iii. 292, cited in Lemmings, 63.

15. J.M. Beattie, *Crime and the Courts in England, 1660–1800* (Princeton: Princeton University Press, 1986).

16. Douglas Hay, "Legislation, Magistrates, and Judges: High Law and Low Law in England and the Empire," in Lemmings, *The British and Their Laws,* 74.

17. See, J.M. Beattie, *Policing and Punishment in London, 1660–1750: Urban Crime and the Limits of Terror* (New York: Oxford University Press, 2003). David Lemmings calculates that, "In the eighteenth century...King's Bench dealt with less than 1 percent of Staffordshire cases, the judges at assize jury trials about 11 percent, judges at quarter session jury trials about 5 percent, and justices out of sessions about 83 percent," (63).

18. It should also be noted that the Toleration Act of 1689 protected the Camisards (and other Dissenters) from being prosecuted as enthusiasts, but did not protect them from common law prosecution for blasphemy and sedition.

19. Francis Bacon, "Of Seditions and Troubles," in *Francis Bacon: The Major Works* (New York: Oxford University Press, 2008), 366.

20. Beattie, *Crime and the Courts*; Peter Linebaugh, *The London Hanged: Crime and Civil Society in the Eighteenth Century* (London: Verso, 2003); Douglas Hay, Peter Linebaugh, John G. Rule, E.P. Thompson, and Cal Winslow eds., *Albion's Fatal Tree: Crime and Society in Eighteenth-Century England* (New York: Penguin, 1975); Frank McLynn, *Crime and Punishment in Eighteenth Century England* (New York: Routledge, 1989).

21. Edward Coke, preface to part 2 of *The Reports of Sir Edward Coke in English in Thirteen Parts Complete*, 7 vols., (London, 1738), ii–iii.Volume 1.

22. Ibid., vol 3, 7a.

23. Matthew Hale, *History of the Common Law in England* (orig. London, 1713, London: 1820, printed for Henry Butterworth), 3.

24. Ibid., 4.

25. J.G.A. Pocock, *The Ancient Constitution and the Feudal Law: A Study of English Historical Thought in the Seventeenth Century* (Cambridge: Cambridge University Press, 1982).

26. Alan Cromartie, *Sir Matthew Hale: Law, Religion and Natural Philosophy* (Cambridge: Cambridge University Press, 1995), 108.

27. See Bradin Cormack's reading of Sir John Davies for an excellent recent complication of the terms of this debate. Bradin Cormack, *A Power to do Justice: Jurisdiction, English Literature, and the Rise of Common Law, 1509–1625* (Chicago: University of Chicago Press, 2007).

28. William Walwyn, *Juries justified or a word of correction to Mr. Henry Robinson,* 1651, quoted in Cromartie, *Sir Matthew Hale,* 109. Michael McKeon, too, has disputed Pocock's analysis of historicism on the grounds that not only was common law becoming demystified by the mid-seventeenth century, but historicity did not move by the kind of instinctive logic of the common-law mind. Rather, for McKeon, historicity was a highly mediated form of knowledge. See Michael McKeon, *The Origins of the English Novel, 1600–1740* (Baltimore: Johns Hopkins University Press, 1987).

29. Henry Home, Lord Kames, *Remarkable Decisions in the Court of Session* (1728; Edinburgh: Bell and Bradfute, and W. Creech, 1799, *Essays Upon Several Subjects in Law* (Printed by R. Fleming: Edinburgh, 1732), and *Principles of Equity* (1760; Edinburgh: Bell and Bradfute, 1825).

30. Shaftesbury, "Sensus Communis," *Characteristics*, 29.

31. Ibid., 30.

32. Geoffrey Gilbert, *The Law of Evidence* (Dublin 1754; repr., New York and London: The Garland Press, 1979). The Camisards were tried both at the French Court at Savoy and at the Court of Queen's Bench.

33. Geoffrey Gilbert, *The Law of Evidence* (Dublin, 1754), quoted in Barbara Shapiro, "Religion and the law: evidence, proof and matter of fact," in Norma Landau, ed., *Law, Crime and English Society, 1660–1830* (Cambridge: Cambridge University Press, 2002), 188.

34. Immanuel Kant, *Critique of the Power of Judgment*, trans. Paul Guyer (Cambridge: Cambridge University Press, 2001), 125.

35. John Guillory, *Cultural Capital: The Problem of Literary Canon Formation* (Chicago: University of Chicago Press, 1993), 304.

36. Ibid.

37. Ibid., 304-305.

38. John Dryden, *Of Dramatic Poesy*, ed. Thomas Arnold (Cambridge: Clarendon Press, 1903), I: 98. On the distinction between wit and judgment, see Ronald Paulson, "Dryden and the Energies of Satire," in *The Cambridge Companion to John Dryden,* ed. Stephen N. Zwicker (Cambridge: Cambridge University Press, 2004); and Roger Lund, "Wit, Judgment, and the Misprisions of Similitude," *Journal of the History of Ideas* 65, no. 1 (January 2004): 53–74.

39. Shaftesbury, "Sensus Communis," *Characteristics*, 33.

40. John Barrell, "'The Dangerous Goddess': Masculinity, Prestige, and the Aesthetic in Early Eighteenth-Century Britain," *Cultural Critique,* 12 (Spring 1989), 104.

41. Ibid., 103.

42. Shaftesbury, "Sensus Communis," *Characteristics*, 30.

43. Ibid.

44. Ibid., 31.

45. Lawrence Klein, "The Third Earl of Shaftesbury and the Progress of Politeness," *Eighteenth-Century Studies* 18, 2 (Winter 1984–1985): 197.

46. Ibid., 200.

47. Ibid. See also Klein's introduction to *Characteristics,* 25, where he states explicitly, that, in "light of Shaftesbury's political colors," the critique of antiquarianism "must be read as a cultural rebellion against a Tory (and possibly Jacobite) Country and a High-Flying Church" in favor of the high culture of Whig aristocrats and the market culture of the city.

48. Klein, "The Third Earl of Shaftesbury," 214.

49. Ibid., 31.

50. Slavoj Zizek, *The Ticklish Subject: The Absent Centre of Political Ontology* (London: Verso, 1993), 13.

51. Shaftesbury, "Miscellany IV," *Characteristics*, 420–421.

52. Zizek, *The Ticklish Subject*, p. 13.

53. In making this argument, I am indebted to the crucial hesitation Michael McKeon introduces into the traditional teleologies of eighteenth-century studies. As McKeon has argued, our tendency to project a coherent "middle class" onto eighteenth-century texts, and to read these text as symptomatic of that class, often obscures the material conditions—and *contradictions*—of eighteenth-century culture more than it illuminates these conditions. See McKeon, introduction to *Origins*.

54. See my discussion of Locke in chapter 1.

55. See Klein's note on 325 of *Characteristics*.

56. Shaftesbury, "Sensus Communis," *Characteristics*, 31.

57. Ibid.

58. The classic text on Mandeville and the political tradition is Albert O. Hirschman, *The Passions and the Interests: Political Arguments for Capitalism Before its Triumph* (Princeton: Princeton University Press, 1977).

59. Bernard Mandeville, The *Fable of the Bees*, or Private Vices, Public Benefits 5th ed. (J. Tonson: London, 1728), Volume II, 244.

60. Ibid., Vol. I, 400.

61. Ibid., 381.

62. See Poovey, *History of the Modern Fact*.

63. Shaftesbury, "Sensus Communis," *Characteristics*, 31.

64. Perhaps Shaftesbury sought to point out that the courts—although prohibited (by the Toleration Act) from ruling on enthusiasm directly—continued to attempt to adjudicate religious matters.

65. Ibid., 32.

66. Ibid.

67. Lieberman, *The Province of Legislation*, 123.

68. Shaftesbury, "Sensus Communis," *Characteristics, 32*.

69. John Locke, *Further Considerations Concerning Raising the Value of Money* (1823), 5:198.

70. For the former position, see Thomas Laqueur, "Crowds, Carnival and the State in English Executions, 1604–1868," in A.L. Beier, David Cannadine, and James M. Rosenheim, eds. *The First Modern Society: Essays in Honor of Lawrence Stone* (Cambridge: Cambridge University Press, 1989), 305–355. For the latter, see Peter Linebaugh, *The London Hanged*, xix–xx.

71. Bernard Mandeville, *An enquiry into the causes of the frequent executions at Tyburn.* (originally published in nos. 128-133 of *The British Journal*, February 27-April 3, 1725; republished by the Augustan Reprint Society, 1964, pp. 18–20).

72. Ibid., 20–22.

73. See, e.g. Hal Gladfelder, *Criminality and Narrative in Eighteenth-Century England: Beyond the Law* (Baltimore: Johns Hopkins University Press, 2001), 168–171 on Mandeville.

74. Henry Fielding, Leader no. 25, in *Covent Garden Journal,* March 28, 1751. See also, Henry Fielding, *An Enquiry into the Causes of the Late Increase of Robbers* (A. Millar: London, 1751).

75. Mandeville, *An Enquiry*, 53.

76. Ibid., 27.

77. This is documented in Linebaugh, *The London Hanged,* in Beattie, *Crime and Courts*, and in EP Thompson, *Whigs and Hunters: the Origin of the Black Act (London: Pantheon, 1976).*

78. James Fitzjames Stephens, *General View of the Criminal Law of England* (London: 1853), 181.

79. Ibid., 182.

80. Benno Teschke, *The Myth of 1648: Class, Geopolitics, and the Making of Modern International Relations* (London: Verso, 2003), 249–250.

81. *The Weekly Entertainer; or Agreeable and Instructive Repository* 25 (1795): 393–394.

82. Fredric Jameson, "The Vanishing Mediator, or Max Weber as Storyteller," in *The Ideologies of Theory: Essays 1971–1986,* vol. 2, *Syntax of History* (Minneapolis: University of Minnesota Press, 1989), 25.

83. Angelo Restivo gives a useful summary of the concept. The vanishing mediator, he argues, occurs when the "historical situation is radically 'open,' and [it] . . . vanishes as

soon as the new order establishes itself and . . . then erases any notion of contingency, i.e., that it could have turned out any other way." Angelo Restivo, *The Cinema of Economic Miracles: Visuality and Modernization in the Italian Art Film* (Durham: Duke University Press, 2002), 23.

84. Recently Etienne Balibar has taken up Jameson's vanishing mediator to describe the constitution of contemporary global politics and statecraft. Balibar's redaction of the vanishing mediator demonstrates this concept's enduring power to spotlight the intimacy of developing capitalism with its residual formations. According to Balibar, "Jameson attempts to show that, at the core of Weber's interpretation of the process of modernization or rationalization (which is basically a European or Eurocentric process), but also of certain Marxian descriptions of revolutionary processes in the past, there lies a dialectical figure that can be called the figure of the vanishing mediator. This is the figure (admittedly presented in speculative terms) of a *transitory* institution (or force, community, or spiritual formation) that creates the conditions for a new society and a new civilizational pattern, albeit in the horizon and the vocabulary of the past, and by rearranging the elements inherited from the very institution that has to be overcome. This is notoriously the case of the "protestant ethic," centered around the paradoxical notion of a "worldly asceticism," or an immanent spiritual calling, where a twist in the meaning of religious beliefs in fact prepares the subjective conditions for a secularized behavior of individuals and the whole society, the emergence of "rational" economic subjects. It creates, therefore, the conditions for its own suppression and withering away. But without this "vanishing" mediation no transition from the old to the new fabric of society would have been possible." Etienne Balibar, "Europe: Vanishing Mediator?," in *We, the People of Europe? Reflections on Transnational Citizenship* (Princeton: Princeton University Press, 2003), 234–235.

85. Jameson, "The Vanishing Mediator," 26.

86. See, for example, Janet Jakobsen and Ann Pellegrini, *Love the Sin: Sexual Regulation and the Limits of Religious Tolerance* (Boston: Beacon Press, 2003).

Chapter 3

1. See, for example, Eric Foner, *The Story of American Freedom* (New York: Norton, 1998).

2. George-Louis LeClerc, Compte de Buffon, *Natural History: General and Particular,* trans. William Smellie (London, 1781), 12:xiii

3. Neil Smith, *Uneven Development: Nature, Capital, and the Production of Space* (Athens: University of Georgia Press, 2008), 67.

4. Ibid., 67-68.

5. On the adaptation of Bakhtin's concept of the chronotope to the history of Atlantic production, see Paul Gilroy, *The Black Atlantic: Modernity and Double Consciousness* (Cambridge: Harvard University Press, 1993).

6. R. Voitle, *The Third Earl of Shaftesbury* (Baton Rouge: Louisiana State University Press, 1984), 177.

7. David Harvey, *The Limits to Capital*, (London: Verso, 2001), 1st ed., 343.

8. Ibid., 344.

9. Shaftesbury, Public Records Office, 30/24/19/2, 48-49; cited in Voitle, *The Third Earl,* 178.

10. Theodore Allen, *The Invention of the White Race*, vol. 2, *Racial Oppression and Social Control* (New York: Verso, 1994), 10.

11. See, for example, Eric Hobsbawn and George Rudé, *Captain Swing* (New York: Phoenix Press, 2001); K.D.M. Snell, *Annals of the Labouring Poor: Social Change and Agrarian England, 1660–1900*, (Cambridge: Cambridge University Press, 1987); Michael Perelman,

The Invention of Capitalism: Classical Political Economy and the Secret History of Primitive Accumulation (Durham: Duke University Press, 2000).

12. Marx, *Capital: Volume 1*, 885.

13. Voitle, *The Third Earl*, 178.

14. Shaftesbury, Public Records Office 30/24/19/2, 82; quoted in Voitle, *The Third Earl*, 190.

15. Allen, *The Invention of the White Race*, 10.

16. John Locke, "Draft of a Representation Containing a Scheme of Methods for the Employment of the Poor. Proposed by Mr. Locke, the October 26th, 1697," in John Locke, *Political Writings*, David Wooten ed. (London, 1993), 449, 452.

17. Bernard Mandeville, *An Essay on Charity and Charity-Schools*, (London: Bathurst, Nourse, Carnan, Newbery, 1795), 179.

18. Christopher Hill, *The Century of Revolution 1603–1714* (New York: Routledge, 2001), 221.

19. Shaftesbury, Public Records Office 30/24/19/2, 100–101; cited in Voitle, *The Third Earl*, 185.

20. This move, too, Voitle describes as evidence of Shaftesbury's "goodwill."

21. Allen, *The Invention of the White Race*, 11. It is for this reason that we might here recall some of the conclusions of chapter 1, and regard what is traditionally termed "secularization" within a somewhat larger context of the proletarianization of England. Allen differentiates the British colonial approach from the Spanish, because Spain did not encourage colonization at the same rate as the English, in large part due to the entrenched aristocracy in Spain, and their resistance to losing their tenants (See Theodore Allen, *The Invention of the White Race*, 4).

22. Voitle, *The Third Earl of Shaftesbury*, 175.

23. Hans Blumenberg, *The Legitimacy of the Modern Age*, trans. Robert M. Wallace (Boston: MIT Press, 1983).

24. Blumenberg, *Legitimacy of the Modern Age*, 10.

25. Shaftesbury, Public Records Office 30/24/19/2, 110; cited in Voitle, *The Third Earl*, 191.

26. Molly McLain and Alessa Ellefson, "A Letter from Carolina, 1688: French Huguenots in the New World," *William and Mary Quarterly* 64, no. 2 (April 2007): 382.

27. See Robert Olwell, *Masters, Slaves, and Subjects: The Culture of Power in the South Carolina Low Country, 1740–1790* (Ithaca: Cornell University Press, 1998), and Bertrand Van Ruymbeke, *From New Babylon to Eden: The Huguenots and Their Migration to Colonial South Carolina* (Columbia: University of South Carolina Press, 2006).

28. McLain and Ellefson, "A Letter from Carolina," 387.

29. Robin Blackburn, *The Making of New World Slavery: From the Baroque to the Modern, 1492–1800* (London: Verso, 1998), 67–68.

30. John Locke, *Fundamental Constitutions of Carolina*, in John Locke, *Political Essays*, ed. Mark Goldie (Cambridge: Cambridge University Press, 1997), 170.

31. Cited in Blackburn, *The Making of the New World Slavery*, 258.

32. Blackburn, *The Making of New World Slavery, 258*.

33. Allen, *The Invention of the White Race*, 14.

34. Allen, *Invention of the White Race*, 12–13.

35. This strategy of fomenting tribal rivalries is well documented as a strategy for developing the Indian slave trade. Allen documents its "grossest development" in the Carolinas in *The Invention of the White Race*, 44.. See also Francis Jennings, *The Invasion of America: Indians, Colonialism, and the Cant of Conquest* (New York: Norton, 1975), and Michael Leroy Oberg, *Dominion and Civility: English Imperialism and Native America, 1585–1685* (Ithaca: Cornell University Press, 1999).

36. Shaftesbury, Public Records Office 30/24/22/2, 24; cited in Voitle, *The Third Earl*, 57; 27 May, 1691.

37. Allen, *The Invention of the White Race*, 44.

38. See Allen, *The Invention of the White Race*, 43. Also, Jon Parmenter, "After the Mourning Wars: The Iroquois as Allies in the Colonial North American Campaign, 1676–1760." *William and Mary Quarterly* 64, no. 1 (January 2007).

39. Shaftesbury, "Sensus Communis," *Characteristics*, 37.

40. Ibid.

41. Ibid., 38.

42. As Giovanni Arrighi points out, "All variants of mercantilism had one thing in common: they were more or less conscious attempts on the part of territorialist rulers to *imitate* the Dutch, to become themselves capitalist in orientation as the most effective way of attaining their own power objectives. The Dutch had demonstrated on a world scale . . . that under favorable circumstances the systematic accumulation of pecuniary surpluses could be a far more effective technique of political aggrandizement than the acquisition of territories and subjects." Arrighi, *The Long Twentieth Century: Money, Power, and the Origins of Our Times* (London: Verso, 2010), 140–141. Arrighi notes this concentration of capitalist power, and the "fusion of state and capital" as a particularly aggressive phenomenon in England's early eighteenth century as it took over from Holland as the leading "regime of accumulation."

43. Benno Teschke, *The Myth of 1648: Class, Geopolitics, and the Making of Modern International Relations* (London: Verso, 2003), 259.

44. Ibid., 250.

45. Marx, *Capital, Volume 3*, 444.

46. Teschke, *The Myth of 1648*, 207

47. Ibid., 3.

48. Shaftesbury, "Sensus Communis," *Characteristics* 39.

49. Ibid., (emphasis added).

50. John Lacy, *The Scene of Delusions, by the Reverend Mr. Owen of Warrington, at his own Earnest Request, Considered and Confuted, By One of the Modern Prophets; and (as it proves) partly by Himself* (Knutsford: S. Noble and Mr Leach, 1722), 6.

51. Shaftesbury, "Sensus Communis," *Characteristics*, 39.

52. Ibid.

53. Ibid.

54. Ibid., 40.

55. Ibid.

56. Roxann Wheeler, *The Complexion of Race: Categories of Difference in Eighteenth-century British Culture* (Philadelphia: University of Pennsylvania Press, 2000), 7.

57. See Lynn Festa, *Sentimental Figures of Empire in Eighteenth-Century Britain and France* (Baltimore: Johns Hopkins University Press, 2006), 62. Also, Ruth Hill, "Towards an Eighteenth-Century Transatlantic Critical Race Theory" *Literature Compass* 3 (2006); G. Gabrielle Starr, *Lyric Generations: Poetry and the Novel in the Long Eighteenth Century* (Baltimore: Johns Hopkins University Press, 2004).

58. Festa, *Sentimental Figures*, 7.

59. On this point, see also David Theo Goldberg, *The Racial State* (New York: Wiley-Blackwell, 2002).

60. The critical literature on this subject is large. See for example Meg Armstrong, "The Effects of 'Blackness': Gender, Race, and the Sublime in the Aesthetic Theories of Burke and Kant," *The Journal of Aesthetics and Art Criticism,* 54, 3 (Summer 1996); Alan Liu, *Wordsworth: The Sense of History* (Palo Alto: Stanford University Press, 1989); Srinivas Aravamudan, *Tropicopolitans: Colonialism and Agency, 1688–1804* (Durham: Duke University Press,

1999); Henry Louis Gates, Jr., "Writing 'Race' and the Difference It Makes," in "'Race,' Writing, and Difference," ed. Henry Louis Gates, Jr., special issue, *Critical Inquiry* 12, 1 (1985): 1–20; and especially, Paul Gilroy's discussion of Cheselden and Burke in *The Black Atlantic*, 9–10.

61. Edmund Burke, *A Philosophical Inquiry into the Origin of Our Ideas of the Sublime and the Beautiful with an Introductory Discourse on Taste* (New York: Oxford Unversity Press, 2009), p. 131.

62. Aravamudan, *Tropicopolitans,* 194.

63. David Harvey, *The New Imperialism* (New York: Oxford University Press, 2003), 115.

64. Harvey, *The New Imperialism,* 109–112.

65. Giovanni Arrighi, "Spatial and Other Fixes of Historical Capitalism," *Journal of World-Systems Research* 10, no 2 (2004): 528–529.

66. Chandler, *England in 1819*, 127.

67. See Raymond Williams, *Marxism and Literature* (New York: Oxford University Press, 1978), 112.

68. Ibid., 40.

69. Shaftesbury, "Sensus Communis," *Characteristics,* 40.

70. Ibid., 40–41.

71. Ibid., 41.

72. Ibid.

73. In order to develop a sense of the stakes of such uneven development, we may refer to Trotsky's original formulation of the concept: "A backward country assimilates the material and intellectual conquests of the advanced countries. But this does not mean that it reproduces them slavishly, reproduces all the stages of their past. The theory of the repetition of historical cycles rests upon an observation of the orbits of old pre-capitalistic cultures, and in part upon the first experiments of capitalist development. . . . The privilege of historic backwardness permits, or rather compels, the adoption of whatever is ready in advance of any specified date, skipping a whole series of intermediate stages. Savages throw away their bows and arrows for rifles all at once, without travelling the road which lay between those two weapons in the past. The development of historically backward nations leads necessarily to a peculiar combination of different stages in the historic process." Leon Trotsky, *The History of the Russian Revolution*, trans. Max Eastman (New York: Pathfinder Press, 2001), 1:26–27.

74. Shaftesbury, "Sensus Communis," *Characteristics,* 42.

75. Ibid., 43.

76. Karl Marx, *Grundrisse: Foundations of Political Economy*, trans. Martin Nicolaus (New York: Random House, 1973),19.

Chapter 4

1. Raymond Williams, *The County and the City* (New York: Oxford University Press, 1975), 7.

2. John Lacy, *Ecclesiastical and Political History of Whig-land, of late years, to which are pre-fixed, the characters of a late ecclesiastical historian, and of the author of this history* (London, 1714), 41.

3. In making this argument, I am building on the excellent and foundational work around "radical enlightenment" done by Margaret Jacob and Jonathan Israel. My point of departure has to do with the status of empiricist knowledge for these critics. Both Jacob and Israel demonstrate the ways in which religious thought partakes of empiricist methods—and thus is bound up with an Enlightenment drive to specify, not only the contours of the natural world, but of the supernatural as well. In some contrast, I want to elucidate the ways in which

religious knowledges, in articulating a critique of empiricism, anticipate and coordinate with a kind of materialist approach is likewise invested in historicizing the forces and relationships underpinning modern social order.

4. Cited in Michael McKeon, *The Origins of the English Novel, 1600–1740* (Baltimore: Johns Hopkins University Press, 1987), 79.

5. See especially the standout volume, *Philosophy, Science, and Religion in England, 1640–1700*, eds. Richard Kroll, Richard Ashcraft, and Perez Zagorin (Cambridge: Cambridge University Press, 1992).

6. For a thorough description of the application of "enthusiasm" to natural science, see Michael Heyd, *'Be Sober and Reasonable': The Critique of Enthusiasm in the Seventeenth and Eighteenth Centuries* (New York: Brill, 1995), particularly Chapter 5. As Heyd points out, "Descartes was not the only new philosopher labeled 'enthusiast' . . . The new experimental philosophers were similarly characterized as enthusiasts by their opponents. Enthusiasm indeed implied a claim to have access to divine secrets not only through direct divine inspiration but—as in the case of the alchemists—by the study of nature" (144).

7. Williams, *The Country and the City*, 7–8.

8. Ibid., 48–49.

9. Ibid., 51.

10. Maximillion Misson, *Le Théâtre sacré des Cévennes* (London: 1707).

11. David Harvey, *The New Imperialism*, (New York: Oxford University Press, 2003), 145.

12. Henri Lefebvre, *The Production of Space*, trans. Donald Nicholson-Smith (Malden, MA: Blackwell Publishing, 1991), 27.

13. Michael Cobb, *God Hates Fags: The Rhetorics of Religious Violence* (New York: NYU Press, 2006); Ann Pellegrini and Janet Jakobsen, *Love the Sin: Sexual Regulation and the Limits of Religious Tolerance* (Boston: Beacon Press, 2003).

14. Misson, *Le Théâtre sacré*, iii.

15. John Lacy, *The Prophetical Warnings of John Lacy, Esq.; Pronounced under the Operation of spirit; and Faithfully taken in Writing, when they were spoken* (London: Printed for B. Bragge at the Raven in Pater-Noster Row, 1707), iii.

16. Ibid. xi.

17. Heyd, *'Be Sober and Reasonable'*, 172.

18. See Heyd, "Shaftesbury and the Limits of Toleration Concerning Enthusiasm," in *"Be Sober and Reasonable,"* 211–240.

19. A very reasonable redaction of the often-convergent political views of Whigs and Tories in the later eighteenth century may be found in Isaac Kramnick, *Republicanism and Bourgeois Radicalism: Political Ideology in Late-Eighteenth Century England and America* (Ithaca: Cornell University Press, 1990).

20. Lacy, *Ecclesiastical History*, 45.

21. John Lacy, *The Prophetical Warnings*, 7.

22. Ibid., 49.

23. Lacy, *Ecclesiastical History*, 49–50.

24. Gerrard Winstanley, "The True Levellers Standard Advanced: Or, the State of Community Opened, and Presented to the Sons of Men," in Gerrard Winstanley, *Law of Freedom and Other Writings* (New York: Penguin, 1973).

25. Henri Lefebvre, *The Production of Space*, 7.

26. Ibid., 8–9.

27. Lacy, *Ecclesiastical and Political History*, 43.

28. Karl Marx, "The Value Form," Appendix to *Capital: Volume. 1*, 1st edition, trans. Mike Roth and Wal Suchtingin in *Capital and Class*.4 (Spring 1978), 142.

29. Nicolas Fatio, "On the Cause of Gravity," cited in Charles Domson, *Nicolas Fatio de Duillier and the Prophets of London* (New York: Arno Press, 1981), 154.

30. Cited in Horst Zehe, *Die Gravitationstheorie des Nicolas Fatio de Duillier* (Gerstenberg: Hildesheim, 1980).

31. See, for example, Matthew R. Edwards, ed., *Pushing Gravity: New Perspectives on LeSage's Theory of Gravitation* (Montreal: Apeiron Press, 2002).

32. Peggy Aldrich Kidwell, "Nicolas Fatio de Duillier and *Fruit-Walls Improved*: Natural Philosophy, Solar Radiation, and Gardening in Late Seventeenth Century England," *Agricultural History* 57, 4 (October 1983): 403.

33. Fatio, "On the Cause of Gravity," cited in Domson, *Nicolas Fatio*, 154.

34. Georges LeSage, *The Newtonian Lucretius,* republished in the *Annual Report of the Board of Regents of the Smithsonian Institution* for the year ending June 30, 1898, proposition XXX, 158.

35. N. Fatio de Duillier to Christiaan Huygens, no. 2465, 24 Juin 1687, in *Oeuvres complètes de Christiaan Huygens*, vol. 1, *Correspondance [de Christiaan Huygens], 1685–1690* (La Haye: M. Nijhoff, 1901), 168–169: "It [the *Principia*] deals generally with the Clockwork of the Heavens; of the way in which circular movements made in a liquid environment spread to the entire environment; of gravity and of a force which he supposes is in all the planets in order to attract each other . . . This treatise which I saw only a part of is most certainly very beautiful, and filled with a great number of beautiful propositions." (Translation by Aaron Winslow.)

36. Fredric Jameson, *Valences of the Dialectic* (London: Verso, 2009), 593.

Chapter 5

1. Daniel Bensaïd, *Marx For Our Times: Adventures and Misadventures of a Critique*, trans. Gregory Elliott (London: Verso, 2002), 35. Bensaid is citing Benjamin here, from *The Arcades Project,* 388–389 K1, 2.

2. Irlam, Hawes and Mee have been our working exempla for this tendency throughout the book, largely because these authors work specifically on enthusiasm.

3. Shaun Irlam, *Elations: the Poetics of Enthusiasm in Eighteenth-Century Britain* (Stanford: Stanford University Press, 1999) 119.

4. Ibid.

5. Ibid., 133.

6. As will be familiar to many readers, Swiftian enthusiasm has been primarily explored in *The Tale of a Tub, The Mechanickal Operation of the Spirit*, and the Academy of Lagado's enthusiastic "projectors" who believe they can directly alchemize excrement into food in Book Three of *Gulliver's Travels.* Swift's poetry—particularly the scatological poems—have also been received as commentaries on enthusiasm's lure.

7. Ronald Paulson, "Swift, Stella, and Permanence," *English Literary History* 27, 4, (December 1960).

8. See, for example, Fredric Bogel, *The Difference Satire Makes: Rhetoric and Reading from Jonson to Byron* (Ithaca, Cornell University Press, 2001); Denis Donoghue, introduction to *Jonathan Swift: A Critical Introduction* (Cambridge: Cambridge University Press, 1969); Dustin Griffin, *Satire: A Critical Reintroduction* (Lexington: University Press of Kentucky, 1994); and Hugh Kenner, *The Counterfeiters: An Historical Comedy* (Champaign: Dalkey Archive Press, 1968).

9. Warren Montag, *The Unthinkable Swift: The Spontaneous Philosophy of a Church of England Man* (London: Verso, 1994), 123.

10. Theodor Adorno, *Negative Dialectics*, trans. E.B. Ashton (New York: Continuum, 1973), 5.

11. Simon Jarvis, *Adorno: A Critical Introduction* (New York: Polity Press, 1998), 165.

12. This is a debate that has been well redacted in Bogel. By way of some departure from that debate, I want to argue that the "Shower" poem's enthusiastic "paddling in" waste is a cipher for the agglomerations of institutional forces and historical change sedimented in the form of the poem itself.

13. Montag, *The Unthinkable Swift*, 119.

14. *Tale of a Tub* in *The Essential Writings of Jonathan Swift*, eds. Claude Rawson and Ian Higgins (Norton: New York, 2010), 144.

15. Michael McKeon, *The Origins of the English Novel, 1600–1740* (Baltimore: Johns Hopkins University Press, 1987), 74.

16. John Brewer, *The Sinews of Power: War, Money and the English State, 1688–1783* (Cambridge: Harvard University Press, 1990). xvii.

17. Sean Moore, "Devouring Posterity: A Modest Proposal, Empire, and Ireland's 'Debt of the Nation,'" *PMLA* 122, 3 (May 2007): 680.

18. Carole Fabricant, *Swift's Landscape* (Notre Dame: University of Notre Dame Press, 1995), 75.

19. See, for example, Laura Brown, "Reading Race and Gender: Jonathan Swift," *Eighteenth-Century Studies* 23, no. 4 (Summer 1990).

20. McKeon, *Origins*, 90.

21. Fabricant, *Swift's Landscape*, 1.

22. McKeon, *Origins*, 120.

23. Ibid., 495.

24. Ibid.

25. *The Essential Writings of Jonathan Swift*, lines 1–18.

26. Ibid., "Stella's Birthday," l. 36.

27. Alexander Pope, *"Windsor Forest," Poetry and Prose of Alexander Pope*, ed. Aubrey Williams (Boston: Houghton Mifflin, 1969).

28. McKeon, *Origins*, 76.

29 *The Essential Writings of Jonathan Swift*, "Stella's Birthday," (ll 55–56).

30. Montag, *The Unthinkable Swift*, 110.

31. Bogel, *The Difference Satire Makes*, 9–10.

32. Bogel, *The Difference Satire Makes*, 10.

33. Hegel. *The Logic of Hegel* from *The Encyclopaedia of the Philosophical Sciences* 3rd ed., trans. William Wallace (Oxford: Oxford University Press, 1975), § 7.

34. Theodor W. Adorno, *Hegel: Three Studies*, 2nd ed., trans. Shierry Weber Nicholsen (Cambridge: MIT Press, 1999), 59.

35. Jarvis, *Adorno*, 167.

36. Fredric Jameson, *Valences of the Dialectic* (London: Verso, 2009), p. 371.

37. For an illuminating reading of secularization and the Stella poems, see Helen Deutsch's claim that: "Swift conceives of his union with his addressee as a kind of secular incarnation of the holy feast." Helen Deutsch, "Swift's Poetics of Friendship," in Claude Rawson, ed. *Politics and Literature in the Age of Swift: English and Irish Perspectives* (Cambridge: Cambridge University Press, 2010), 151. In proposing this incarnation of the friend (Stella) as a site of futurity and futural-thinking, Deutsch highlights the problem of secular and theological forms of poetic mediation, albeit from a slightly different angle than our own. Insofar as the Stella poem appears to be about the impossible rendering of the mortal body in poetic form, critics have been tempted to range their readings of the poem around that relationship (body of Stella/body of poem). But Deutsch reminds us that this apparently immediate relationship

(however vexed or impossible) between body of person and body of poem, is itself the mediation of another relation that conditions both body and poem: the social one. We may understand this triple-jointing as a very satisfying and productive Swiftian reminder that the poem's anguished limnings of the always-receding possibility of the transubstantiation of Stella's body into poetic form do not only spectacularly and poignantly fail but, in doing so these limnings point to the social field within which the body/language relation is itself embedded and made legible. In Deutsch's argument that Stella's friendship represents the possibility and potentials of futurity, we see that what appears to be an unresolved circling around the difficulty of linguistic memorialization, turns out to engrave the contours of the social field within the form of the poem itself. In this way, the question of the past and its future resonance becomes less a progressive, narrative problem—what Swift might call the impossible "long schemes of life"—and rather a different kind of social temporality etched within the lyric form itself.

38. Roncaglia, 5. Quoted in Moore, "Devouring Posterity," 689.

39. Moore, "Devouring Posterity," 689.

40. Laura Brown, *Fables of Modernity: Literature and Culture in the English Eighteenth Century* (Ithaca: Cornell University Press, 2003), 23.

41. Fabricant, *Swift's Landscape*, 56-57.

42. Ibid., 72.

43. Swift, *The Run Upon the Bankers*, 1–4; quoted in Fabricant, *Swift's Landscape,* 72.

44. Jonathan Swift, "The Bubble," in *The Poems of Jonathan Swift*, ed. Harold Willams (Oxford: Clarendon Press, 1958), ll.23-25.

45. Fabricant, *Swift's Landscape,* 73.

46. Ibid.

47. *The Prose Works of Jonathan Swift,* 14 vols., ed. Herbert Davis (Oxford: Basil Blackwell, 1939–1968), quoted in Fabricant, *Swift's Landscape.* 84–85.

48. Marx, *Capital: Volume 1*, 799.

49. See Eric Rothstein, "'Ideal Presence' and the 'Non Finito' in Eighteenth-Century Aesthetics," *Eighteenth-Century Studies* 9, 3 (1976).

50. See Nina Schlief, "Dreaming about the Renaissance," in *Art History* 26, no. 5 (December 2003).

51. Rothstein, "'Ideal Presence,'" 307.

52. Rothstein, "Ideal Presence," 309.

53. Swift, "A Description of a City Shower," *The Essential Writings of Jonathan Swift*, eds. Claude Rawson and Ian Higgins (Norton: New York, 2010).

54. Rothstein argues that "Kames's position . . . was widely held by critics of eighteenth century poetry and painting; second, that this position probably represents real reading behavior, as well as a fashion of expressing enthusiasm; third, that although it does not entail the non-finito, it does entail an imaginative expansion of the text; and fourth that this expansion . . . was by no means exclusively visual" (310).

55. *An Act of Common Council: together with certain orders, rules, and directions touching the paving and cleansing the streets, lanes and common passages with the city of London, and liberties thereof: and other things relating thereunto* (Printed by Andrew Clark: London, 1671).

56. Ibid.

57. See, for example, Nicholas Rogers, "Policing the Poor in Eighteenth-Century London: the Vagrancy Laws and their Administration," *Social History,* XXIV, 47 (May, 1991).

58. *Act of Common Council for Paving and Cleansing, and Preventing Nuisances in the Streets of London and the Liberties Thereof,* (London, 1671), microfilm.

59. David Harvey, "The Urban Process Under Capitalism, a Framework for Analysis," in *Urbanization and Urban Planning in Capitalist Society*, ed. Michael J. Dear and Allen John Scott (New York: Routledge, 1981), 111.

60. "[O]verinvestment [in infrastructure] . . . is in relation solely to the needs of capital and has nothing to do with the real needs of people which inevitably remain unfulfilled," Ibid., 101.

61. I wish to thank Aaron Winslow for his provocations on the commodity form in "The City Shower," graciously articulated in my graduate seminar in 2007.

62. Marx, *Capital,* Volume I, 128.

63. Moishe Postone, *Time, Labor and Social Domination: A Reinterpretation of Marx's Critical Theory* (Cambridge: Cambridge University Press, 1993), 144.

64. Marx, *Capital: Volume 1*, 1st ed. (1867), 224; quoted in Postone, 144.

65. In England, the institution of beer making was undergoing an enormous transition, as the peasantry, newly without land, were no longer able to brew at home, as they traditionally had, and proto-industrial brewing had found a relatively swift foothold domestically. The transformation of beer-production represented quite vividly the larger-scale reconfigurations of English production, and because beer registered very quickly and thoroughly the expropriation of the land from the people, the result was that beer production was rapidly standardized, and beer prices became one of the most stable commodity prices in the early eighteenth-century. See Fernand Braudel, *Capitalism and Material Life, 1400–1800* (New York: Harper Collins, 1973).

66. Marx, *Capital Volume 1*, 132.

67. It will come as no surprise that it is labor's double character that supports the doubleness of the commodity form: "commodity-producing labor is both particular—as concrete labor, a determinate activity that creates specific use-values—and social general, as abstract labor, a means of acquiring the goods of others" (Postone, *Time, Labor,* 151).

68. Marx, *Capital,* Volume I, 165.

69. Ibid., 164-165. Indeed, the stink of doubleness achieves its strongest waft, shall we say, when we consider that the entire poetic exchange is grounded in the pairing of service work with an imported good.

70. Both are subjected to what Marx describes as the "trinity formula," the overarching field of production that manages to cover its own tracks, as it were, to obscure the labor by which commodities are produced: "Capital-profit (or better still capital-interest), land-ground-rent, labor-wages, this economic trinity as the connection between the components of value and wealth in general and its sources, completes the mystification of the capitalist mode of production, the reification of social relations, and the immediate coalescence of the material relations of production with their historical and social specificity" (Marx, *Capital: Volume 3,* 968–969).

71. Harvey, *Urbanization.*

72. This phenomenon has been most thoroughly described in John Brewer, Neil McKendrick and J.H. Plumb, eds., *The Birth of a Consumer Society: The Commercialization of Eighteenth-Century England* (Bloomington: Indiana University Press, 1982), and in the essays contained in John Brewer and Roy Porter, eds., *Consumption and the World of Goods* (London: Routledge, 1993).

73. Harvey, http://titanus.roma1.infn.it/sito_pol/Global_emp/Harvey.htm

74. I thank my colleague Steven Harris for his comments delivered during a faculty seminar meeting, encouraging this connection.

75. *Capital: Volume 1,* 143

76. Moishe Postone,"Theorizing the ContemporaryWorld,"%3cahref=http://209.85.207.104/search?q=cache:owokmbKvhgQJ:platypus1917.home.comcast.net/~platypus1917/postone_brennerarrighiharvey2006.pdf+david+harvey+falling+rate+of+profit&hl=en&ct=clnk&cd=6&gl=us&;client=safari

77. *The Essential Writings of Jonathan Swift*, "City Shower," ll. 33-34.

78. Peter Linebaugh, "(Marxist) Social History and (Conservative) Legal History: A Reply to Professor Langbein," *New York University Law Review* 60 (1985), 222.

79. Cited in Brendan O'Hehir, "Meaning of Swift's 'Description of a City Shower,'" *ELH*, Vol. 27, no. 3 (September 1960), 204.

80. Ibid.

81. Linebaugh, "(Marxist) Social History," 241.

82. *The Essential Writings of Jonathan Swift*, "City Shower," ll.61–63.

83. Trevor Bark, review of *The London Hanged*, *Capital and Class* 22 (June 2007), 489.

84. Marx, *Capital: Volume 1*, 896.

85. *An Act of Common Council* (1671).

86. Laura Brown, *Fables of Modernity: Literature and Culture in the English Eighteenth Century* (Ithaca: Cornell University Press, 2001), 43.

87. The continuation of these claims are quite helpful in determining the relationship between the literary study of consumption and that of production and development: "We have, secondly, to consider the consumption aspect. Here we can usefully distinguish between the consumption of revenues by the bourgeoisie and the need to reproduce labour power. The former has a considerable impact upon the urban process, but I shall exclude it from the analysis because consideration of it would lead us into a lengthy discourse on the question of bourgeois culture and its complex significations without revealing very much directly about the specifically capitalist form of the urban process. Bourgeois consumption is, as it were, the icing on top of a cake which has as its prime ingredients capital and labour in dynamic relation to each other. The reproduction of labour power is essential and requires certain kinds of social expenditures and the creation of a consumption fund," Harvey, "Urban Process," 103.

INDEX

29 Sects, 53
abstraction
   commodity, 80, 84, 125–126, 143, 173, 175–176
   Derrida on, 24, 143
   land rent, 102
   Marx on, 4–6, 23–24
   religion as form of, 4–6, 185n3
accumulation. *See* capital accumulation
accumulation by dispossession, 28, 132, 172, 177–178
   See also Harvey, David
Adorno, T.W., 153–154, 163
Allen, Theodore, 102, 107–108
Aravamudan, Srinivas, 118
Arrighi, Giovanni, 15–17, 53, 109, 119, 200n42
Astell, Mary, 43
Atlantic circuit, 4, 25, 28, 98, 101, 105, 108–110, 124, 126

Bacon, Francis, 69–70
Bacon, Matthew, 68
Bacon's Rebellion, 107, 109
Badiou, Alain, 21
Balfour, Ian, 48
Balibar, Etienne, 198n82
Barrell, John, 77
Bartholomew Fair, 54–55
Baucom, Ian, 15–16, 19, 53, 188n27

beer production, transformation of, 206n64
Benjamin, Walter, 149
Bensaïd, Daniel, 149, 152
Blackburn, Robin, 17–18, 58, 100, 107, 172
Blackmore, Richard, 169
Blount, Charles, 50
Blumenberg, Hans, 104
Bogel, Fredric, 162
Brewer, John, 17, 155, 183
Brown, Laura, 29, 160, 183–184
Buffon, George-Louis LeClerc, Compte de, 98, 166
Burke, Edmund, *see* race *entries*.

Calamy, Edmund, 91
Camisards
   and developments in English political geography, 98, 119, 131–132, 135–136
   and enthusiasm, 26, 28, 64–68
   and Fatio, 128, 145, 151
   as focal point for debate about state power, 58, 65, 68
   and geography, 98–99, 131
   and Lacy, 131–132, 135–136
   and millenarianism, 54, 66
   and prophesy, 67, 113, 121, 128–136
   "Satyr" on, 66
   Shaftesbury on, 41–43, 54–55, 58, 85, 121
   trial of, 42–43, 64–68, 74–75, 110, 137

Cavilier, Jean, 64, 134
  See also Camisards
capitalism. *See* capital accumulation
capital accumulation
  and colonialism, 111–112, 137–138
  and commodity form, 22–25, 144–148
  contradictions of, 4–9, 22–26
  and country and city, 166–167
  and criminalization of non-wage-labor, 178, 181
  Egypt as metaphor for, 56–59, 63
  and enthusiasm, 12, 68, 121, 131, 152–153
  fugitive form of, 17–22
  hermeneutics of, 14–17, 93–94
  and London sanitation reform, 170–173, 184
  and mediation, 155–157
  origins of, 34–36, 60–63
    See also primitive accumulation
  and religious transformation, 36
  and race, 116–117
  Shaftesbury on, 92–94, 126
  transatlantic, 15, 27, 53–54, 97, 99–101, 104, 107, 109–110, 112
  and transformation of English national identity, 71
  and Weber, 34–36
  and world history, 58–59
  and waste, 176–177, 180–181, 184
capital punishment. *See* executions, public
Carolina Colony, 27–28, 100, 105–107, 109
Cartesian *cogito*. *See* Descartes
Chakrabarty, Dipesh, 13, 58
Champion, J.I.A., 45
Chandler, James, 48, 100–101, 120–121
Charles II, 69, 105, 194n4
civil theology, 50–51
cognitive mapping, 47, 192n41
Coke, Edward, 26, 71–72
Collins, Anthony, 57
colonialism, 27, 101, 155, 176–177
commodity
  contradictions of, 21–22
  Derrida on, 24
  doubleness of, 173–174, 206n66
    See also Swift *entries*
  exchange of, 23, 163, 175, 179–180
  fetishism, 23–25, 143–144
  land as, 102–103
  Marx on, 22–24, 173, 179

  and Shaftesbury, 59, 102
  and Swift, 173–176, 178–181, 184
commodity form. *See* commodity
common sense, 110–113, 126
Coppe, Abiezer, 10
Craig, John, 128
Cromartie, Alan, 73
Cromwell, Oliver, 139–140

Derrida, Jacques, 23–24, 143
Descartes, René, 79–81, 128, 147, 202n6
dialectic, 3–5, 21–23, 97, 101, 124, 150–155, 163
Dissenters, 6, 41, 86
Donatello, 168
Dryden, John, 76, 182

East India Company, 49
Edict of Nantes, 26, 41, 131
empiricism, 38, 48, 52, 111, 127–129, 140, 201–202n3
enchantment, 7, 8, 13, 93
  See also enthusiasm
enclosure, 17, 58, 101, 166, 168
English Civil War, 7, 10, 15, 41–42, 139
enthusiasm
  Camisards. *See* Camisards *entries*
  and capital accumulation. *See* capital accumulation *entries*
  and civil society, 10, 41–42
  as civic virtue, 52
  and commodity, 22–25
  critique of enthusiasm, 7, 37–40
    See also Locke *entries*
  as discourse, 5, 13, 70
  and economic transformation, 14, 40
  and empiricism, 36–39, 48
    See also Locke *entries*
  and ethics, 44
  and English Civil War, 10
  and existential commitment, 20
  and feminine fantasy, 159
  and geography, 28, 98–99
  and historicity, 6–9, 12–14, 19–22, 31–34, 39, 40–41, 169
  and Islam. *See* Islam *entries*
  as judgment, 44
  Lacy on. *See* Lacy, John, *entries*
  and law. 68–71
  and legislative transformation, 97, 141

and mediation, 163–164
as metadiscourse, 36, 52
and millenarianism, 7, 41
and moral philosophy. *See* moral philosophy *entries*
passion as a form of, 7, 10–11, 13, 45–47
and politics, 7
Platonic form of, 9
and poetry. *See* poetry *entries*
prophesy. *See* prophesy *entries*
and religion. *See* religion *entries*
and Romanticism, 11
and sedition laws, 64–65
secularization. *See* secularization *entries*
Shaftesbury on. *See* Shaftesbury *entries*
and social order, 36–39, 42–44
and sovereignty. *See* sovereignty *entries*
and space, 128–148, 152
and state, 20, 97, 188–189n38
and time, 38–39
and social whole, 44–47
and Swift. *See* Swift *entries*
and universalism, 9–10, 45–47, 151–152
See also Shaftesbury *entries*
Wit. *See* wit *entries*
enthusiastic transport, 113–114, 119–120
See also enthusiasm
executions, public, 55, 67–68, 86–89, 140–141, 181

Fabricant, Carole, 153–154, 166–167
Fage, Durand, 64, 134
See also Camisards
Fatio de Duillier, Nicolas
and Camisards, 42, 64–66
and enthusiastic physics, 144–146, 169
LeSage on, 146
and Newton, 147
"On the Cause of Gravity," 128, 144–145
poetic form of writings, 144–146
and space, 145–147
See also Camisards
feelings, 4, 129
Festa, Lynn, 116
Fielding, Henry, 88–89
Free Mart, 88–90
freemarket. *See* market

geography
critical, 183
critique of empirical geography, 127–131, 140, 144, 147
political, 28, 120, 153
Gilbert, Geoffrey, 75
Glorious Revolution, 49, 112
Guillory, John, 45, 47, 75

Hale, Matthew, 26, 71–73, 90
Harvey, David, 16, 101–102, 118–119, 132, 172–173, 176–177, 184, 207n86
See also accumulation by dispossession
Harvey, William, 176
Hawes, Clement, 147, 162
Hay, Douglas, 69
Hegel, G.F.W., 5, 21–22, 38, 163
Heyd, Michael, 41, 135
Hill, Christopher, 52, 103
Hill, Ruth, 116
history. *See* historicism
historicism, 25, 28, 33, 39, 99, 47–48, 52–53, 57–58, 63, 68, 74, 83–84, 97, 99, 127, 150–151, 160–161
historicization. *See* historicism
Hobbes, Thomas, 48, 124–125, 190n7
Huguenots, 42, 106, 191n23
Hume, David, 10, 26, 34, 40
Hutchinson, Francis, 41

Inquisition, 84–86, 90, 110
international relations, 17, 35, 111–112, 121
Irlam, Shaun, 10, 121 147, 150–151
Islam
as allegory of the birth of British economic might, 53
and anti-trinitarianism, 50
anxieties surrounding conversion to, 49
and British expansion into the Atlantic, 53
and English Civil War, 49
and enthusiasm, 48–51
as figure of past, 53
and orientalism, 50
practiced in early modern London, 49
and trade with Britain, 49
Israel, Jonathan, 52, 191n23

Jager, Colin, 20
Jameson, Fredric, 19, 59, 93, 147, 164, 192n41
Jarvis, Simon, 154, 163

Kames, Lord (Home, Henry), 74, 169
Kant, Immanuel, 20, 21, 75, 80–81, 147, 189n39
Kaul, Suvir, 47, 160
Klein, Lawrence, 47, 56, 77–78, 81
Knights Templar, 122–123

Labor
   accumulation by dispossession, 132, 137, 176–177
   Adam Smith on, 62, 98–99
   and capital accumulation, 17, 27, 102, 118–119
   and colonialism, 100–106, 116–117
   creation of reserve army of, 166–170, 172–174
   division of, 35, 83–85, 90, 175
   and empiricism, 38
   Locke on, 38
   Mandeville on, 83–85, 89–90
   philosophical labor, 9
   and poetry, 150–179
   and primitive accumulation, 60–62
   and race, 14, 16, 28, 100–101, 107, 121
   Shaftesbury on, 59, 85, 90, 103–105
   and Swift, 149–179
   theory of value, 59
   and uneven development, 120
   wage, 4, 18
Labor-power, 17, 163
Lacy, John
   colonialism, 138–140
   critique of empiricist geography, 28, 42, 127–133, 134–135, 138, 140, 144
   A Cry from the Desart, 28, 142, 131–136, 140
   An Ecclesiastical and Political History of Whig-Land, 28, 127, 136–137, 141–143
   excess, 140
   enthusiasm, 37, 91, 113–114, 136, 129, 140–141, 144
   nationalism, 138–141
   prophesy, 114, 135–136
   Prophetical Warnings, 133, 138–139
   supernatural science, 128–129
   value, 144
Laqueur, Thomas, 87
law
   common, 26, 68–76, 86, 110, 112, 114, 124, 195n27
   expansion of, 68
   positive, 86, 91–92
   statute, 14, 25–26, 66–67, 71–72, 91, 172, 177
   See also Shaftesbury
Lefebvre, Henri, 132–133, 140
Lemmings, David, 66
   See also Camisards
LeSage, George, 146–147
Levellers, 41, 65
liberalism, 17, 34, 43, 62, 88, 121, 144
Lieberman, David, 68
Linebaugh, Peter, 87, 97 172, 180–181
Locke, John
   association with Islam, 50
   belief in necessity of death penalty to state sovereignty, 87
   critique of enthusiasm, 10, 36–39
   empiricism, 37–39
   Essay Concerning Human Understanding, 34, 37–39
   Fundamental Constitutions of Carolina, 26–27, 100, 105–107
   Reasonableness of Christianity, 48
   and revelation, 37–38
   Shaftesbury's critique of, 81, 103
Louis XIV, 41
   See also Edict of Nantes
Louis-Lesage, George, 128
Lucretius, 55–56
Lyotard, Jean-Francois, 21

Macaulay, Aulay, 168
Mandeville, Bernard
   on division of labor, 82–84
   Fable of the Bees, 67–68, 82–83
   An enquiry into the causes of the frequent executions at Tyburn, 68, 88
   and the market, 82
   on public executions, 88–89
Marion, Elie, 42, 64
   Prophetical Warnings of Elias Marion, 64–65
   See also Camisards
market, 10, 26–28, 35, 62, 78–79, 82–85, 92–94, 100–102, 112, 115–119, 143–144, 176, 183, 196n46
Marx, Karl
   on accumulation, 16, 112, 126
   accumulation as Mosaic law, 70

on commodity, 173, 175, 179
on commodification of land, 102
Capital, 5, 35, 61, 64, 102, 167, 174–175
Contribution to the Critique of Hegel's Philosophy of Right, 60
critique of Adam Smith, 62
Grundrisse, 62, 126, 143
"On the Jewish Question," 4
on religion, 4–5, 59–60, 186n7
political economy as narrative, 62
on primitive accumulation, 60–63, 97, 167, 182, 190n3
Theses on Feuerbach, 5
trinity formula, 206n69
on value, 143
Matar, Nabil, 49
McKeon, Michael, 39, 155–156, 159
mediation, 21–22, 25, 29, 98, 110, 155–161, 163–164, 184, 198, 204n37
Mee, John, 11
Michelangelo, 168
modernity, 3–4, 7–8, 11–13, 24, 27, 33–34, 47, 61, 70, 105, 132–133, 135, 150–151
modernities, alternative, 186–187n17
Montag, Warren, 153–154, 162
Moore, Sean, 155, 165
moral philosophy
  and colonialism, 27–28, 100
  and commercial society, 33–34
  And discourse, 187n21, 191n32
  and enthusiasm, 14, 33–34
  and legal theory, 67, 71
  and limits of jurisdiction, 71
  as model of historical change, 8–9
  and racialization, 100
  and secularization, 33–34, 63, 76
  Shaftesbury on, 100, 124–126
  and sovereignty, 67, 126
  totalizing tendency of, 45–47

nature, production of, 98–99, 129, 133
natural science, 127–129, 202n6
Newton, Isaac, 66, 128, 145–147
Nicholson, Colin, 183

O'Hehir, Brendan, 181
over production, 118, 176–177
over accumulation. *See* capital accumulation and waste
Owen of Warrington, Reverend, 113

Parker, Samuel, 43
Paulson, Ronald, 152
periodization, 3, 6, 12, 26, 34, 47–48, 50, 58–59, 63
Pinch, Adela 183
Pocock, J.G.A., 10, 26, 40, 52, 73
poetry
  Augustan, 6, 151–153
  and enthusiasm, 145–153, 155–156, 205n53
  and history, 28–29, 150–151, 156
  and religion, 149–151
  and Romantic sublime, 11
  as vehicle for expressing early modern change, 8–9, 18, 160, 162, 183
  See also Swift *entries*
poetics. *See* poetry.
Poovey, Mary, 26, 46–47, 83–84
Pope, Alexander, 158, 182–183
Postone, Moishe, 173–174
primitive accumulation, 26, 34–35, 59–63, 97–102, 132, 136–137, 164, 188n29, 200n42
  and Camisards, 98
  and colonization, 104–105
  and Lacy, John, 137
  and London infrastructure development, 165–167
  Marx on, 60–62, 190n3
  and moral philosophy, 60–61
  and secularization, 59, 63, 104–105
  and Shaftesbury, 61, 63, 104
  And Swift, 164–165
production, capitalist, 16–18, 22–26, 60–62, 69, 79, 83–85
prophesy
  Camisard, 54, 121, 131, 133–136
  enthusiastic, 6–7, 93–94
  and Islam, 50, 53
  Locke on, 38
  as mediator of historical change, 93
  See also vanishing mediator.
  and Shaftesbury, 66–68, 93–94
  and bureaucracy, 66–67
Protestantism, 35, 38, 93, 138, 145
public sphere, 70, 78–79
Pynchon, Thomas, 188n35

race
  and free market ideology, 115–117

race (*countined*)
  and moral philosophy, 27, 100
  and nationalism, 117
  and secularization, 116
  and transatlanticism, 117
  and Burkean sublime, 117–118
  and management of labor, 107–110
radical enlightenment, 201–202n3
Reed, Joel, 57
religion
  civil, 7–8, 50
  and commodity form. *See* Marx on Religion.
  Enlightenment critique of, 5
  enthusiastic, 25–26, 49, 149
  Hegel's critique of, 21
  and Hobbes, 192n44
  Marx on, 3–6, 23–24, 60, 185n3, 186n7
  and modernity, 12
  monotheistic, 50–52
  and poetry, 149–150
  and science, 128
  Shaftesbury on, 54–55, 104, 110
  and slavery, 107
  Stubbe on, 51–52
  as threat to state, 42
  Toland on, 57
residual and emergent social forms, 25, 53, 101, 103, 109–110, 119–124
Roach, Joseph, 183
Roncaglia, Catherine, 164–165
Rosenheim, Edward , 162
Rothstein, Eric, 168, 205n53

Schneewind, J. B., 46
Schwartz, Hillel, 42
secularism. *See* secularization
secularization
  of enthusiasm, 22–23, 29, 47–48
  of fanaticism , 70
  as fantasy, 186n9
  Locke on, 37–39
  Marx on, 5
  and modernity, 33–34
  as a narrative, 3–4, 7–8, 25, 33–34, 37, 47–48, 57–59, 63, 93, 104–105, 121, 144, 149–151, 187n18
  and poetry, 149–151
  and primitive accumulation, 104–105
  and proletarianization, 199n21
  and public sphere, 70
  and race, 116
  Shaftesbury on, 43, 47, 57–59, 63, 93–94, 104–105
  and sovereignty, 68–70, 94
  studies, 3, 12–14
  thesis. *See* secularization as a narrative.
  and uneven development, 121
Shaftesbury, Anthony Ashley Cooper, Third Earl of
  on accumulation, 57–61
  and aesthetics, 77
  on aristocracy, 77
  and Camisards, 41–43, 54–55, 58, 85, 121
  on the Cartesian cogito, 79–80
  Characteristics of Men, Manners, Opinions, Times, 41, 42, 45–47, 53, 100, 122, 124, 110
  Christ as model enthusiast, 54
  and civil society, 41
  common sense, 112–113, 124
  common law, 74–76, 82, 90–92, 110, 112, 114
  and critique of common law courts, 75
  and critique of millenarianism, 41
  and critique of Lockean empiricism, 111
  and critique of priestcraft, 56
  on credit, 82
  on custom as superstition, 74–75
  and enthusiasm, 87, 92, 110, 113–114, 123–124, 63, 121–122, 160, 53–54, 93, 191n31
  and enthusiastic transport, 113–114, 119
  and excess, 77–78, 85, 134
  and exchange, 56
  on Egypt as allegory for secularization, 56–58
  on ethics, 81
  and Hermeticism, 56–58
  historicism, 122
  and Indian policy, 108–109
  and inquisitorial law, 86, 110, 121
  and concept of the *Je ne sais quoi*, 46, 56, 111
  and Judaism, 54–56
  on the Kantian subject, 80–81
  and the law, 45–46, 67, 122–124
  "A Letter Concerning Enthusiasm," 34, 41, 42–44, 56–57, 70, 92

Letters of, 102–103, 108–110
and 'likenesses', 56
on the Magi, 122–124
on Mosaic law, 36, 54–57, 92
and physiognomy, 115
and periodization, 58
and politeness, 47, 78–79
and plantation management, 102–104
on public executions as form of state power, 86–87
on racial difference, 117
and self-reflection, 79–81
and self-regulation, 81–82, 92, 110, 122, 159
"Sensus Communis," 41, 42, 67, 74, 77–78, 85–86, 92, 94, 100, 110–111, 113, 114–115, 122–124
on the state, 55, 92–93, 192n36
and statute law, 92, 97–100
on theocracy, 53, 55, 57–58, 74, 92, 122
wit, 113, 82, 84–85, 78
Siskin, Clifford, 48
slavery, 18, 27, 100–109, 103, 116, 120, 132, 183
Smith, Adam, 35, 44, 62–63, 103
Smith, Neil, 98–99
sovereignty
of Carolina Colony, 108–109
and enthusiasm, 22, 43, 69, 101, 121–123
individual, 22, 52, 67, 94, 100, 126
  See also Shaftesbury
state, 25–26, 68–73, 85–89, 91–92, 97, 99–101, 112, 114, 142, 155, 184
  See also law, statute
space, 99, 101, 110, 120, 128, 127–133, 135, 138–140, 144, 147–148
spatiality. *See* space.
spatio-temporal fix, 28, 101, 118–119, 126, 184
  See also Harvey, David
Spencer, John, 50
Steele, Richard, 137, 142
Stephens, James Fitzjames, 90–91
Stern, Laurence, 190n14
Stubbe, Henry
  An Account of the Rise and Progress of Mahometanism, 34, 50–51
  enthusiasm as civic virtue, 26, 53–54
  on Islam, 10, 50–54
subject, 33, 38–39, 79–80, 111–112
sublime, 11, 21, 45, 81, 118, 121, 189n39

Sutcliffe, Adam, 57
surplus value, 18, 60, 62, 112, 119, 165, 172–173, 177, 184, 194n80
Swift, Jonathan
  critique of consumer culture, 155, 166, 176, 180, 183
  "Description of a City Shower," 29, 151–152, 156–157 164–165, 167–169, 173–183
  and enthusiastic form, 152–153, 162–163
  and enthusiasm, 156, 159, 162, 202n6
  and enthusiastic excess, 152–154, 162, 176
  and mediation, 155–160, 163
  and moral comportment, 158–159
  and non-finito, 168
  and overproduction, 176–177
  and poetic form, 156, 168, 178, 203n12
  The Run Upon the Bankers, 166
  and satire, 162, 165, 173, 180
  "Stella's Birthday," 29, 152, 157–159, 161, 164
  A Tale of a Tub, 154, 162
  and the transatlantic, 178–179
  and transatlantic studies, 29, 183–184
  and urban georgic, 164, 173–175
  and waste, 152–154, 165, 168, 171–173, 176–178, 181–182, 204n12

Taylor, Charles, 187n18
Teschke, Benno, 91, 111–112
Thomson, James, 150, 160, 183
Toland, John, 26, 35, 45, 50, 53, 57, 193n64
  Letters to Serena, 34, 57
  Nazarenus, or Jewish, Gentile, and Mahometan Christianity, 50
Toscano, Alberto, 4–5, 23–24, 185n3
transatlanticism as a field of study, 15, 27, 29, 183–184
Trotsky. *See* definition of uneven development

uneven development
  aesthetics of, 124–125, 132
  definition of, 120–121, 201n73
  and British state, 59
  and race, 118, 120
  and Shaftesbury, 120–121
urban development, 98–99, 156, 161, 164, 183–184

value
　and capital accumulation, 15
　and the city, 136–141, 173–180, 184
　and the commodity, 23–24, 173–174
　Mandeville on, 89
　Marx on, 175, 179
　surplus, 60, 62, 165, 194n80
　Shaftesbury on, 59, 79–81, 102, 112
　and Swift, 173–175, 179–180, 184
　and literature, 141–144
　and taste, 79
vanishing mediator, 92–94, 197–198n81
　　See also Jameson, Fredric
Virgil, 165, 168
Voitle, Robert, 103, 104

wage labor, 4, 18, 132, 172
Walwyn, William, 73

Wheeler, Roxanne, 116
Whigs, 137, 139
Williams, Raymond, 25, 119, 122, 127, 129, 132
Winstanley, Gerrard, 10, 139
wit
　as aesthetic form, 75–77
　and economic transformation, 76
　and enthusiasm, 74–78, 113–115
　and judgment , 76–77
　and the market, 82, 85–86, 119
　and self-regulation, 74–78, 90–91, 122–123
　"Sensus Communis," 41–42
　　See also Shaftesbury
Wordsworth, William
　"Tintern Abbey," 11

Zizek, Slavoj, 20, 80

www.ingramcontent.com/pod-product-compliance
Ingram Content Group UK Ltd.
Pitfield, Milton Keynes, MK11 3LW, UK
UKHW042006230426
12048UKWH00009B/585